NOBODY CAN GIVE YOU FREEDOM

THE POLITICAL LIFE OF
MALCOLM

KEHINDE ANDREWS

BOLD TYPE BOOKS

NEW YORK

Hachette Book Group supports the right to free expression and the value of copyright. The purpose of copyright is to encourage writers and artists to produce the creative works that enrich our culture.

The scanning, uploading, and distribution of this book without permission is a theft of the author's intellectual property. If you would like permission to use material from the book (other than for review purposes), please contact permissions@hbgusa.com. Thank you for your support of the author's rights.

Bold Type Books
Hachette Book Group
1290 Avenue of the Americas, New York, NY 10104
www.boldtypebooks.org
@BoldTypeBooks

Printed in the United States of America
First published in Great Britain by Allen Lane 2025
First US Edition: September 2025

Published by Bold Type Books, an imprint of Hachette Book Group, Inc.
Bold Type Books is a co-publishing venture of the Type Media Center
and The Basic Books Group.

The Hachette Speakers Bureau provides a wide range of authors for speaking events. To find out more, go to www.hachettespeakersbureau.com or email HachetteSpeakers@hbgusa.com.

Bold Type books may be purchased in bulk for business, educational, or promotional use. For more information, please contact your local bookseller or the Hachette Book Group Special Markets Department at special.markets@hbgusa.com.

The publisher is not responsible for websites (or their content) that are not owned by the publisher.

Library of Congress Cataloging-in-Publication Data has been applied for.
ISBNs: 9781645030706 (hardcover); 9781645030713 (ebook)
Printing 1, 2025

CONTENTS

For Assata, Kadiri, Omaje, and Ajani
In memory of Brother Malcolm X

PREFACE

I have only ever once stood before an awaiting crowd and been unsure if I would be able to deliver. Looking out at the packed church, my only audience was my children, who were expecting me to do justice to their mother and my wife, Dr. Nicole Andrews, whose life had been cut tragically short by cancer at just thirty-seven years of age. Aside from having to break the news of her passing to them, these were the hardest words I have ever had to summon up. I stumbled through thanking so many people for turning out and outlining her achievements: She was the first person I met to achieve a PhD with no corrections at all, and is still the only one I've met who, while heavily pregnant, has chased crackheads out of a community building, one we were renovating, in order to make sure it stayed on track. I only really found my footing in the eulogy when I joked that "Nicole is probably looking down rolling her eyes, but to make this make sense I am going to have quote Malcolm." Nicole definitely would not have been surprised. I quote Malcolm so frequently that I was once dubbed by a disgraced comedian as a "devotee." Speaking to the congregation, I certainly found a strength in spreading his gospel, and I implored the crowd to remember Malcolm's words, "It's already too late," to inspire them to live their lives to the absolute fullest, as Nicole had done. At this point my children were probably numb to the Malcolm references. By then, after their protests, I had stopped playing his speeches during dinner. At two years old, my eldest son thought the X-Men toys were in honor of Malcolm. In my house it is not an exaggeration to say that it is all Malcolm all the time. When I ended the eulogy by asking Nicole to "say hello to Malcolm for me," it wasn't just to put a rhetorical bow on the speech but a genuine expression of my personal and political connection to Malcolm and his work. The purpose of this book is to outline why the politics of Malcolm became the foundation of my worldview and how he is the intellectual we need to reshape the future.

I was fortunate to grow up in the wake of the Black Power movement in Britain. My parents' bookshelves were teeming with classic texts that they had smuggled into the country. As I am typing these words, I am sitting in the shadow of many of the titles I liberated from my family home when I moved out. *The Philosophy and Opinions of Marcus Garvey*, *The Black Jacobins* by Trinidadian intellectual C. L. R. James, and various books by James Baldwin were the background to my upbringing. I was volunteered to work in the Harriet Tubman Bookshop that my parents started as part of the Harambee Organisation they founded in 1973. By the time I picked up *The Autobiography of Malcolm X* as a teenager, I was well acquainted with Black political literature and had already had my transformative moment, when picking up *Stokely Speaks: From Black Power to Pan-Africanism*, by Stokely Carmichael (later Kwame Ture). Malcolm talks about how, when he started to read in prison, his thinking was changed as suddenly as the fall of "snow off a roof."[1] That was the impact of *Stokely Speaks* on my confused teenage mind, which had been convinced that being a good student meant being (or at least acting like) a White one. I will always credit *Stokely Speaks* for jolting me awake, but it was Malcolm who wiped the crust from my eyes and provided the cold splash of water to truly bring me to consciousness.

Decades after he died, thousands of miles from where he lived, Malcolm's voice came through with such clarity it felt as though he were talking directly to me. His words resonated because they explained so much of what I was feeling and experiencing at the time, so that it was at once comforting and a little eerie. Ever since then, and especially with the more that I have read and listened to, Malcolm's vision has become the basis of my worldview.

Perhaps the most annoying challenge that I get to Malcolm's thinking being the basis of my approach is that, living in Britain, it is wrong to seek inspiration from an American. This is wrongheaded on so many levels, but the assumption that there is a "British" way to understand the problem of racism is particularly questionable given that almost all Black people living here can trace our heritage to a former colony within a couple of generations. Part of the reason we are wary of embracing Americans is because the idea of American exceptionalism holds on so strongly over there. It is an odd approach to attempt to replace that with a British version. I promise you: We have no equivalent of Malcolm who is "British," if by that you mean born or raised on this cold, rainy little island. This shouldn't really come as a surprise, given that we haven't been here in large numbers for very long and most of us still live in the former colonies. In the Caribbean, Europe managed slave plantations by remote control, whereas America was a settler colony, meaning that slavery predated the founding of that nation. The result is that there are more than four times as many Black people in America as there are in the whole of Europe. America is also home to almost twice as many Black people as there are in the Caribbean. The only region in the diaspora with more Black people is Latin America, due to the number of enslaved people being taken to Brazil, which makes that nation's Black population greater than any country other than Nigeria. In the English-speaking African diaspora, there is little point in denying that America is the epicenter of the Black world, which is why, culturally and politically, its impact is outsize. Of course, this doesn't mean that we should blindly follow the American lead, but we shouldn't turn away out of some misguided national pride.

It felt like Malcolm was speaking to me because of the connection of his words to my experiences. Racism is a global system, not a national one. The Black Lives Matter protests of 2020 were sparked because we watched George Floyd die in circumstances all too similar to the fate of a disproportionate number of Black people in Britain. In housing, education, health care, and employment, we can see the same inequalities as in America playing out on our shores, and the same is true across the world. In the last year of his life, Malcolm traveled across Africa and Europe, and he was in my hometown, Birmingham, just nine days before he was murdered. Malcolm was surprised to discover how popular and well-known he was around the world. He was treated like a foreign dignitary in the Middle East and Africa, holding meetings with heads of state and speaking at the Organization of African Unity (OAU) summit in 1964.[2] His popularity has not waned. I have spoken to young people in Brazil, South Africa, and Ethiopia, where his impact was as profound as it was on me. Malcolm was not speaking solely to America: he was (and still is) speaking for the Black world.

Malcolm X is the perfect example of the problem of seeing Black Americans as being an exceptional, separate part of the diaspora. His mother was born on the Caribbean island of Grenada, and both of his parents were members of the Universal Negro Improvement Association (UNIA) founded by Marcus and Amy Ashwood Garvey in Jamaica in 1914.[3] The UNIA was the largest ever Black political organization, building a membership of between two and eight million members across more than forty countries.[4] It was hugely influential on African American politics, the United States being the nation where the majority of its members resided. The Nation of Islam (NOI), which Malcolm joined while in prison, took much of its organizational style from the UNIA. Radical and liberal groups drew inspiration from the Garvey movement. Malcolm's father would take him to UNIA meetings as a child, and so profound was the impact of the organization on Malcolm's politics that Kwame Ture would argue Malcolm's "basic ideology was Garveyism."[5] One of the few Black leaders Malcolm publicly praised in speeches was Marcus Garvey, whom he described as a "bold, brave great Black man who came to America to try and unite Black people," while comparing him to Jesus and Moses.[6] Malcolm's political blueprint coalesced after international trips, and he was particularly influenced by his discussions with first Ghanaian President Kwame Nkrumah. Malcolm's vehicle for revolutionary change, the Organization of Afro-American Unity (OAAU), took its name from the Organization of African Unity, with the explicit intention to directly connect the struggles on the continent with the whole of the diaspora.

To classify Malcolm's politics as "American" is frankly ludicrous. As with Black political thought around the world, he was influenced heavily by Africa and the diaspora. In a very real way Malcolm *was* speaking to me, as a Black citizen of the world, which is why his ideas had such a profound effect upon me and continue to do so.

None of this is academic to me. I am trying to make Malcolm's blueprint a reality through the Harambee Organisation of Black Unity, which takes its constitution from the OAAU. I have put my money where my mouth is by using the proceeds from this book to fund the Harambee OBU to try to build a global organization in his honor. We are going to hold the Convention of Afrikan People to mark what would have been Malcolm's one-hundredth birthday in May 2025. To say I am invested in Malcolm is an understatement.

Like most people, I came to Malcolm through *The Autobiography of Malcolm X*, the powerful story of Malcolm's life (ghostwritten by Alex Haley), which then framed Spike Lee's biopic *Malcolm X* in 1992. The book is a masterpiece of storytelling, showing us the young Malcolm, whose family was devastated by the racist murder of his father and his mother's mental health struggles, which saw her institutionalized. Young Malcolm ends up living with his sister Ella Collins in Boston and falling into the life of a street hustler, escalating up the ladder of criminality until he is imprisoned for burglary in 1946. At his lowest moment in prison, he transforms his life, devouring books and joining the Nation of Islam. The NOI was a small, cultlike organization with deeply questionable beliefs, but it allowed Malcolm to express his frustration with White society. He embraced the NOI's anti-White, hateful rhetoric that all White people were devils, and he became the violent yang to Martin Luther King's yin, arguing for the complete separation of the races.

According to Spike Lee's version of the story, it is only when he leaves the clutches of the NOI (after finding out the group's leader is sexually abusing his young secretaries) that Malcolm can become the true civil rights spokesperson he was meant to be. His visit to Mecca in 1964 and adoption of orthodox Islam is meant to signify his evolution into the mainstream. According to this narrative, before his tragic assassination he was supposedly ready to embrace King and the civil rights struggle to redeem America and the world. But like all movie narratives, this is a fairy tale, and a very dangerous one at that. Malcolm was murdered on February 21, 1965, just a few months shy of his fortieth birthday, because he had laid out the blueprint for Black liberation. Now, a hundred years after his birth, it is the perfect time to rid ourselves of the Malcolm myths and truly engage with his politics of liberation.

1

MAKE IT PLAIN

I have lost count of the amount of times during Black History Month that I have heard complaints that people are tired of hearing about "Martin, Malcolm, and Rosa Parks." It is true Malcolm is one of the most well-known Black political figures, a household name and icon whose autobiography continues to sell millions of copies. Spike Lee's film starring Denzel Washington was a hit, and in 2020 Netflix created a miniseries called *Who Killed Malcolm X?* But the biggest irony about Malcolm is that, although he remains a cultural idol, he is one of the most misunderstood and misrepresented figures in history. Reverend Albert Cleage, who organized with Malcolm, warned that: "Malcolm has become a symbol, a dream, a hope, a nostalgia for the past, a mystique, a shadow sometimes without substance, 'our shining prince' to whom we do obeisance, about whom we write heroic poems. But Malcolm is in danger of being lost in a vast tissue of distortions which now constitute the Malcolm myth."[1]

The Malcolm myth has two sides, which were being formed even before he died. Malcolm shot to national prominence when the Nation of Islam was featured on Mike Wallace's five-part series *The Hate That Hate Produced* in 1959. Although he always pledged fealty to his leader Elijah Muhammad, Malcolm was the star of the show, with his intelligence, wit, and charisma leaping out of the television screen. But the documentary framed the NOI and Malcolm as peddlers of hate, fiery preachers who wanted America to burn in vengeance for the evils done to African Americans. Wallace described the series as an examination of "Black racism" and "Black supremacy," setting the tone for how Malcolm would be viewed in the mainstream. At the same time as the nonviolent civil rights movement was making legislative inroads, Malcolm became viewed as the violent "evil twin" of the peaceful Martin Luther King.[2] The press vilification of Malcolm was so thorough that it became a common theme of his speeches, often warning his audiences not to let the press distort their view of his personality. He recounted a story of having a conversation with a White woman on a plane for almost an hour before she noticed his suitcase was marked with the initials M. X. and asked what surname he could have that started with an *X*. When she finally realized she was talking to *the* Malcolm X, she was stunned and exclaimed, "You're not what I was looking for." Malcolm had a similar conversation with a White student at Oxford and explained their surprise was due to their "looking for the horns that had been created by the press. Someone who was out to kill all White people, [who] was a segregationist, rabble rouser, extremist, subversive, seditious and someone who couldn't hold a conversation with just anyone."[3] But Malcolm did not find this demonization of him problematic; in fact he reveled in his role, wearing his "hate teacher" badge of honor with pride.

He laughed off his misrepresentation in the press, telling a group of White students at Michigan State that it would not have the desired effect of turning the Black masses against him, but the opposite:

> The only one this type of propaganda alienates is this Negro who's always up in your face begging you for what you have or begging you for a chance to live in your neighborhood to work on your job or marry one of your women.[4]

In an interview before he died, Malcolm said that he understood "the only person who can organize the man on the streets is the one who is unacceptable to the White community, they don't trust the other kind," and, as we will see in this book, he spent a lot of time lambasting Black spokespeople who defended White supremacy.[5] Malcolm's appeal was precisely because he was unapologetic, and *The Hate That Hate Produced* sparked a wealth of admiration for his speaking the hard truths. He was someone who never ducked controversy, declaring at the London School of Economics: "I come here to tell the truth, and if the truth is anti-American, then blame the truth, don't blame me."[6]

The more insidious myth than that of "Malcolm the fiery hate preacher" that sought to alienate him from the masses is the version that tried to co-opt him into the American project.[7] After Malcolm's assassination, the figure of the angry martyr for the revolution was a dangerous one, and therefore his image was recreated to be more palatable. The new myth was that Malcolm died on a path of evolution to embracing civil rights, having rejected his wicked ways. Esteemed academic Michael Eric Dyson was relieved that Malcolm was "finally to make his rage work in the best interests of black folk . . . learning to work with people like Martin Luther King and other civil rights leaders."[8] The academic text that best captures the later Malcolm myth is Manning Marable's *A Life of Reinvention*, which caused an uproar on publication in 2011. The book is a detailed memoir that is seriously undermined by engaging in personal gossip—speculating among other things that Malcolm was gay, bad in bed, and had affairs—based on the flimsiest evidence. It was so poorly received that a collection of activists and academics, including those who knew Malcolm, responded with *A Lie of Reinvention*.[9] If you are interested in the beef, then I recommend reading that book; but for our purposes I want to focus on the truly damaging aspect of the myth that Marable feeds into: the notion that Malcolm reinvented himself into "a quintessentially American" civil rights leader. In a telling passage, Marable argues that "despite his radical rhetoric, the mature Malcolm believed that African Americans could use electoral rights and the voting system to achieve meaningful social change."[10] The use of the word "mature" is a patronizing judgment of Malcolm's radical, supposedly childish prior incarnation before he embraced democracy.

We will discuss the fallacious idea that using the electoral system is at odds with radical politics later on, but it is clear from Marable's work that Malcolm was supposed to have emerged from his radical, separatist, extremist cocoon to become a civil rights butterfly. In order to uphold this lie, the clear revolutionary program that Malcolm devised had to be erased from public consciousness. In service of this aim, or more generously, as a result of it, we have an academic consensus that "Malcolm X was eloquent and relentless in his analysis of the problems facing Black America, but he never spoke a solution"; that he did not "formulate any programmatic response to America's racial strife."[11] We are left with a Malcolm who was strident, unapologetic, but who rejected his violent ways and was in search of a fresh political program for his new self. That is a Malcolm that can be put on an American postage stamp and one who offers no concrete revolution for the Black masses. Ironically, given how important *The Autobiography of Malcolm X* has been to so many, including myself, it is that book that is most responsible for this dangerous Malcolm myth.

Underlying the problems with the *Autobiography* is that it was ghostwritten by Alex Haley, who had interviewed Malcolm for *Playboy* magazine before they worked on the memoir. The pair took part in hours of interviews, and Malcolm would write chapters and send them over to Haley for review, so he was clearly heavily involved. The book was unfinished when Malcolm died, so we will never know what he thought of how Haley put it together. But author Ishmael Reed quotes his editor, who worked with the book's original editor, Anne Freedgood, who told him that "an angry Malcolm X burst into the offices of Doubleday and threw the manuscript of *The Autobiography of Malcolm X* across the room shouting, 'This manuscript has nothing to do with me.'"[12] Having read the book after reflecting on Malcolm X's life and legacy, I would not be surprised if this account is true. The more times I read it, the angrier I become about the final version.

To be charitable to Haley, the aim of the book changed as it was being written. When Malcolm started the project, he was a member of the Nation of Islam and wanted to use the book to help spread the word and solidify his standing with the leader of the sect, Elijah Muhammad. The focus on his transformation from a street hustler who ended up in jail to an upstanding member of the NOI was meant to demonstrate the power of the organization (and its leader). Much of the book is about Malcolm's days on the street, the gritty details of life as a hustler; in fact, you could argue that is the real emphasis of the project. But by the end of his time working on the book, Malcolm had completely split with the NOI and was openly condemning the hypocrisy of Muhammad and the limits of the organization. Malcolm was charting a new course, having established the Organization of Afro-American Unity in 1964, and no doubt would have liked to use the book to promote his vision for racial justice. But there really is no worse source than the *Autobiography* if you are looking for the real Malcolm's practical program.

You get as much information on the OAAU as you would from reading a *Black Panther* comic. Consider the fact that the organization that Malcolm had dedicated his life to building, which he was recruiting members for and traveling around the world promoting while he was writing his autobiography, Malcolm mentions once in the original book. It is impossible that he did not discuss his work with Haley. In fact, it was Marable who revealed there are pages of notes on the OAAU taken by Haley in the process of writing the book.[13] Marable recounted being given brief access to these pages by the private collector who owns them in the trunk of the man's car. The Schomburg Center for Research in Black Culture announced that it had purchased the "missing pages" from the autobiography, and I was very excited because I thought these were the OAAU notes. When I visited, I found out they were actually a chapter called "The Negro," which had been omitted and was fascinating to read, and which we will explore in Chapter 7. But it wasn't those missing pages. They may never see the light of day, but there is no chance that Malcolm didn't want the OAAU to feature widely in his autobiography.

Haley has become a controversial figure after the *Autobiography* because of the fiasco relating to his book *Roots*, which was also immortalized into a TV miniseries, telling the story of Kunta Kinte, who is meant to be Haley's direct ancestor from Senegambia. The book and

TV series were a cultural phenomenon, catapulting Haley to fame. One of the most prominent books on my parents' bookshelves was a first edition of *Roots*. But the truth of Haley's account was undermined when he was accused of plagiarizing sections of the book and had to pay the equivalent of half a million dollars in damages.[14] Haley admitted that the book was what he called "faction," a blurring of fact and fiction, but always maintained that the overall story was true and that he *was* descended from Kunta Kinte, although there is debate as to how truthful even this history was. I will avoid leaping into the debate about *Roots*, but it is notable that both of Haley's important works raise serious questions about his credibility.

Haley was an odd choice to ghostwrite the *Autobiography*, as he fit firmly into Malcolm's category of a "bourgeois type [of Negro] who blinds himself to the conditions of his people and is satisfied with token solutions."[15] Haley was a supposedly "liberal Republican" at a time when the party was opposed to even the modest gains of the civil rights movement.[16] This made Marable skeptical of Haley's reading, believing that his political views impacted the writing. Marable revealed that Haley had written more than one note on the draft that described Malcolm as a "demagogue." Given Malcolm's original intention for the *Autobiography* to be about his own personal redemption at the hands of Elijah Muhammad and the NOI, Haley's political views might not have mattered originally. In fact, the Nation of Islam embraced both the American Nazi Party and the Ku Klux Klan, so Haley was more progressive than many of the NOI's bedfellows. But once the purpose became to showcase Malcolm's political views and program, there was perhaps no more inappropriate author to do the translation. As we will discuss later, Malcolm was least trusting of Black people who did the work of White supremacy.

Haley put a Black face upon the misrepresentation of Malcolm X. In case you think I am being paranoid about Haley's work and intentions, he was recently accused of having fabricated quotes from Martin Luther King in his 1965 interview with the icon in *Playboy* magazine to make it seem as though the civil rights leader was directly criticizing Malcolm. Historian Jonathan Eig has compared a transcript of the interview between Haley and King to what was published in the magazine. He found that Haley had completely made up the line he attributed to King: "I feel that Malcolm has done himself and our people a great disservice." Haley directed Martin Luther King's condemnation of "fiery, demagogic oratory in the black ghettos, urging Negroes to arm themselves and prepare to engage in violence" directly to Malcolm, when King never does this in the transcript.[17] There is little doubt that Haley's politics influenced his misrepresentation of Malcolm.

The only real question is whether this was a case of doing a hidden master's bidding of his own accord or if there was a hand on the whip coercing him into it. We know that the FBI was surveilling Black activists (and continues to do so), with a particular focus on King and Malcolm. There is a whole book called *Malcolm X: The FBI File* that includes some of the released surveillance notes. Malcolm even went public about a time when the FBI approached him to give them information about the Nation of Islam.[18] We also know that, as part of the FBI's "counterintelligence program" (COINTELPRO), the bureau would plant agents within organizations and fake correspondence between groups to create discord. Part of the criticism of Marable's *Life of Reinvention* is that he relies on letters that we cannot trust were genuinely written by the protagonists, given the Feds' practice of faking correspondence between people to sow distrust. The FBI's infiltration of the Black freedom struggle was so total that, after Malcolm's body-guard, the first person to tend to him after he was shot was an informant. There is no doubt that the FBI was aware of the *Autobiography*, its contents, and the danger it presented if Malcolm's political program was acted upon. This was particularly true after he died. The director of the FBI at the time, J. Edgar Hoover, was obsessed with stopping the "rise of a Black messiah," and in death Malcolm could have become the martyr that rallied the Black nation around his radical vision.[19] It is widely accepted that the FBI arranged for Chicago Black Panther Fred Hampton to be drugged and then murdered in his sleep in 1969, so I have absolutely no trouble believing the Feds would have a hand in editing the *Autobiography* to present a palatable Malcolm myth.[20] The alternative reading of the situation is actually still more depressing: that you don't need a conspiracy to produce the revised Malcolm myth, given how efficiently the system of White supremacy works on its own. Whatever the case, the *Autobiography* laid the framework for the Malcolm we celebrate today: the angry, reformed man with no political program.

Spike Lee's 1992 film *Malcolm X* only compounded the issue. Based on the *Autobiography*, it perpetuated the myth with a feature-length focus on Malcolm the hoodlum and convert. It also reduced Malcolm to a symbol: the *X* that was slapped on hats, T-shirts, and jackets. The film became a classic due to Denzel Washington's virtuoso performance as Malcolm. If you have sat through the more than three-hour epic, imagine it with pretty much any other actor in the lead role, and I promise you it would have been lost to the dustbin of history. It was an empty gesture, a "prestige project" that pioneered movie marketing by packaging and selling the "dangerous Malcolm made safe" myth.[21] You leave the marathon movie with absolutely no insight into what Malcolm offered the world, other than a tragic redemption story.

The end of the film perfectly sums up the limits of the project. Lee decided to ask South African President Nelson Mandela to end the film by reciting the lines from Malcolm's 1964 speech at the second founding rally of the OAAU. It demonstrates the power of the Malcolm myth that someone who spent years making a film about him thought Mandela would be a good spokesperson for his message. As we will discuss later on, Malcolm savagely condemned the 1963 March on Washington for being a sellout of the radical feelings of the Black masses. He chastised its integrated nature, asking: "[Who] ever heard of angry revolutionists all harmonizing 'We Shall Overcome . . . Sum Day . . .' while tripping and swaying along arm-in-arm with the very people they were supposed to be angrily revolting against? Who ever heard of angry revolutionists swinging their bare feet together with their oppressor?"[22]

If Malcolm had this to say of the minority Black population in America, I can only imagine what he would have said about Mandela, who was fighting a White minority. Apartheid was the most vicious, violent, and open system of racial oppression in the postwar period. There was an armed struggle, which Mandela was a part of and which landed him in prison on Robben Island. Mandela admitted that he unilaterally negotiated with the apartheid leaders and sold out the revolutionary struggle in order to have a smooth transition to a so-called democracy.[23] He made a show of embracing F. W. de Klerk, the last apartheid president, who served as vice president in Mandela's initial government. Mandela is celebrated by the West *because* he was a puppet master who sold out the revolution and led South Africa merrily singing down the continued path of colonial exploitation it is still on. Mandela was so far gone in approval seeking that he actually flew into an all-White settlement to have tea with Betsie Verwoerd, the wife of the architect of apartheid.[24] Malcolm would have savaged Mandela as nothing but a modern-day Uncle Tom African leader, but Lee chose him to conclude the message of the film. If that wasn't bad enough, the final line of the Malcolm speech Mandela was supposed to quote about the anti-apartheid struggle ends with the words, "By any means necessary," but he actually refused to utter those words because he was so committed to nonviolence. You couldn't make this up. Spike Lee actually asked the African equivalent of Martin Luther King to close the film about Malcolm X and had to edit in footage of Malcolm saying his infamous line because it went against Mandela's sellout sensibilities! Ironically, given the dubious nature of the source material in the *Autobiography*, this may have been the most fitting ending for this timid and inaccurate film.

It was wrong to expect anything from the movie. Kwame Ture fiercely argued Lee was "selling his people for a fistful of dollars. Malcolm X was a revolutionary. . . . 'Can you imagine for one minute Hollywood giving Malcolm X a hand? You might as well ask Zionists to make a film about [Palestinian leader Yasser] Arafat.'"[25]

The almost total acceptance of the "tamed" Malcolm myth has meant that he can now be claimed by anyone to suit their own purposes. Betty Shabazz, Malcolm's wife, just a few years after he died, warned that the "constant refrain that my husband was changing his beliefs" had allowed "some people to invoke Malcolm's name to justify some highly unorganized, anarchistic ventures that he would never have dreamed of becoming involved in."[26] It is worth stating from the outset that Malcolm was not a civil rights leader; he was the fiercest critic of the civil rights movement you will ever hear. Unlike the civil rights leaders, Malcolm did *not* believe that America could be redeemed if only Black people could access the levers of power through voting rights so that they could reform racism out of the system. He was also not in favor of violence for the sake of violence, and in fact never committed any political violence during his career. Just because he spoke to some left-wing organizations after he left the Nation of Islam didn't mean he was a Communist. Perhaps the most bizarre claim to Malcolm's legacy is by the ultra-right-wing African American Supreme Court Justice Clarence Thomas, who dubbed himself Clarence X.

I came across this nonsense when I saw a podcast episode, "Clarence X," and thought it must have been about a member of the NOI. It is difficult to explain my confusion when I realized it was about a Supreme Court judge. I assumed it must have been some misplaced White liberal joke.[27] The podcast took a deep dive into Thomas's life, talking to people who knew him when he was younger and charting his rise to become the most powerful Supreme Court justice in the United States. If Malcolm would have laid into Mandela, only God knows what he would have had to say about Thomas. The second ever Black Supreme Court justice was picked for the role because George H. W. Bush needed a Black person to replace the legendary Thurgood Marshall, who had retired due to ill health. Marshall was the lawyer who argued in front of the Supreme Court against racial segregation in the infamous *Brown v. Board of Education* case in 1954, which he successfully won. On a related sidenote, Marshall thought Malcolm was a "low-life" and refused to even acknowledge him in the street.[28] This was likely because Malcolm spent so much time slamming that court victory as nothing but an empty token gesture.

When Marshall retired, Bush wanted a strong conservative judge to join the Supreme Court but needed to replace the first, and only, Black justice with another brother (this was 1991; they were not ready to even consider a Black woman). In selecting Thomas, Bush started a new era of affirmative action, placing Black conservatives in positions of power to be the Black faces of White supremacy, regardless of their qualifications. Even after Donald Trump packed the court with archconservatives, Thomas remains the most extreme example. He consistently votes to weaken voting rights protections, voted against affirmative action, and even voted to allow the state of Texas to execute a Black defendant before the DNA evidence against him could be tested (thankfully, he was in the minority on that issue).[29] Just days before Bush nominated Thomas, Marshall warned at his retirement press conference that he didn't want a Black justice picked as a "ploy . . . to do wrong." As if predicting the future, he explained that "there's no difference between a White snake and a Black snake, they both bite."[30] It is so routine to call Clarence an Uncle Thomas, there is no chance that Malcolm could have resisted the poetry.[31] I struggle to think of any Black public figure so clearly the antithesis of Malcolm, so I couldn't fathom how on earth the Clarence X label had stuck as anything other than parody.

Apparently, in college Thomas was obsessed with Malcolm, constantly playing his recordings and fashioning himself as a supposed Black nationalist. The crux of this appears to have been a misreading of Malcolm so bad you wonder whether those who indulge in it are literate. For instance, we are assured by American so-called legal scholar Stephen Smith that "for anyone who cares to listen, Justice Thomas's opinions thunder with the strong black-nationalist voice typically associated with one of Thomas's personal heroes, Malcolm X."[32] Such illogic is only possible because of the Malcolm myth that removes any serious understanding of his political framework. Just because Thomas and Malcolm were both anti–civil rights does not mean that they were in unison. Malcolm thought civil rights could never provide freedom because they do not go far enough. Thomas is against civil rights because he feels that they stand in the way of Black people pulling their sleeves up and making progress without support from the state. Malcolm didn't believe we should rely on White people (e.g., affirmative action) because the Western system was incapable of providing justice for Black people. Thomas sets store on self-sufficiency because he has been deluded into believing that America is the land of milk and honey for all those who work hard and pull themselves up by their bootstraps. Malcolm called for a revolution that would have started with knocking people like Thomas off their White-supremacy-appointed perches. Malcolm would have denounced Thomas as one of those "Negroes who have been put in that position by the White man himself. They're not speaking for Black people, they're saying exactly what the White man who put them in the position wants to hear them say."[33] It is utterly ludicrous to connect the two. As respected legal scholar Patricia Williams explains, "Thomas invokes a mythical image of Malcolm X to serve his own needs."[34] Unfortunately, he is by no means the only one, and hopefully this book will help you to weed out the false prophets claiming links to Malcolm's legacy.

NINCOMPOOP WITH A PHD

Malcolm's story has fascinated authors and publishers since the publication of the *Autobiography*. The numerous reprints of his memoir were joined by a number of biographies, notably Marable's in 2011, which was followed by Les Payne and Tamara Payne's *The Dead Are Arising*, which aimed to give context to Malcolm's life and won the Pulitzer Prize for Biography.[35] But for all of the millions of words and hours of film and documentary dedicated to Malcolm, his political message remains hidden. This is not a biography; there are plenty of places you can go to learn about the man. My aim is to simply outline Malcolm's political ideas, his program for revolution, which was clear and spelled out before he died. There have been scant attempts to do this work previously. The most recent demonstrates the problem of Black intellectual thought being co-opted into the university.

When I saw title of the book *Black Minded: The Political Philosophy of Malcolm X*, by Michael Sawyer, I was both excited and intrigued. But as soon I opened the book, I understood why I needed to write this one. In the first few pages, Sawyer explains that his project was "employing the discipline of philosophy to examine the thought of Malcolm X."[36] He wanted to recognize the importance of Malcolm as a political philosopher and to elevate his theory into the academic canon. I can attest to the allure of this idea, as Malcolm's ideas are the theoretical basis for all my work, and I have felt the need to justify his work to my colleagues. Sawyer raises the issue of the lack of writing from Malcolm, because academia conflates intellect with written production. Just like Sawyer, in the past I have stressed the importance of Malcolm's spoken words as being just as legitimate as if he had written those words down. While writing this book, I gained even greater appreciation for just how much intellectual work Malcolm produced. *The Last Speeches*, a book that compiles only the speeches and interviews from the last three weeks of his life, is 266 pages long. This doesn't even include everything. I know of at least two missing speeches from his time in Birmingham during this period. I have based my book on reading and listening to over fifty speeches and interviews spanning 1959 to 1965. There is no doubt that Malcolm has a robust body of work that can measure up to anything produced by academia. If I had written this book a few years ago, my intention might well have been to argue that Malcolm's work be allowed legitimacy within academia. But I now realize that is the wrong way to treat his scholarship. While his work is certainly just as credible as anything produced by the esteemed academics, he is not a political philosopher because his work is far more important than that. In fact, the discipline of political philosophy has no credibility to examine Malcolm's work.

In Sawyer's book, as in most academic texts on Black thinkers, the tendency is to evaluate Black political thought in relation to the established (mostly White) scholars. The problem with academia is not just that the curriculum is White, but that the entire framework of knowledge is White. The founding fathers of the disciplines are dead White men who didn't just hold racist beliefs; their whole intellectual world was shaped by White supremacy.[37] Academia may have belatedly opened up to Black students and to a lesser extent welcomed more Black academics into faculty, but the foundations and practices remain deeply rooted in White supremacy. If Malcolm were alive today, there is a good chance that with his passion for reading and intellectual brilliance he would have become an academic. But if he'd done so, he would not have been *Malcolm*. Malcolm's intellectual production is so groundbreaking precisely because he was *not* an academic. To explain this, we need only consider Sawyer's "difficulty of disentangling the activist Malcolm X from the political philosopher."[38]

As much as we would like to think that academic notions of knowledge have been transformed, they remain rooted in a belief that thought must be separated from action. That is why the university exists, to host the esteemed intellectual who theorizes the world at a distance. The idea that there is an "activist" and a "philosopher" and these two positions are somehow distinct sums up the problems with academia. I was listening to a speech made by Malcolm at Michigan State University in 1963, and there is a telling moment when he catches himself while speaking and says, "If I raise my voice, please forgive me. I'm not doing it out of disrespect. I'm just speaking from my heart and you get it exactly how the feelings let it out."[39] In 1963, Malcolm was the second most sought-after speaker on American college campuses (after racist US Senator Barry Goldwater), so he spoke at enough universities to know that the students were used to their dispassionate professors outlining the "facts." I have lost count of how many times I have been told, "You are so passionate," as though caring about your work is somehow an aberration. I have almost completely stopped attending academic conferences because I cannot sit through people reading out densely written, deeply boring papers. I am not exaggerating when I say to do so actually hurts my soul. Contrast the standard academic performance with a Malcolm speech and they could not be more different. If you want to understand Malcolm, the place to go is the speeches, but you need to really *listen* to them. The pitch, the cadence, the jokes (Malcolm was hilarious), but just as important are the audiences, who are not passive but constantly participating with interjections—"Preach, Malcolm!"—applause, laughter, and affirmation. Maya Angelou explained that when Malcolm would turn up to speak "he couldn't talk for the first four or five minutes, the people would be making such a praise shout to him."[40] It's impossible to imagine Malcolm the academic having that effect. We academics can barely get our students to turn up at all! This relationship with the audience is not just incidental; it goes to the heart of Malcolm's importance and the limits of academic knowledge. To be able to consistently draw hundreds of people to speeches, carrying the crowd along in agreement, is a testament to the power of the ideas being conveyed. It is even more so when we consider who made up those audiences.

Malcolm drew his legitimacy from representing the masses, the grassroots. These are exactly the people who are excluded from the university. The academic bubble means that at conferences and in articles we are only speaking to other university-trained elites. Even the student body is highly selective. Depending on where you work, you can spend your entire career speaking and writing to mainly White staff and mostly White students, with a sprinkling of those Black people lucky enough to enter the hallowed halls of your institution. But even if you work at a historically Black college or university, your career will be determined by how well you can engage with the Whiteness of academia. That means avoiding or ignoring the audiences that sustained Malcolm. But it is this organic connection to Black communities that makes Malcolm's intellect so vital. There have been attempts to incorporate these kinds of approaches into the university. For instance, Patricia Hill Collins explained that for a Black feminist approach, scholars must have an "ethic of personal accountability," where the community knows they can trust you.[41] But any academic reading this will have to admit that this is *not* standard practice and that the fundamentals of our jobs—writing, teaching, admin—largely keep us away from Black communities. Your promotion or application for tenure will depend on how much time you have committed to the academic bubble. This is the reason that Malcolm distrusted Black academics so much, because we are ultimately in bourgeois positions defined by and in service to Whiteness.

Malcolm's work was, and remains, better than that produced in the academy because it was rooted in the reality of the struggle. His activism *is* his philosophy; they are utterly inseparable. It is impossible to theorize about the struggle without being engaged in it. You cannot understand a concept like Blackness separate from the communities and activism that define it. There is no way to comprehend White supremacy without appreciating the standpoint of those suffering the harsh end of it, or "catching hell" as Malcolm would say. So, I am not going to try to justify Malcolm to the academy. I am not going to give you Malcolm via dead White men like Marx or Sartre or even dead Black men like Du Bois. I am going to give you Malcolm through Malcolm, his speeches and interviews. But the obvious question this raises after everything I have just said is, How can you trust this author, this particular "nincompoop with a PhD," when you can't rely on the rest?

It is true. I am a recovering academic and bear the title of "professor," which I view in a similar way to that of "chief of police." I've been trained in the ways of Whiteness and sold my soul to the academic industrial complex to reach where I am today. But I was also fortunate enough to avoid being taught about race, racism, and Blackness in the university. My parents' bookshelf and activism were my introduction to ideas about Blackness and fights against White supremacy. British school curricula are allergic to talking about racism, and I graduated with the Whitest psychology degree in human history at the University of Bath. By the time I took a sociology second-year class on "race and racism," I had already formed the framework of my thought, which was so deservedly scornful of the mainstream view, the professor had to give me a great grade. Although I have all the White credentials, just like Malcolm I would say that "my alma mater was books."[42] Malcolm's intellectual ideas, along with those of a host of other Black radical thinkers, have been nurturing me for as long as I can remember being able to think. Of everything I am paid to teach and write about now, I learned none of it in a university. I learned it all from Malcolm.

Theory generated in struggle is simply better than that produced in the bubble of academia. Often these ideas travel into the university, but they are slower to do so and their radical impulse is removed. When I heard about critical race theory (CRT) for the first time, its ideas sounded like an echo. That's because I had already heard that racism is a permanent feature of society and the so-called civil rights gains are actually mirages. Those are two of the key premises that Malcolm had been testifying to decades before they reached the halls of academia. So far behind were universities that they made Malcolm look like a prophet. I never take the label of critical race theorist because his work is my theoretical basis, and once the ideas make it into the academy they are lacking Malcolm's radical solution. CRT embraces the critique but ignores the obvious remedy. If racism is a permanent feature of Western society, then the only solution is revolution.

Academic Cedric Robinson is much praised for his book *Black Marxism*, where he is credited with developing the idea of racial capitalism. I promise this notion was circulating long before in Black movement circles. One of the concepts that I always teach, which *is* from Robinson, is that the Negro, with no history, culture, or civilization, was a creation of White supremacy in order to justify slavery.[43] The Negro is more than just an identity; it is an essential creation that made the West possible through our unpaid labor and torture. But as valuable as Robinson's work is, I struggle to recommend it to students, let alone share it among communities off campus. It is a dense academic treatise that is clearly written to try to "elevate" Black thought to the White academy. But when I visited the Schomburg Center, I found the missing chapter was on Malcolm's articulation of the Negro, and I realized it was written more than twenty years before Robinson's book. I was delighted to find Malcolm's words. They outlined the same concept but in ways that were readily understandable. Not only is the theory better, but it is more accessible. This goes back to the importance of the audience. Malcolm was speaking to the masses and so had to present his ideas in ways they could understand. The academic's default audience is the university, which is framed by Whiteness. The convoluted, jargon-filled, unnecessarily complex, and deeply boring style of presentation is the standard by which we are judged. I remember when I wrote my PhD, my supervisor said it was unscholarly to use the phrase "Marcus Garvey never set foot in Africa." I dread to think what he made of the shrug emoji I put in my last book. Malcolm told us to "make it plain" to ensure that we are reaching the right people, not the esteemed White people.[44] I have also tried, with varying degrees of success, to put that politics into action. Following my PhD and learning about the OAAU, I founded the Organisation of Black Unity using the constitution of Malcolm's organization. This has now become Harambee OBU, and, as I will explain later, we are trying to build the organization following Malcolm's blueprint. This includes a website called *Make It Plain*, where we attempt to popularize Black radical ideas in an effort to help develop the program of political education that Malcolm saw as so vital. For me this is not an abstract theoretical discussion but a living theory that I am applying in the real world. One of my main motivations for writing this book is to convince people to join the movement to make Malcolm's vision a reality.

Malcolm left behind the most important intellectual analysis and practical program to overturn White supremacy. The Malcolm myth has distorted how we understand him to such an extent that he has become an empty symbol. For those looking to bring freedom to Black people worldwide, Malcolm is the first person we should look to for a framework to move forward. The purpose of this book is to make plain Malcolm's diagnosis and his solution so that we can pick up the mantle and create the revolution, which is as necessary as it has ever been.

I also stress that there was only evolution in Malcolm's thought after his departure from the Nation of Islam, and that you can see similar themes in his speeches from his time both in and outside of that organization. Therefore, you will find no chronology of events. I have picked out the key parts of Malcolm's ideas, and for the most part I have drawn on his speeches interchangeably (from when he was in the NOI *and* after he left). When necessary, I have indicated where there were departures from earlier thought or an evolution in his ideas, but for the most part I have used quotations from both time periods without making a distinction between them. The fact that this is possible is testament to the continuity in his thought.

Inevitably, in a book like this I am attempting to speak for Malcolm, drawing on his work to outline what his position would have been if he were alive today. I obviously cannot know what Malcolm would actually say had he lived. Martyrdom has frozen him at his most revolutionary, uncompromising best. The depressing lesson of history is that the longer people live, the more they disappoint. It may well be that an older Malcolm would have ended up a fully fledged member of the civil rights fraternity, running for elected office and leaving Betty to marry a White woman. I strongly doubt it with all my being, but I honestly cannot tell you what might have gone on in his head in his later life; I don't profess to be a medium. What I can do with certainty (and a whole load of receipts) is give you the real mission of Malcolm X based on his impressive body of work. If you are serious about fighting for racial justice, it is a political program that, whatever your views are, you must genuinely engage with. Once you cut though the noise of the Malcolm myth, you will find a legacy that either terrifies or inspires you.

2

THAT WICKED RACE OF DEVILS

Contrary to the Malcolm myth, the only real transformation in Malcolm X's life was during his time in prison. In 1946, he was convicted for burglary and went in as a drug-addicted street hustler but came out a committed member of the Nation of Islam in 1952. At the time, the NOI was a small organization led by the Honorable Elijah Muhammad, who claimed to be the Messenger of Allah, meant to lead Black people to the promised land. The NOI drew some inspiration from the Garvey movement, insisting on economic self-reliance and believing in strict segregation of the races. It was founded in 1930 by Wallace D. Fard, who claimed to be the reincarnation of Noble Drew Ali, who founded the Moorish Science Temple in 1913, which blended Islamic ideas and Black politics. Fard also claimed to be the human incarnation of Allah, and the Nation of Islam teaches believers that Fard will return in a spaceship and wipe out the White race. The NOI is shunned by orthodox Islam because it departs so drastically from the teachings of that religion.[1] To be admitted to Mecca, on his famous trip there, Malcolm had to prove he had fully embraced a recognized version of Islam. In reality, the NOI is a cult, complete with dress code (men wear suits and bow ties, women white Islamic dress), segregated living, and fanciful doomsday beliefs. When Malcolm joined, it was a marginal sect, and had he not been recruited, it would probably have remained so. The NOI transformed Malcolm, but he also did the same to the organization. By the time he left, after tirelessly building chapters around the country, it was a national organization with more than seventy-five thousand members.[2] Current estimates put the number of members at between ten thousand and fifty thousand.[3] As I will explain in further detail below, it was in the Nation of Islam that Malcolm began condemning White people as the "wicked race of devils" whose time was up. The myth holds that when he emerged from the NOI cocoon as a civil rights butterfly, he had dropped the negative rhetoric and embraced White people. As with the rest of the myth, this is a dangerous misunderstanding. The Malcolm in the Nation of Islam and the one outside were not two different people; he developed his radical politics while within this regressive organization. To understand Malcolm's politics, we need to trace the evolution of his views, because his eventual position is fundamental to radical Black politics.

The strength of the Nation of Islam was that it reached out to the most neglected members of society, recruiting heavily from those in prison. The NOI sought to rehabilitate those who were lost, clean them up, and bring them into the fold. Prison took Malcolm away from the streets, and he eventually spent his time diving into reading. He described the change in his thinking as being as swift as the fall of melting "snow off a roof," with reading lifting the scales from his eyes.[4] His sister introduced him to the NOI, which truly transformed his life.

As he explained: "I was a very criminal, wayward, backward, uneducated, illiterate, and whatever other negative type of person you could think of until I heard the teachings of Elijah Muhammad. Because of the impact it had on me in giving me the desire to rehabilitate and reform myself . . . and instill such a high degree of racial pride and racial dignity that I realized I wanted to be somebody."[5]

Not only did the teachings of Muhammad reach Malcolm, but they exchanged letters while he was in prison, and Malcolm credited Muhammad with "chang[ing] my whole world."[6] Malcolm was close to Muhammad. He looked up to him as a father figure, recounting that "my faith in Elijah Muhammad was more blind and more uncompromising than any faith that any man has ever had for another man."[7] Malcolm helped build the Nation of Islam into a national, mass organization, becoming its most famous spokesperson until March 1964, when, as he described, he was "put out" of the group by Muhammad.[8] In the Malcolm myth, this split from the NOI is the second transformation, when he abandoned the group's extremist, anti-White, separatist views and began his journey into civil rights international statesmanhood. Nothing could be further from the truth. As he accepted in perhaps his most famous speech, in August 1964, "The Ballot or the Bullet," "I still credit Mr. Mohammed for what I know and what I am. He's the one who opened my eyes."[9]

Malcolm was alive for less than a year outside of the NOI, and the majority of his speeches and interviews were delivered as the group's most prominent minister. Malcolm was initially suspended from the NOI in December 1963 and banned from preaching or speaking to the press for ninety days. The reasons for his suspension speak volumes about why his split from the group was inevitable. After President John F. Kennedy was assassinated, Elijah Muhammad, who led the NOI, declared sorrow for the loss of the president and ordered his ministers to say nothing about his assassination. Muhammad knew how popular Kennedy was, and he did not want to rock the boat or draw negative attention to the organization. Given how controversial and maligned the group was by the mainstream, it might seem strange that their leader would be so conscious of popular appeal. Muhammad was already viewed as an extremist hate teacher, so reveling in the death of the president would have been on-brand. But the secret of the Nation of Islam is that it was never a radical organization that wanted to bring revolution to America or anywhere else. Muhammad's vision was strictly a religious one, and Malcolm explained that his leader prophesied that the time of the White man was at an end, declaring that "before God can set up his new world, God himself must first destroy this evil Western civilization."[10] Due to this approaching divine intervention from God, the NOI did not get its hands dirty in the business of trying to change society, because there was no point. While still in the Nation of Islam, Malcolm remarked that "we rely on God to fight our battles for us."[11] The solution to the problem was to separate from the wicked Whites and wait for God to step in and restore Black people to their rightful place. While they were waiting, Muhammad wanted to spare the NOI and its members any unnecessary attention from White society, which is why he prohibited any comments on Kennedy's assassination. But Malcolm, being Malcolm, couldn't resist speaking his mind.

On December 1, 1963, just nine days after the president's assassination, Malcolm gave a speech entitled "God's Judgment of White America." In the speech, he explicitly called out the "late president" a number of times for his role in watering down the struggles of the Black masses. According to Malcolm, Kennedy was guilty of placing the nonviolent civil rights leaders at the forefront of the struggle by "building them up, and propping them up, in order to hold the Black masses in check, keep them in his grasp, and under his control."[12] He laid responsibility for the failure of America to embrace the divine solution of racial separation squarely at the feet of the "late president" and then promised God's wrath and Armageddon upon those who blocked the righteous path. There was no subtlety whatsoever conveyed in how he thought about the death of Kennedy. But in the Q&A he removed all doubt by responding to a journalist's question about the president's assassination by explaining that, "being an old farm boy myself, chickens coming home to roost never did make me sad; they've always made me glad."[13] Malcolm was suspended from the NOI for being Malcolm, making it plain and telling the truth as he saw it. During his suspension, he also learned the details of Muhammad's infidelities with his secretaries, that he had fathered a number of children and then shunned the women from the NOI because of *their* apparent sin. This shook Malcolm, who had total devotion to the image of the man. He said that he had "believed 100 per cent in the divinity of Elijah Muhammad. . . . I always thought that he believed it himself. And I was shocked when I found out that he himself didn't believe it. And when that shock reached me, then I began to look everywhere else and try to get a better understanding of the things that confront all of us."

Once he started to look, he understood the limits of the Nation of Islam, and when announcing his departure he admitted that the organization had "gone as far as it can" in dealing with the problems confronting Black people.[14] Malcolm's realization did not come to him suddenly during his suspension, but his tension with the NOI's laissez-faire approach to the situation of Black people in the real world was evident for years. Alongside his religious duties, he held "unity rallies" in Harlem where he would invite civil rights leaders and encourage the crowd to agitate for their interests. Malcolm was furious with Muhammad when he prevented him from taking more direct action after the police shot dead Black Muslim Ronald Stokes in Los Angeles in 1962.[15] Stokes had been in a group of unarmed members of the NOI who were coming to the aid of one of their own and a dry cleaner who were being harassed in the streets by the police. Although Stokes approached officers with his hands up, the police shot and killed him and also wounded a number of other NOI members. They then went on to raid the local NOI mosque. Malcolm wanted to back up the rhetoric of the Nation of Islam and retaliate against the police but was ordered to remain calm.

Although he is remembered for invoking violence in his speeches, he never did so in practice, largely because he was constrained by the nonviolent NOI. Once out of the organization, he laid bare his frustration, declaring in 1964 that he had sent a memo to George Lincoln Rockwell, the head of the Ku Klux Klan,

> to warn him that I am no longer held in check from fighting White supremacists by Elijah Muhammad's separatist Black Muslim movement. And that if Rockwell's presence in Alabama causes harm to come to Dr. King or any other Black person in Alabama who's doing nothing other than trying to enjoy their rights, then Rockwell and his Ku Klux Klan friends would be met with maximum retaliation from those of us who are not handcuffed by this nonviolent philosophy.[16]

Given his politics, Malcolm's break with the NOI was inevitable, but the one criticism of Malcolm I would make is that he stayed in the sect for far too long. It was a cult, built around a flawed leader with deeply problematic and fanciful beliefs. Even so, Malcolm never left of his own accord and had to be forced out before he would fully understand that the Nation of Islam's policy was a dead end. Once he had left, he realized his error, regretting that "I was a zombie then, hypnotized. . . . It cost me twelve years."[17] Malcolm's departure from the NOI allowed him the freedom to say and act exactly how he wanted. He rejected the false teachings of Elijah Muhammad, embraced Sunni Islam, and traveled to Mecca and across Africa. This newfound freedom led Malcolm to express that "I feel like a man who has been asleep somewhat under someone else's control. I feel what I am thinking and saying now is for myself."[18]

It is these expressions of freedom that led to the mistaken belief that Malcolm's departure heralded a transformation in his politics. In truth, they mark the beginning of the development of the next chapter in the same book. Malcolm did not abandon any of his analysis, developed over his twelve years in the Nation of Islam. As I lay out his political analysis through this book, you will find that there is a remarkable continuity in his diagnosis of the problem, even if some of the metaphors change. The evolution that was most seemingly dramatic was the shift in how Malcolm saw White people. He admitted to being regretful about shunning White people who were interested in change, and when he broke away from the NOI, he acknowledged that "I find that most White students are more attuned to the times than their parents and realize that something is fundamentally wrong in this country."[19] Under NOI orthodoxy, there was to be no redemption for any White person, but upon leaving the sect Malcolm did leave open the possibility of White people being involved in the struggle. However, the extent of this involvement and how far it changed from his analysis in the NOI have been grossly overstated.

BLOND-HAIRED, BLUE-EYED DEVILS

When Malcolm was in the NOI, he preached the teachings of Elijah Muhammad, including his foundational creation myth. It is a testament to the delusions of the Nation of Islam that members believed that the world is sixty-six trillion years old and was originally a paradise for Black people. At this time, so they said, the moon was part of the earth, and Mars was a satellite of our planet. This was apparently until a dispute broke out between the prominent scientists, who apparently were an essential part of civilization, and one of them decided to try to destroy civilization by drilling to the center of the earth and filling it with explosives. It was the result of that explosion that propelled the moon into orbit around the earth (believe it or not, this is *not* the most ridiculous NOI belief). While recounting this story, Malcolm assured us that "you can't destroy the Black man. . . . The Black man has the most powerful brain in the universe. He is indestructible."[20] The result of the so-called explosion six thousand years ago was that only twelve of the original thirteen tribes on the planet remained, so the evil scientist Dr. Yacub decided to create a new wicked race that he "could teach to lie and rob and cheat and thereby become the ruler of all of the rest of the world."[21] Yacub and his followers were exiled to the Island of Pelan, where he instituted a strict eugenic society to breed the lighter-skinned people together until he reached his goal of "the pale skinned, blue-eyed, blond-haired thing that you call a man."[22] Malcolm went into vivid and elaborate detail, most of which I will spare you, about how they discarded any dark-skinned offspring: "They had to murder off the Black, Brown and Yellow in order to get to the White. And right to this very day the White man by nature wants to murder off the Black, Brown and Yellow. You don't have to teach him how to kill the Black man. He does it for sport. He does it for kicks. He does it because it's in his nature to do it."[23]

Malcolm made it clear that "you're not using the right language when you say the White man. You call it the devil."[24] Apparently, Yacub next taught his creation a "science called tricknology, which is a science of tricks and lies, and this weak man would be able to use that science to trick and rob the world."[25] Tactics of tricknology included that of divide and conquer in order to set the rest of world against each other. The Nation of Islam frequently referred to "dark mankind," and Malcolm explained that the White man is "a minority, and the only way a minority can rule a majority is to divide the majority."[26]

Despite this creation myth's ridiculous aspects, it should be obvious why it is appealing. It offers a history of the world that explains a lot and restores pride to the "indestructible" original Black people. Looking at the history of White supremacy, it is not difficult to believe that White people are evil. As Malcolm declared, "God won't forgive [the White man] for a killing [of] 80 million Black people" through slavery and colonialism. And that is a low estimate. One of the founders of Black psychology, William Cross, used Malcolm as an example in his "Nigrescence" model of Black identity.[27] He argued that Malcolm was originally—"pre-encounter" with prison and the Nation of Islam—just a hustler not thinking about race and acting out the stereotype. He then had his "encounter" with racism in prison and it lifted the scales from his eyes. Once he "immersed" himself in reading, he saw the atrocities committed by White people around the world and became understandably anti-White. This is the NOI, stuck in the anti-White phase. Cross argued that Malcolm eventually stopped being anti-White when he internalized his Blackness and committed to the uplift of the Black people.

Importantly, Cross gives us a way of understanding the Nation of Islam's condemnation of White people as devils, one very different from the racism about Black people that lies at the foundation of White supremacy. For a start, this critique of White people is not a genetic one; it is based on prophecy and their devilish deeds. While in the Nation of Islam, Malcolm admitted that "no one can give biological evidence to show the Black actually is the stronger or superior of the two if you want to make that kind of comparison."[28] There was never any prohibition on serving White customers in NOI stores, nor were they ever treated unequally. The complaints were always about what White people have done—and continue to do. In a speech to an audience in Harlem in 1963, Malcolm described how

> he breaks your legs and then calls you a cripple. He puts out your eyes and says you can't see. Unemployment has forced many of our people into crime, but the real criminal is in the State House. You're not poor accidentally. He maneuvers you into poverty. You're not ignorant accidentally. He maneuvers you into ignorance. You're not a drug addict accidentally. Why this White man maneuvers you into drug addiction. You're not a prostitute accidentally. You have been maneuvered into prostitution.[29]

As I have argued (to bemused-looking academic colleagues), denouncing all White people as devils in this way is in actual fact an *anti-racist* form of argument: We have to set ourselves against White people in order to build ourselves up and to get freedom. Malcolm specifically rejected any comparison of the NOI's views with those of the Klan because their purpose was entirely different: "The Klan in this country was designed to perpetuate an injustice upon Negroes, whereas Muslims are designed to eliminate the injustice."[30] Malcolm repeatedly denounced those who accused the Nation of Islam of spreading hate. After leaving the NOI, he contended that "I don't think that the Black Muslim movement and its hate can be classified as the same degree or type of hate you find in the American society itself, because the hate, so-called, that you see among Black people is a reaction to the hate of the society which has rejected us. In that sense, it is not hate."[31]

Of course, writing off an entire group of people as devils because of their skin color is problematic. But even when he was teaching Black people to distrust, fear, and dislike all White people, the purpose was in order to protect the community, its collective self-esteem, and to foster the ability to separate from White society.

In the Nation of Islam creation myth, once Yacub's devils had tried to infiltrate Black civilization, they were rebuked and forced to march through the desert, eventually settling in the caves of Europe. Malcolm described how

> they didn't have clothes, so by being out there in the cold their hair got longer and longer. Hair grew all over their bodies. By being on all fours, the end of their spine began to grow. They grew a little tail that came out from the end of their spine. . . . And just like a dog, he was crawling around up there. He was hairy as a dog. He had a tail like a dog. He had a smell like a dog.[32]

The references to White people as dogs are commonplace for Malcolm; for example, he pointed out, "They still like to eat raw meat, 'rare,' that's raw. That's the dog in them, that's the animal in them, brother."[33] Malcolm's NOI speeches are peppered with references to some variation of the "blue-eyed, string-headed, bad-smelling" White man.[34] But

Malcolm explained that "this isn't hate teaching, this is love teaching. If I didn't love you I wouldn't be telling you what I'm telling you," because "he's nothing but a walking, talking blue-eyed devil and the day you realize it you'll stop looking to him for a solution to your problems."[35] It's important to understand that the purpose of this preaching was not so that Black people would go and attack, oppress, or colonize White people, but the exact opposite. The Nation of Islam was advising us to avoid the devil altogether. Malcolm rationalized that integration was a dead end, because White people had "no morals, no conscience, so don't waste your time."[36] He warned of the coming Armageddon and that Black people had a choice: "If we integrate, we will be destroyed along with them. If we separate, then we have a chance for salvation."[37]

IT'S THE JEWS

Malcolm has been accused of anti-Semitism because of his disparagement of Jewish people in his speeches. Anti-Semitism is a common charge against the NOI and one of the areas of consensus between the sect and the American Nazi Party.[38] Louis Farrakhan, who has led the cult for over thirty years, is frequently condemned for his anti-Semitism, which includes statements like, "Those who call themselves 'Jews,' who are not really Jews, but are in fact Satan . . . the Arch Deceiver, the enemy of God and the enemy of the Righteous."[39] There is no doubt that anti-Semitism was rife in the Nation of Islam, and while he was a member and its foremost spokesperson, Malcolm would have reflected the beliefs of the organization. But look a bit more closely at Malcolm's condemnation of Jewish people, and you will see he is not criticizing them *because* they are Jewish, but reminding his audience that Jews are White. In a speech in Harlem in 1959 he told the crowd, "If you listen to Elijah Muhammad, the Jew will go broke, the Irishman will go broke, the Italian will go broke. Everyone who is in Harlem robbing you right now will go broke. . . . The Jewish merchant won't have any business, the Italian dope peddler won't have any customers, the cop won't have any skulls to crack."[40] There are some very clear stereotypes being drawn here: the Jewish shopkeeper, Italian mobster, and Irish cop. But the purpose is to remind the audience that they are all White and they are all therefore the devil. The above section of the speech reflects the part of Malcolm that railed against the general economic exploitation of the Black ghetto and is quickly followed with a warning that "money is power and the White man is tricking you out of your money. He does it with whiskey. He does it with cigarettes. He does it with nightclubs and oh boy he does it with churches."[41]

In a later Harlem speech, he argues that "it's the Jews selling you that bad food" who "control the economy of Harlem for the benefit of Israel."[42] Malcolm was peddling in anti-Semitic tropes here, associating Jews with money and a global Zionist conspiracy. But the reason he drew specific attention to Jewish people was not because there was something wrong with being a Jew. His point was that "many of our people would rather believe that the Jews are God's chosen people than to believe that *they* are God's chosen people. . . . Nobody else would put everybody else above him but the Negro."[43] He was reminding the audience that no matter the difficulties Jewish people had faced, however close they were to the bottom of that particular pile, they were still White. They acted like the rest of the wicked race: "They know how to rob you, they know how to be your landlord, they know how to be your grocer. . . . They know how to control everything you've got."[44]

In addition, many Jewish people were part of the civil rights struggle, which made Malcolm even more convinced of the need for the reminder. He specifically chided his audience that "they know how to be your lawyer," in reference to those defending Black civil rights activists, and even more tellingly, "They know how to join the NAACP [National Association for the Advancement of Colored People] and become the president."[45] Jewish people were being painted as the natural ally to Black people, having suffered their own persecution and now standing shoulder to shoulder with them in the struggle for civil rights. Malcolm's intent was to burst that delusional bubble of allyship. Malcolm criticized Jewish Supreme Court Justice Arthur Goldberg, who was seen as a champion of civil rights when he was appointed in 1962. Malcolm took exception to Goldberg's public call for the three million Jews in the Soviet Union to be addressed by the United Nations, while he had stayed silent on the issue for Black Americans: "How can the plight of three million Jews in Russia be qualified to be taken to the United Nations by a man who is a justice in this Supreme Court, and is supposed to be a liberal, supposed to be a friend of Black people, and hasn't opened up his mouth one time about taking the plight of Black people down there to the United Nations."[46]

Malcolm undoubtedly engaged in a number of anti-Semitic stereotypes that were common at the time and prevalent within the Nation of Islam. But there was no specific malice against Jewish people in particular. The message was not that you could not trust Jews because they were Jewish, but that you shouldn't expect anything but trickery from them because they were White.

SOUTHERN WOLF AND NORTHERN FOX

In many ways, Malcolm's warning about Jewish people was very similar to his distinction between the Southern Wolf and the Northern Fox. In 1963, he explained that the Southern Wolf "will show their teeth in a snarl that keeps the Negro always aware of where he stands with them."[47] The Wolf was responsible for the open, vicious hostility toward Black people that was making news around the world: lynchings, police dogs, church bombings, and mobs harassing schoolchildren trying to integrate. This was racism that was easy to see and provoked a response, but Malcolm warned that the Northern Fox was more cunning than the brazen Wolf and instead "show their teeth to the Negro but pretend that they are smiling." In fact, he argued that the Fox, the "White liberal," was the far more dangerous predator because "they lure the Negro, and eagerly run from the growling Wolf, he flees into the open jaws of the smiling Fox."[48]

At the time, the discussion of racism in America was heavily framed around the Wolves in the South. Mamie Till choosing an open casket to display the brutality inflicted on her fourteen-year-old son Emmett, for offending a White woman in Mississippi, is credited with sparking off the civil rights movement in the 1950s. The Montgomery bus boycott in Alabama in 1955 brought Martin Luther King and Rosa Parks into the national spotlight. Civil rights campaigns focused heavily on the issue of desegregation, with a high-profile student sit-in movement launched in North Carolina in 1960. Black and White people from the North took "freedom rides" throughout the South to challenge segregated seating on buses. Alongside desegregation, the key victory of the civil rights movement was on voting rights, which aimed to enfranchise the millions of Black voters who were barred from casting ballots in the South. All the attention was focused on the snarling Southern Wolf's backlash against these mobilizations.

In contrast, the North was the place that Black people fled *to*, away from the evils of the South. During the Great Migration, millions of Black Americans abandoned the former slave states to seek better lives in the North.[49] But Malcolm was keen to remind the refugees that when they reached the North, they would not find the promised land. Instead, in Northern cities Black Americans found themselves "trapped in a vicious cycle of inferior jobs, inferior housing, inferior education which again leads to inferior jobs."[50] While the world was focused on the images of White mobs attacking children trying to integrate Southern schools, Malcolm explained that the efforts in the North were "an even more miserable failure." White families didn't protest, they just "evacuated the schools and built modern schools for themselves out in the suburbs."[51] He frequently railed against the appalling conditions facing people where he lived and laid the blame squarely at the feet of the "White liberals who own the rat-infested apartments in Harlem."[52]

A much more foundational difference than violence between the politics of Malcolm and Martin Luther King is that one organized in the North and the other in the South. Malcolm's firebrand, uncompromising approach would have gotten him lynched in the South. While King's nonviolent, mass-marching tactics completely failed in the Northern context. Malcolm was keen to ensure that people did not fall into the trap of thinking that the North was any less racist than the South. He chastised the "White liberals" that were "making a great fuss over the South only to blind us to what is happening to us here in the North."[53] He rebuked his audiences: "Stop talking about the South. As long as you're south of the Canadian border, you're South." He went on to explain that there was no substantive difference between Northern and Southern politicians, telling the crowd that "in the South, they're outright political Wolves. In the North, they're political Foxes."[54]

In an indication of why Malcolm could not hold his tongue when JFK was assassinated, he had, earlier in that year, singled out the president as a target of his ire: "That 'F' stands for Fox. He's undoubtedly more foxier than any of the others because any time a man can become president and be in office three years and do as little for Negroes as he has done despite the fact that Negroes went for him 80% and he can still maintain the friendly image in the mind of Negroes, I'll have to say he's the foxiest of the foxy."[55] For Malcolm, the White liberal posing as a friend was the embodiment of Yacub's "tricknology," using tricks and lies to control the world. He thought that the Fox was "more cruel and more vicious than the White Wolf in the South" because at least "the Southern Wolves always let you know where you stand." This honesty meant there was no need to convince the Black community that the Wolf was the enemy. But the Fox could literally get away with murder, while deceiving the community into believing they were only trying to help: "These Northern Foxes pose as White liberals, as your friends, as your benefactor, as your employer, as your landlord, as your neighborhood merchant, as your lawyer. They use integration for infiltration. . . . By joining you, they strangle your militant effort towards true freedom."[56] For Malcolm, this was the greatest danger, allowing the Fox to water down the struggles for freedom. It was better to condemn all Whites and keep them out of the movement than to trust the seemingly well-meaning ones and allow yourself to be tricked and controlled. These blanket warnings against the "White man" were attempts to ensure that the urgent needs of the Black masses could not be denied.

This is one of the reasons he was opposed to the civil rights movement, charging that "the job of the Negro civil rights leader is to make the Negro forget that the Wolf and the Fox both belong to the same family. Both are canines; and no matter which one of them the Negro places his trust in, he never ends up in the White House, but always in the doghouse."[57] The closeness of the civil rights leaders to the president was, therefore, not a sign of their power and political influence but rather that they were being controlled like puppets by the cunning Fox who was pulling their strings. This is an analysis Malcolm further developed after he left the Nation of Islam, with the "doghouse" line a recurring theme of his speeches. In the last speech he gave before he died, demonstrating further the continuity of this thought, Malcolm couldn't resist invoking the canine metaphor by joking that before Black people embraced pride in ourselves, "we wanted those long, dog-like noses."[58] Notwithstanding the canine references, there was a further, important shift in his theory of Whiteness after he left the NOI.

WHITE IS AN ATTITUDE

For the Nation of Islam, there was no salvation for the wicked White race of devils. Elijah Muhammad taught that, due to their natural wickedness, White people were barred from entering the Islamic holy city of Mecca. Malcolm learned that this was not true, and when he made the pilgrimage, he recounted that he had "eaten from the same plate, drunk from the same glass, and slept on the same rug—while praying to the same God—with fellow Muslims, whose eyes were the bluest of blue, whose hair was the blondest of blond, and whose skin was the whitest of white."[59] He admitted that this experience had "forced me to rearrange much of my thought-patterns previously held, and to toss aside some of my previous conclusions."[60] "Rearrange" is the perfect word to describe how this experience changed Malcolm's theory on Whiteness and White people. Seeing White people in Mecca and sharing such intimate moments with fellow Muslims meant that he had to "toss aside" the NOI proscription that all White people were by their nature wicked devils. If individual Whites could accept Islam and join in the brotherhood, then they could not all be devils. When

he was asked in 1965 if he still believed that all White people were devils, he replied, "No, I don't believe that. I believe as the Qur'an teaches,
that a man should not be judged by the color of his skin but rather
by his conscious behavior, by his actions, by his attitude towards others and his actions towards others."[61] On his pilgrimage, he had seen
that for his White comrades "their belief in one God had removed the
White from their minds, the White from their behavior, and the White
from their attitude."[62] They were redeemable, after all.

Rather than seeing Whiteness as an inextricable feature of White
people, Malcolm now understood that "White is an attitude more
than it is a color," a way of thinking produced by the need to maintain
White supremacy.[63] In his last recorded speech, given in Detroit, he
explained that

> in Asia or the Arab world or in Africa, where the Muslims are,
> if you find one who says he's White, all he's doing is using an
> adjective to describe something that's incidental about him. . . .
> He's just white. But when you get the White man over here in
> America and he says he's White, he means something else. You
> can listen to the sound of his voice. When he says he's White,
> he means he's boss. . . . He's up there. So that when he says he's
> White he has a little different sound in his voice.[64]

This is an important evolution, the move from condemning all
White people and instead locating Whiteness in a set of attitudes and
actions. After leaving the NOI, Malcolm explained that "I myself do
not judge a man by the color of his skin. The yardstick that I use to
judge a man is his deeds, his behavior, his intentions."[65] In the Nation
of Islam this was partially true, too, in that White people were written

off as devils because of the collective evils of White society. As Malcolm justified it, "I have never heard Muhammad preach hate against anyone. He teaches hate against evil."[66] But in locating that evil within the individual, it misdiagnoses the problem. In the Nation of Islam, it always led to a political powerlessness. The belief that all White people were devils and God was going to annihilate them and redeem the Black masses actually worked to paralyze the believers, keeping them trapped in thinking there was nothing they could do to change the world, other than to have faith. The other problem with the anti-White-people approach is that Whiteness becomes the center of your philosophy. In the NOI creation story, the White devil is the central character around which everything revolves. Being anti-White keeps you focusing on the very thing you say you want to separate from. After leaving the Nation of Islam, Malcolm became anti-Whiteness instead of anti-White. He never stopped castigating the evils of White society but understood that the problem was one that lay beyond individual wicked devils. In a post-NOI speech at Harvard in 1964, he assured the students that "I'm not here to condemn all White people. I use the word 'White people' because it's short, it cuts to the point."[67] But he did still have to use the words "White people," and his fundamental analysis about the ills of society never changed. Relieved from the shackles of being anti-White, Malcolm was able to develop a political program truly based around Blackness.

The notion that this represented a dramatic transformation in Malcolm's thinking about Whiteness is misguided. At least as far back as 1959, Malcolm acknowledged that he was using the description of Whites as a metaphor, explaining: "If he's not a devil then he's the closest thing to one that you'll ever find. . . . [That] man has robbed you deaf, dumb, and blind. Deprived you of civil rights, deprived you of everything a man is supposed to have."[68] In a speech in 1963 at the University of California, Berkeley, he responded to a question about why Cuba had success with overturning racism if White people are devils by outlining how the "Cubans don't refer to themselves either as White people or Black people. . . . The American White man is the one who has laid such stress on being White or being Black." He also stressed that context was central, and that in America "you're dealing with the man who used to have total possession over the Black people in this country as a farmer has possession over his cow, his chicken, his fox. This created an attitude among American Whites that they themselves find almost impossible to eliminate. . . . I personally don't think it will ever be eliminated."[69]

Malcolm didn't come to his understanding of Whiteness as an attitude as some sort of post-NOI epiphany; it was a thread in his thinking the entire time. If context matters, and Cuban Whites were not White devils because of their deeds, then the same was true of American Whites. He just felt there was very little chance of those in America being able to eliminate the devilish attitude. You can certainly criticize the NOI Malcolm for being unaware that the slavery context in Cuba was little different from that of America, as both were slaving nations. But the point about Whiteness was clear, even while he was in the NOI, and so was the fact that his using the phrase "White devil" was a metaphor.

All religions have fanciful creation myths that include stories that aren't taken as absolute truth but that are used to tell us something about the present. You will find very few Christians who believe every story in the Bible as though it is real, and we should look sideways at anyone who does so, just as we would at those who embraced the Nation of Islam tales literally. There is no contradiction between Malcolm teaching the NOI creation story in all its vivid detail while he was part of that movement and his using the White devil as a meta-phor after he left: both have symbolic meaning. The purpose of the metaphor was to warn Black people against integration, infiltration, and being tricked into thinking that there was any freedom possible in wicked Western society. None of this changed for Malcolm once he left the Nation of Islam and supposedly became enlightened.

The attitude of Whiteness is the foundation of Western society, and the result is a devilish social order that must be overturned. Remember, Malcolm was never deluded enough to believe that God was going to bring a rupture that erased the wicked devils, and even when he was still in the NOI he was organizing and urging others to take up the liberation struggle. While he was still a minister, Malcolm often prefaced his remarks with, "The Honorable Elijah Muhammad teaches us," but it is telling how directly he attributed the divine solution to his leader. In a debate with civil rights stalwart Bayard Rustin, who was most responsible for organizing the 1963 March Farce on Washington, Malcolm was pressed on what he believed the solution to the problem of racism was. He stressed Nation of Islam orthodoxy and that "Mr. Muhammad does not believe in a political solution. He says that the primary solution is God. . . . Our entire approach is a religious approach."[70] Even then it was clear this was not a position he was entirely comfortable with, but he toed the party line. Malcolm's attitude to revolution and White people did not dramatically transform when he got out of the NOI. He was just free to express his philosophy on Whiteness without the shackles of the cult and its leader.

WE ARE AGAINST INTERMARRIAGE

Malcolm's shift from the metaphor of White devils to that of Whiteness as being principally an attitude of mind did not lead to any kind of embrace of integration. Where the continuities are clearest is on the issue of integrated relationships. While in the NOI, his distaste for mixed relationships couldn't have been spelled out more clearly: "We are against intermarriage. We don't want to see no Black man with a White woman. We don't want to see no White man with the Black woman. When you see a Black woman out here running around with a White man, straighten her out. I should say straighten her up and straighten him out."[71] This rhetoric was strongly tied to the idea of the White man polluting Black women with their devilish ways and is connected to the need for Black men to "protect *our* women," which we will discuss in Chapter 6. The sentiment is also based on the continued exploitation of Black people and White people's wicked ways:

> These Negroes who go for integration and intermarriage are linking up with the very people who lynched their fathers, raped their mothers, and put their kid sisters in the kitchen to scrub floors. Why would any Black man in his right mind want to marry a lyncher, a murderer, a rapist, a dope peddler, a gambler, a hog eater. . . . Why would any Black man want to marry a devil?[72]

The need to reject interracial relationships went to the core of the political message that Malcolm was expressing in the Nation of Islam and once he left. In an interview with the journalist Louis Lomax in 1963, Malcolm asked, "How can any Negro, man or woman, who sleeps with a White person speak for me?" and then scoffed, "No Black person married to a White person can speak for me!"[73] When Lomax asked him to explain, he replied, "Because only a man who is ashamed of what he is will marry out of his race. There has to be something wrong when a man or a woman leaves his own people and marries somebody of another kind. Men who are proud of being Black marry Black women; women who are proud of being Black marry Black men."

Reclaiming pride in ourselves as Black was an essential ingredient to Malcolm's revolutionary politics. Prior to the transformation from hustler to Malcolm X, he not only dated White women but revered them for their pale skin and straight hair.[74] Once he had committed to Black politics, he understood that to hold a White person as your standard of beauty and object of love demonstrated that a Black person was not loving themselves. Authentically loving Blackness has to mean loving Black people. In a forerunner to the feminist notion that the "personal is political," Malcolm argued that the most intimate choice a person can make is rooted in their political position. He used the example of Black celebrities who were supporting the civil rights movement: "All of those who are used to finance the program of the integrationists, the average so-called Negro celebrity, put all of them in one pile. And as fast as you name them off, you'll find that every one of them is married either to a White woman or a White man." He specifically brought up a meeting between JFK and Black celebrities—including Harry Belafonte, James Baldwin, Lena Horne, and Lorraine Hansberry—who all had White partners, and accused them of "representing their own personal desires" so that they "can mix and mingle" in White society. Their attachment to White people made them inauthentic, meaning that they had a stake in the wicked society that Whiteness has created. Therefore, they could not be trusted to advocate for the masses. Malcolm went on to say that the impact this had was to distance those Black celebrities from the community: "Subconsciously a Negro doesn't have any respect or regard or confidence, nor can he be moved by another Black man who marries a White woman or a Black woman who marries a White man."[75] Personal desire was such an important indicator of political authenticity that it meant embracing interracial relationships was a disqualifying act for Black leadership.

In the Malcolm myth, his departure from the Nation of Islam meant that he "changed his mind on interracial marriage."[76] This inaccuracy is based on an interview Malcolm gave in Canada a few weeks before he died, when he responded to a question about whether he was still against intermarriage: "I believe in recognizing every human being as a human being, neither White, Black, Brown, nor Red. When you are dealing with humanity as one family, there's no question of integration or intermarriage. It's just one human being marrying another human being, or one human being living around and with another human being."[77] However, this is no ringing endorsement of either integration or intermarriage. While in the NOI, Malcolm talked about not judging anyone solely by the color of their skin, and what he appears to be saying here is that, in theory, if there were true equality, then the question of interracial relationships wouldn't be a pressing one because we would all just be part of the human family. He quickly went on to remind the interviewer that "it is the White man collectively who has shown that he is hostile towards integration and towards intermarriage and towards these other strides towards oneness."

In his last speeches, Malcolm clearly outlined how American society was nowhere near being in a place where he could talk in ideal terms of humanity, and that White supremacy was the framework for all interactions from the largest to the most intimate. It is a complete misreading of his position therefore to argue that he was suddenly in favor of interracial relationships after freeing his mind from the NOI. In an interview just eleven days before he was murdered, Malcolm's position couldn't have been any clearer. When asked about interracial relationships, he responded: "Mixed marriages don't solve anything. What are Black men trying to prove? Such Toms need psychoanalysis."[78] The use of the Uncle Tom figure here is telling because, as he explained, the Tom is someone "who wants to identify himself with Whites," and there was no better way to do so than marrying a White person. So against the idea was Malcolm, even after he left the Nation of Islam, that he declared, "We are as against intermarriage as we are against all of the other injustices that our people have encountered."[79] To marry White was to hold back the progress of Black people.

One true evolution in Malcolm's thinking, once he was free of the NOI, was to stop condemning all individual White people, while continuing to relentlessly indict the wicked ways of Whiteness. This was a far more subtle shift than the Malcolm myth has misled us to believe. It was an important move because, ironically, being anti-White centers the very people that you are railing against in your mind. Free from the limits of individualizing racism, Malcolm was more able to explore its structural problems and to devise an actual solution. He maintained the warnings against integration for the whole of his life and never had faith that White people in the West would ever give up their Whiteness. Malcolm left open the opportunity for White people to "help, if they're progressive minded." He also made it clear that his position "doesn't mean that we're anti-White, but it does mean we're anti-exploitation, we're anti-degradation, we're anti-oppression. And if the White man doesn't want us to be anti-him, let him stop oppressing and exploiting and degrading us."[80]

3

STOP SINGING AND START SWINGING

In the Malcolm myth, after leaving the NOI he transformed from a bloodthirsty, anti-White hate teacher into a nonviolent, integration-minded civil rights statesman. The main way this caricature is drawn is through Malcolm's relationship to Martin Luther King. The two are forever linked in the collective memory, trapped in a tragicomic relationship like that of the X-Men's peaceful Professor X and warmongering Magneto. (So powerful is this representation that in 2024 *National Geographic* made an eight-part miniseries, *MLK/X*, dedicated to exploring the relationship between the two.) The historical contrast is not, in itself, a misstep. The two were contemporaries, working on the same issue at the same time and were killed at the same age for their activism. Notwithstanding, they only met once and never worked together because there was a stark contrast between the political visions of the two, who are representatives of fundamentally different ideologies. King is the epitome of the liberal civil rights struggle for justice and recognition, whereas Malcolm is the purest example of the Black revolutionary tradition. The mistake by academics and commentators has been to draw the distinction between the two around the question of violence or nonviolence. This is an easy error to make, considering how directly Malcolm's critique of King revolved around the civil rights leader's complete embrace of nonviolence. Malcolm was so opposed to King on this issue that he privately belittled his opposite number as "Reverend Dr. Chickenwing," suggesting he was too afraid to stand up to the Southern Wolf.[1] But as often as Malcolm chastised those who were nonviolent, violence was *not* a defining feature of his political thought. Violence was simply a tactic made necessary by his radical understanding of the problem facing Black people.

SELF-DEFENSE

In America, Malcolm advocated violence only in terms of self-defense. He was crystal clear when he explained that "I have never said that Negroes should initiate acts of aggression against Whites but where the government fails to protect the Negro he is entitled to do it himself."[2] After leaving the restrictions of the Nation of Islam, he vowed to send in people to protect civil rights demonstrators from the mobs. As part of the revolutionary organization which he founded, the Organization of Afro-American Unity, he promised that the organization would

> train you, show you how to protect yourself. Not so that you can go out and attack someone. You should never attack anybody. But at the same time, whenever you, yourself, are attacked you are not supposed to turn the other cheek. . . . If Martin Luther King was teaching White people to turn the other cheek, then I would say he was justified in teaching Black people to turn

the other cheek . . . but as long as they're not nonviolent, don't you let anybody tell you anything about nonviolence. No. Be intelligent.[3]

Malcolm was stressing the need to address the violence coming from White people that was (and is still) a feature of Black people's lives. Responding to accusations of advocating violence in 1961, he told a journalist: "If a man is putting a rope around my neck, or being violent, when I violently struggle against this lyncher to try and keep him from putting a rope around my innocent neck? Why, you'd be insane to call me violent."[4]

Malcolm used these examples to indict the civil rights leaders' approach to nonviolence, complaining that when "someone comes at you with a rope, when someone comes at you with a gun, despite the fact that you've done nothing, he tells you to suffer peacefully."[5] However, this criticism of the civil rights movement is somewhat unfair. The nonviolence of civil rights was confined to the protests, where the marchers were trained to take the verbal and physical abuse of the White mobs and police and not to respond. But away from the public stage, many self-defense precautions were taken to protect the activists. Robert F. Williams formed an armed defense unit in his North Carolina chapter of the NAACP in 1961, which provided support for nonviolent protests.[6] Williams inspired groups like the Deacons for Defense, which was founded in 1964 to protect civil rights protesters in Jonesboro, Louisiana. The armed group was formed by Earnest Thomas and Frederick Douglass Kirkpatrick, who was part of King's Southern Christian Leadership Conference.[7] In *This Nonviolent Stuff'll Get You Killed*, Charles E. Cobb, a Student Nonviolent Coordinating Committee member who marched with King, explained that the civil rights movement would not have been possible without guns.[8] Once public attention was off the marchers, they were at the mercy of the bloodthirsty Southern Wolves. The civil rights leaders knew their lives were in serious danger, and so armed guards were a necessary feature at the places where the activists were staying. Even if the leaders had objected, the residents would never have let either the activists or themselves be put in mortal danger by not committing to armed self-defense.

Guns were (and remain) a common feature of the South, and many of the residents were army veterans. The locals, and by extension the civil rights activists, could survive only by being prepared to protect themselves. Cobb recalls a time when he witnessed King himself sleeping with a gun under the sofa cushion he was resting on. King referred to self-defense as a "false issue," when he explained that "the right to defend one's home and person when attacked has been guaranteed through the ages in common law."[9] Nonviolence was a demonstration *tactic*; it was not a philosophy that left the activists at the risk of death. In this sense, Malcolm's embrace of violence in self-defense is exactly what he described as "intelligent" and well within the mainstream of Black political thought. Both he and King agreed with the sentiment that "if someone comes knocking on your door with a rifle, you walk out of your door with a rifle."[10]

Given how widespread the use of armed self-defense was in the South by the nonviolent protesters, it is clear that Malcolm's position on violence has been grossly exaggerated. He accused the press of this at the time, complaining that "they call us racist and people who are 'violent in reverse.' This is how they psycho you. They make you think that if you try to stop the Klan from lynching you, you're practicing 'violence in reverse.'"[11] The press highlighting Malcolm's violent rhetoric was a key mechanism for building the foundation of the Malcolm myth of the violent, hate-preaching demagogue.

Although there were, in practice, synergies with the civil rights movement on self-defense, Malcolm did depart strongly from their thinking on the idea of nonviolence as a strategy. He could not believe that the civil rights leaders would take the beatings, police dogs, and even murders without fighting back. For Malcolm, there was no use in taking abuse, as it would not lead to any meaningful change. He declared that "you can't ever reach a man if you don't speak his language. If a man speaks the language of brute force, you can't come to him with peace."[12] Thus Malcolm believed that civil rights supporters supplicating themselves on the altar of nonviolence was pointless, and the armed self-defense they practiced in private should have been adhered to on the marches as well. He vowed to send protection to the civil rights marchers in the South in order to maintain their human dignity.

It wasn't just the principle of nonviolence that angered Malcolm but the very nature of the tactics themselves. Sit-ins, where groups would go into segregated places and refuse to move, were a common feature of the civil rights movement. But Malcolm couldn't have been much more scornful of the tactic:

It's not so good to refer to what you're going to do as a sit-in. That right there castrates you. Right there it brings you down. What goes with it? What? Think of the image of someone sitting. An old woman can sit. An old man can sit. A chump can sit, a coward can sit, anything can sit. Well, you and I been sitting long enough and it's time for us today to start doing some standing and some fighting to back that up.[13]

The idea that a sit-in "castrates you" goes to the heart of much of the feminist criticism of Black Power in general and Malcolm's politics in particular. Black movements have often been reduced to a one-dimensional quest to reclaim "Black manhood," and Malcolm's appeal to stand up and show some testicular fortitude could certainly be read in that light.[14] In his 1961 debate with James Baldwin, he explained that the "Honorable Elijah Muhammad's" program differed from the sit-in movement because "he's trying to make us men. . . . Students around the world are standing up for their rights, fighting for their rights, but here in America the so-called Negro will allow themselves to be maneuvered under a tag of sit-in. . . . The name describes its nature. It's a passive thing."[15]

We will critique Malcolm's views on women and gender politics in Chapter 6, but there is little doubt that the patriarchal outlook of the NOI framed Malcolm's positions even after he left. Real men don't turn the other cheek; they punch back. Being awake to the hell that had been wrought on the Black man in America meant rejecting the subservient, eyes-down approach to the White man. To claim our dignity we had to meet strength with strength. Malcolm was against the politics of nonviolence, but he was not promoting violence for the sake of violence. He never suggested picking up the gun or striking back as a way to reclaim a lost so-called manhood. He famously declared, "Be peaceful, be courteous, obey the law, respect everyone; but if someone puts his hand on you, send him to the cemetery."[16] This was crucial to gaining Black personhood, to demand the respect that was our right at birth.

The rejection of nonviolence was also connected to his religious differences with leaders like Martin Luther King, whom he rebuked for their "wishy-washy love thy enemy" approach.[17] He contrasted the passive approach of the Christian church leaders with the message from Islam, which he marked out as a "good religion, that old-time religion . . . that Ma and Pa used to talk about: an eye for an eye, and a tooth for a tooth, and a head for a head, and a life for a life."[18] Malcolm liked to throw jabs at Christianity for its role in pacifying Black resistance. He once drew laughter and shouts of approval from a crowd for pointing out that "when he's [the White man] putting a rope around your neck he calls for God and you call for God. And you wonder why the one you call never answers you." But he also frequently spoke in churches and counted preachers such as Reverends Milton Galamison and Albert Cleage as brothers in the struggle. The problem for Malcolm was not a theological disagreement but a political one. He saw the insistence on nonviolence as a tactic of White liberals to water down the revolutionary passion of the Black masses, warning them not to "struggle with the ground rules that the people you're struggling with have laid down."[19] This was particularly true given the fact that these were not rules that White society followed when under attack.

Malcolm reminded his audiences that "he's only nonviolent when he's on your side. . . . But when he's on his side he loses all that patience for nonviolence."[20] This theme was cited as early on as 1961 in a debate with James Baldwin and then in his classic "Message to the Grassroots" speech in 1963. Speaking of the Second World War, Malcolm quipped that "when the Japanese attacked Pearl Harbor, he didn't say get nonviolent. He said praise the Lord but pass the ammunition."[21] Worse than the hypocrisy of America preaching nonviolence "on Sunday but not practicing it any day," Malcolm chastised, was his audience's role in exporting American violence overseas but refusing to stand up for their own people at home: "The White man sent you to Korea, you bled. He sent you to Germany, you bled. He sent you to the South Pacific to fight the Japanese, you bled. You bleed for White people. But when it comes time to seeing your own churches being bombed and little Black girls being murdered, you haven't got no blood."[22]

Malcolm truly could not believe that people would not go to any means to defend their communities. He explained that the reason Black people fell for the trick of embracing nonviolence was the belief that they needed to keep White people onside in order to join them at their abundant table. It was "dangling this integration goal" in front of those struggling for freedom. The tantalizing thought of being able to achieve equality in White society "disabled them, nullified their ability to fight like a man for something that is their right, rather than to just sit around and beg and wait for the White man to make up his mind that they are worthy."[23] Ceding our power to those who had ill intentions was the ultimate betrayal of the Black population, and this is the essential context for the notion of a sit-in being an act of castration.

To "castrate," in Malcolm's words, is to take away the vitality and strength of the movement. It is notable that in the same speech he specifically invoked the image of an "old man" and an "old woman" sitting, highlighting youth as a key indicator of the movement's power and success. After he left the Nation of Islam, he explained that his new organization would deliberately have an "accent on the youth," because "they have less stake in this corrupt system."[24] The young were the "dissatisfied, uncompromising element" that would not be led astray by the powers that be.[25] This was the real danger of nonviolence for Malcolm: that it weakened the movement at the behest of the White benefactors of the civil rights struggle. Castration was just one of the many metaphors Malcolm used to talk to this neutering or pacifying of the revolutionary demands of the grassroots.

A RACIAL POWDER KEG

For Malcolm, the masses of Black people were so disillusioned by both the situation they found themselves in and the slow pace of change that they were ready to explode. He accused civil rights leaders of "sweet talking" the White man and downplaying the ill feelings of those trapped in the ghetto. Both in and out of the NOI, he staked his credibility on representing the most downtrodden, and he explained that "the only way to get support of the Black masses is to say how they think and how they feel."[26] Integral to achieving this was to tell the White man "about the hell you've been catching and let him know that if he's not ready to clean his house up, he shouldn't have a house. It should catch on fire and burn down."[27]

While in the Nation of Islam, Malcolm represented the anger of the masses in fiery speeches and warned of the coming racial Armageddon. Responding to the redemptive spirit of the civil rights leaders, Malcolm chided, "You're really out of your mind if you want to forgive him. . . . Ask God to kill him, to do unto him what he has done unto you."[28] These condemnations of White people were where Malcolm's anti-White reputation was burnished. At a funeral for Muslims who had been killed by the police in LA in 1962, he referred to the recent crash of a plane full of White people from the South as divine justice. Later, scoffing at the idea of integrated toilets, he said, "The only way I want to go to the toilet with them is to flush them down with the rest of that stuff. Flush him right down the drain with the rest of his kind."[29] Malcolm used this rhetorical anger to represent the feelings of the masses. He sensed the power of their animosity and predicted that "1964 will be America's hottest year, a year of much racial violence and much bloodshed."[30] With all the tensions building up, he believed that there was no way it could not explode.

They're fed up. They've become disenchanted. They've become disillusioned. They've become dissatisfied, and all of this has built up frustrations in the Black community that makes the Black community throughout America today more explosive than all of the atomic bombs the Russians can ever invent. Whenever you got a racial powder keg sitting in your lap, you're in more trouble than if you had an atomic powder keg sitting in your lap. When a racial powder keg goes off, it doesn't care who it knocks out the way.[31]

Violence was the authentic representation of the masses, their legitimate anger that demanded to be expressed. Nonviolence was inauthentic, because it aimed to control the fury, to put out the fires burning in the hearts of the Black community. He believed that these violent urges were produced by the oppression of White supremacy and therefore should not be resisted. Malcolm accused the civil rights leaders of being sent in to anesthetize the masses:

It's like when you go to the dentist, and the man's going to take your tooth. You're going to fight him when he starts pulling. So he squirts some stuff in your jaw called novocaine, to make you think they're not doing anything to you. So you sit there and 'cause you've got all of that novocaine in your jaw, you suffer peacefully. Blood running all down your jaw, and you don't know what's happening. 'Cause someone has taught you to suffer—peacefully.[32]

Malcolm defended the violence that erupted onto the streets in the urban rebellions that hit major cities in the 1960s. He rejected the idea that the riots were "mindless" and destroying their own neighborhoods. He reminded his audiences that the houses and properties in the ghetto were not owned by Black people but by those who were oppressing them. So when the fuse was lit and the powder keg went off, "the merchant is not there, the landlord is not there; the one he considers to be his enemy isn't there. So they knock at his property . . . knock down store windows and set fire to things." Though Black people lived in these neighborhoods they didn't own them, so they were "attacking White property."[33] The violence on the streets was the product of "a corrupt vicious hypocritical system that has castrated the Black man and the only way the Black man can get back at it is to strike it in the only way he knows how."[34] Not only was this expression of violence justified, but it was necessary, to let the White power structure know just how dire the situation was. We see the same rage erupt every so often on the streets, in urban rebellions that I can never call riots. When the powder keg explodes, you have to blame the society involved for creating those explosive conditions.

Listening to hours of Malcolm's speeches, I can't think of anything that made him angrier than the thought of puppet civil rights leaders pacifying the rowdy masses. His denunciation of the March on Washington as a "farce," "a circus with clowns and all," was due to how civil rights leaders put a brake on the militancy of its mobilization. I once thought Malcolm must have been exaggerating when he recounted the story, but British journalist Gary Younge has since corroborated his retelling of events.[35] There had been talk of a major march on Washington for years. Malcolm said that the first explosion was in Birmingham, Alabama, in 1963, where he had seen that the people had "beg[u]n to stab the crackers in the back and bust them upside their head." President Kennedy sent in the National Guard to quell the trouble, which revealed the feelings of the would-be marchers. When there was further resistance from Congress to Kennedy's civil rights bill, this lit the fuse for the masses. They were ready for action and started saying, "We're going to march on Washington, march on the Senate, march on the White House, march on the Congress, and tie it up, bring it to a halt; don't let the government proceed. They even said they was going out to the airport and lay down on the runway and don't let no airplanes land."[36]

The prospect of civil disorder on the streets of the capital terrified the president, who told the major civil right leaders that they needed to call off the march. But the leaders couldn't stop it because they didn't start it, and they explained to their benefactors that "these Negroes are doing things on their own. They're running ahead of us." In keeping with the cunning of other White liberals, Kennedy knew exactly what to do, reassuring King and the rest that "I'll put you at the head of it. I'll endorse it. I'll welcome it. I'll help it. I'll join it." Kennedy then proceeded to get White wealthy backers to support the march, and the fuse on the racial powder keg was put out, allowing the barrel to roll safely through the streets of Washington. Malcolm decried the fact that the integration of Black and White in the organization and in the march itself weakened the protest: "It's just like when you've got some coffee that's too Black, which means it's too strong. What you do? You integrate it with cream; you make it weak. If you pour too much cream in, you won't even know you ever had coffee. It used to be hot, it becomes cool. It used to be strong, it becomes weak. It used to wake you up, now it'll put you to sleep."

This is why he steadfastly argued that our activism needed to be Black, and to avoid White people. Not because there was something genetically wrong with the devils but because it would dilute the militancy of Black politics. He explained of the march that "they didn't integrate it; they infiltrated it," and once it was under White people's control, the Black masses "ceased to be angry. They ceased to be hot. They ceased to be uncompromising." In fact, Malcolm says, "it even ceased to be a march. It became a picnic, a circus." This criticism made it into the *Autobiography*, where Malcolm was incredulous: "The marchers had been instructed to bring no signs—signs were provided. They had been told to sing one song: 'We Shall Overcome.' They had been told how to arrive, when, where to arrive, where to assemble, when to start marching, the route to march. First aid stations were strategically located—even where to faint!"[37] Malcolm was exasperated because the march organizers had taken the legitimate anger of the masses and turned it into a "performance that beat anything Hollywood could ever do."[38] He warned that no matter how much the powers that be tried to dampen the fuse, the powder keg would explode.[39]

He was keen to stress that he was not advocating for the violence that would erupt, only that it was inevitable given the conditions under which people had to struggle. Although he was not inciting violence, unlike the civil rights leaders he was neither condemning nor trying to prevent it. Violence on the streets was the "chickens coming home to roost," and Malcolm hoped that the "racial explosion" in the United States could "ignite the racial powder keg that exists all over the planet that we call Earth."[40]

THE BLACK REVOLUTION

A consistent feature of Malcolm's political ideas was the international nature of both the oppression of White supremacy and its antidote. One of the reasons he was so keen that the desperate urges of the Black community should not be watered down was because he saw them as part of the worldwide "Black revolution" that could topple Western society. He reminded his audiences of the violence committed by America and other colonial powers across the globe to protect their interests: "They're violent in Korea, they're violent in Germany, they're violent in the South Pacific, they're violent in Cuba, they're violent wherever they go."[41] He drew particular attention to Congo, where the CIA, in league with the French and Belgians, facilitated the murder of the first elected prime minister, Patrice Lumumba, in 1960.[42] Lumumba became a martyr and iconic figure for the Black revolutionary cause because he wanted the African nation to control its vast mineral resources rather than to continue to allow the West to steal its wealth out of the ground. When Lumumba's supporters rose up, Malcolm described how "planes were dropping bombs on African villages. When these bombs strike, they don't distinguish between enemy and friend. They don't distinguish between male and female. When these bombs are dropped on African villages in the Congo, they are dropped on Black women, Black children, Black babies."[43]

Hopefully, it should by now be clear how Malcolm saw the violence at the heart of White society as connected to his NOI denunciation of White people as devils. There were so many historical and contemporary examples of the evils that the West spread across the world that it was difficult to avoid the wickedness of the White man. He understood that painting it in such simple terms reduced the nuances of the situation, but these broad brushstrokes were an essential part of his ambition to make it plain. He repeatedly insisted, "We're not for violence, we're for peace, but the people we're up against are so violent you can't be peaceful when you're dealing with them."[44] The difference between Whites being irredeemable devils hell-bent on oppressing dark mankind and Whiteness being a system of meaning necessary for neocolonial domination really is purely semantic if you are on the harsh receiving end of it. For the Congolese villagers being blown to pieces by American bombs or the thousands lynched for the crime of being Black in America, the White man might just as well have been a blond-haired, blue-eyed devil. This is why Malcolm never dropped the references to the "fork-tongued" White man, whom he accused of "talking out both sides of their mouths" by practicing horrendous violence and telling Black people they had to be nonviolent.[45] This trickery was a key feature of the devilish ways of White society.

Malcolm pointed out that American society was built on violence and reveled in it. Chiding the school system for the lessons he was unlucky enough to receive there, he recalled how the founders of America, Patrick Henry and George Washington, went to war to liberate themselves from the English Crown: "There wasn't nothing nonviolent about ol' Pat, or George Washington. 'Liberty or death' is what brought about the freedom of Whites in this country."[46] He explained that the American Revolution was achieved through "bloodshed," because that is a feature of all revolutions, including the French, Chinese, and Russian. He rebuked and reminded the audience that "you haven't got a revolution that doesn't involve bloodshed. And you're afraid to bleed." At the time, much was being made of the civil rights so-called revolution that was reshaping America through nonviolent protest. But Malcolm scoffed at this: "Many of our people are using this word 'revolution' loosely, without taking careful consideration of what this word actually means." The civil rights reformist approach of trying to modify the American system did not qualify as revolutionary in the least for Malcolm: "Revolution is bloody. Revolution is hostile. Revolution knows no compromise. Revolution overturns and destroys everything that gets in its way. . . . Whoever heard of a revolution where they lock arms, as Reverend Cleage was pointing out beautifully, singing 'We Shall Overcome'? Just tell me. You don't do that in a revolution. You don't do any singing; you're too busy swinging."

Malcolm implored those in America to join the real Black revolution that was "sweeping Asia, sweeping Africa, is rearing its head in Latin America."[47] The worldwide movement against racial oppression was always the solution for Malcolm, and he told his audiences that independence was not won in places like Kenya with passive resistance. The world order was shifting because people across the globe were taking up arms against the same oppressor with his boot on the neck of the Black American population: "The dark people are waking up. They're losing their fear of the White man. No place where he's fighting right now is he winning. Everywhere he's fighting, he's fighting someone your and my complexion. And they're beating him. He can't win any more. He's won his last battle."[48]

The only times when Malcolm advocated the use of violence other than for self-defense was in the context of liberation struggles in the former colonies. In those nations where Black people were the majority, he argued that violence was not only justified but the only solution for a true revolution. He praised the guerrilla tactics of freedom fighters in the Global South.

Guerilla action takes heart, takes nerve, and he [the White man] doesn't have that. [Cheering.] He's brave when he's got tanks. He's brave when he's got planes. He's brave when he's got bombs. He's brave when he's got a whole lot of company along with him. But you take that little man from Africa and Asia; turn him loose in the woods with a blade. [Cheering.] That's all he needs. All he needs is a blade. And when the sun comes down—goes down and it's dark, it's even-Stephen.[49]

This embrace of violence in the homelands is testament to Malcolm's understanding of violence as a tactic and not a philosophy. He recognized that, with a Black minority in America, there was no point in trying to start an armed insurrection. This would, of course, be defeated by the might of the majority society, which was the most bloodthirsty that ever existed. But in the former colonies it was possible to overthrow the corrupt system and build anew. Malcolm was calling on his audiences in America to draw inspiration from those revolutionary movements and to adopt their spirit of uncompromising action. Taking up the mantle of the Black revolution meant expanding the scope from the "American scene" and seeing ourselves as part of a global "majority" and White people as the "microscopic minority."[50] To do so meant that we would not be confined to the national struggle and demonstrated why there was no need to "fight a battle like the odds are against us."[51] Malcolm explained that, due to the divide-and-conquer tactics of the imperialists, dark mankind was separated like fingers on an open hand. The result was to rob us of our power: "If I take my hand and slap, you won't even feel it . . . because all these digits are separated." The solution to regaining a position of strength was simple: "All I have to do to put you back in your place is bring those digits together."[52] In the West, this did not mean guerrilla warfare but embracing a militancy of attitude that would scare governments into treating their Black subjects with dignity. In 1964, Malcolm argued for the creation of a guerrilla group like the Mau Mau who fought against the British in Kenya, stating, "In Mississippi we need a Mau Mau. In Alabama we need a Mau Mau. In Georgia we need a Mau Mau. Right here in Harlem, in New York City, we need a Mau Mau."[53] But this was in his introduction to civil rights legend Fannie Lou Hamer, who was recounting the torture she had been through in Mississippi. The role of the Mau Mau in America would have been to ensure that Black people were not being brutalized, rather than to topple the government there.

Malcolm used the threat of violence in the racial powder keg to pressure the government into making meaningful changes. In 1964, rumors were rife that there was a gang of Black Muslims, the "Blood Brothers," formed with the intent to violently attack White people. Malcolm was, at the very least, seen as the inspiration for such a group, and when he returned from his first trip to the Middle East and Africa he addressed the issue. He made it clear that he did not "know why anybody should be sad in any shape or form if such a group does exist" and argued that the question should rather be, "If they do not exist, should they exist?" He had just visited Algeria, which had recently liberated itself from French colonial rule in a violent and bloody struggle. Connecting the two colonial situations, he pointed out that the

> same conditions . . . that forced the noble people of Algeria to resort eventually to the terrorist-like tactics that were necessary to get the monkey off their back, those same conditions prevail today in America in every Negro community. . . . You'll see terrorism that will terrify you and if you don't think you'll see it you're trying to blind yourself to every historic development that is taking place on this earth.[54]

Malcolm knew that he didn't create the coming flood of violence but, with his apocalyptic warnings of bloodshed, he acted as the canary in the coal mine for the United States, and his predictions came to pass with the urban rebellions that rocked America during the 1960s. Malcolm conveyed the simple message that it would be either "freedom for everybody, or freedom for nobody."[55]

Malcolm's use of violence was in the form of metaphor, most eloquently expressed in his "Ballot or the Bullet" speech, where he offered America an olive branch, a way to avoid racial Armageddon. He argued that the United States was the "only country in history, in the position actually to become involved in a bloodless revolution. . . . All she's got to do is give the Black man in this country everything that's due him, everything."[56] If the government failed to deliver freedom through the "ballot," then it would have to deal with the consequences of the "bullet," which was the exploding racial powder keg. He expanded on this metaphor in a later address when asked if he would encourage Black people to register to vote. Malcolm replied that he was setting up a voter registration drive, and this became a key activity of his Organization of Afro-American Unity. He explained:

> Registering is all right, that only means "load your gun." Just because you load it doesn't mean you have to shoot it. You wait until you get a target and make certain that you're in a position to put that thing up next to the target, and then you pull the trigger. And just as you don't waste bullets at a target that's out of reach, you don't throw ballots just to be throwing ballots.[57]

Malcolm argued that Black people could sway elections with their voting power and therefore needed to use it as a resource to pry leverage. This use of violence as a metaphor to encourage voting has been wildly misread in the Malcolm myth as evidence of his supposed transformation into a civil rights reformist before his tragic death. But in fact, he had managed to persuade Elijah Muhammad to allow the NOI "to announce the possibility of Muslims voting" in 1963, worked with local civil rights leaders, and praised Harlem Congressman Adam Clayton Powell, even while he was still in the NOI.[58] Malcolm met with Cuban President Fidel Castro in 1961 because he was part of a delegation organized by the mayor, with the support of the police, to welcome dignitaries to Harlem.[59]

The Nation of Islam was based on a religious and economic Black nationalism, which sought to build financial and physical independence for Black people. Malcolm never abandoned those aims; he just radicalized them. He never saw the ballot as a solution to the problem of racism, but it was a lever that could be pulled to gain some more control over the communities we were trapped in. We will explore Malcolm's solutions more fully later, but he aimed to link up the African American struggle with those of Black people in Africa and embraced the solution of a physical return to the continent to build a new future. But that was his "long-range program" that he knew could not happen for years. So in the "short range," he demanded "that we must eat while we're still here, we must have a place to sleep, we must have clothes to wear, we must have better jobs, we must have better education."[60] The ballot was not going to heal the wounds of racism but could provide a bit of pain relief. It would not solve the problem, but Malcolm expressed a belief that "through politics and through the politician you can actually change the deplorable school situation in Harlem."[61] This was an idea later picked up by the Black Panther Party, which instituted food, medical, legal, and educational programs to aid the community in their "survival pending revolution."[62] It is a grave mistake to confuse Malcolm's efforts to support the community with his attempt to liberate it. The violent metaphors helped to infuse the politics with militancy and connect the domestic struggle with the worldwide uprisings against White supremacy.

The other misreading of Malcolm's relationship to violence is to drain it of all its intent. In this version of the myth, he was just a fiery preacher and his calling wrath on the White man was nothing more than empty rhetoric. I even read one academic article that tried to intellectualize his "lack of organized, violent attack against White America" as rooted "in his earlier experiences as a hustler and confidence man. After all, a hustler may sometimes succeed by threatening violence, but seldom are such threats realized."[63] If the publishers let me include a "face palm" emoji, I certainly would have put one here. It is true that Malcolm never committed any acts of political violence, but that was entirely consistent with his program. As I have already explained, organizing a violent attack would have gone against the very basic principles of that program. In the Malcolm myth, "by any means necessary" captures the essence of his views, and is taken to center violence at the heart of his message. But little could be further from the truth when understanding his politics. Malcolm saw self-defense as necessary because we are dealing with the most violent, bloodthirsty wolf of a society that has ever graced the earth. Malcolm diagnosed violence as part of the condition facing Black people across the world. The revolutionary struggle in the former colonies had to pick up the gun to dislodge the violent oppressor. Violence was, and remains, ever present, the backdrop that both defines and maintains our oppression. The issue was simply a matter of fact for Malcolm: "I believe it's right to be nonviolent with people who are nonviolent. But when you're dealing with an enemy who doesn't know what nonviolence is, as far as I'm concerned you are wasting your time."[64] In fact, his main use of violence was actually to reject nonviolence, not to make the case for armed insurrection. As we discussed above, he saw the militant non-violent approach of the civil rights movement as a con, a game played by White liberals to take away the power from the angry Black masses.

Contrary to the Malcolm myth, violence was not a major part of Malcolm's political program for building revolutionary politics in the West. Malcolm's discussions of violence were central to his analysis of the system and stemmed from his critique of Whiteness and also his understanding of racism as a permanent feature of Western society. He believed that White society was the most violent one that had ever existed and we therefore had to defend ourselves from brutality, that we shouldn't worry about keeping White people onside because the system could never give us freedom. Malcolm was not advocating violence but completely rejecting nonviolence because of his radical understanding of the world.

4

A CHICKEN CAN NEVER LAY A DUCK EGG

To fully understand Malcolm's rejection of nonviolence, we need to explore his analysis of the problem of racism in society. In trying to comprehend the nature of White supremacy, he insisted that "dealing with the condition itself is not enough. We have to go to the cause of it all, to the root of it all."[1] This quotation is reminiscent of Angela Davis explaining that "radical simply means grasping things at the root."[2] To make it plain meant more than to communicate in a simple manner—it was also to strip the analysis down to the basics. Malcolm's theory is so insightful because it gets to the heart of the matter, ignoring the distractions and diversions that can lead us astray when trying to understand the world. For Malcolm, the West was irredeemable, with racism being the basic operating system. This fundamental truth about society shaped his analysis and necessitated a revolutionary solution.

In developing this theory, he predated much of the academic literature that emerged decades after his death. Critical race theory has come to prominence because of its diagnosis of the "permanence of racism" in American society.[3] The idea that the nation was founded on and is perpetuated by racism has turned the stomachs of the patriots proud of America. The backlash against CRT has been shocking; in America, the first Trump White House ramped up the campaign by banning "un-American" ideas from receiving federal funding.[4] Since then, more than thirty states have limited schools and universities' teaching of supposedly dangerous ideas in their curricula, with more than one thousand books banned.[5] In Britain, so little about racism is taught in the curriculum that we have had decades-long campaigns just to include the nuts and bolts. Despite this, in the aftermath of the Black Lives Matter summer of 2020, the then equalities minister, Kemi Badenoch, felt the need to explain to schools that teaching "critical race theory as fact . . . is breaking the law."[6] CRT has become the bogeyman haunting the dreams of the narrative about progress. I came across this school of thought as an undergraduate, but on reading the literature, I knew it was an idea I had heard before. It didn't take me long to locate the source of the original in the work of Malcolm. From his days in the Nation of Islam until his death, he diagnosed racism as lying at the heart of the Western system. This is the building block upon which the rest of his theory is built.

CATCHING HELL

As a member of the Nation of Islam, Malcolm spent a good deal of time chastising his Black audiences for their moral failings and vices. Part of the appeal of the NOI to the Black community was that it cleaned up those on the street. As a Nation of Islam minister, he told a crowd in LA in 1962 that "we take the dice out of your hand and whiskey out of your head."[7] Some respected commentators, like Professor Robin Kelley, have interpreted this inclination as "part of a movement that tried to turn the most lumpen Negroes into respectable (by bourgeois standards, at least), well-mannered, 'civilized' Black men and women."[8] There is no doubt that while Malcolm was in the NOI his rhetoric overlapped with right-wing personal-responsibility arguments that laid the blame for the problems facing Black people upon their ghetto lifestyles.

Louis Farrakhan—who has denied being involved in Malcolm's assassination, saying that he may have "created an atmosphere" that led to the murder, but insisting he played no role in the killing—eventually became the leader of the Nation of Islam, and the high-water mark of his reign was the Million Man March in 1995. The march took a crowd of Black men to the Washington Monument so that Farrakhan could help them to "atone to God for our failure to be the providers, the protectors, the defenders of our women and children."[9] Apparently, all we needed to do was to work hard, to stop gambling, drinking, and doing drugs, and, of course, to get married to the mothers of our children if we wanted to end the problems in our communities. The march was like cotton candy to White Republicans, who supported the focus on moral virtues that meant they could ignore the actual problem of racism.[10] No doubt, for the NOI, bourgeois respectability and civilizing the savages in the urban jungles was a major step toward liberation. But remember, Malcolm's departure from the cult was because his politics were ultimately opposed to their so-called solutions. Given Malcolm's evisceration of the Farce on Washington, I struggle to think how strongly he would have blasted the Million Man March. I'm actually laughing thinking about it. At least the 1963 march aimed for "jobs and freedom." It might have been a circus, but the leaders were trying to persuade the White man into granting some concessions. But marching with the backing of White Republicans to apologize for *our* lack of morals? I've never heard Malcolm swear but now I can imagine it! When he wanted the NOI to get involved in some action, I can absolutely guarantee that Farrakhan's parade was not what he had in mind. He said that Hollywood couldn't have produced the Farce; I doubt his worst nightmares could have conjured up the jamboree.

When Malcolm drew attention to the afflictions harming the Black community, he was not doing so to urge us to save ourselves by becoming bourgeois. He made it clear in his speeches that those in the ghetto were "trapped in a vicious cycle," decrying how "we are forced to live in the poorest section of the city, we attend inferior schools, we have inferior teachers, we get an inferior education. The White power structure downtown makes sure that when we do graduate, we won't be good for anything but the dirtiest subservient poorest-paying jobs that no one else wants."[11]

Unlike Farrakhan, he was not blaming Black people for our situation because of moral failings; he was indicting the system for creating the conditions where immorality can fester. He frequently railed against the "rat-infested dens" and overcrowded conditions in places like Harlem that bred "ignorance, poverty, disease, sickness," where it "seems like there is no escape so we turn to drugs and crime."[12] This was a trap to keep the community down, which was caused by the government creating the conditions for crime and thus the opportunities for them to arrest Black people: "You can't get into a whiskey bottle without getting past the government seal. You can't crack open a deck of cards without getting past the government seal. The White man makes the whiskey and then puts you in jail for getting drunk.

He sells you the cards and the dice and then puts you in jail when he catches you using them."[13]

Malcolm decried the failure of the police to deal with "drug trafficking," "gambling," plus "prostitution and all of these evils that are destroying the moral fiber of our community." He thought this was by design: the conditions were a key mechanism to hold the Black community back. Once out of the NOI, he continued to demand that the community clean up its act, take the situation into our own hands by rejecting the poison and criminality being foisted onto us by our oppressors.

Rather than embrace the savages in the urban jungle stereotype that was behind the Million Man March, he challenged the notion that the Black community was defined by criminality. He indicted the White press, which, he said,

> inflames the White public against Negroes and the police are able to use it to paint the Negro community as a criminal element. Then this automatically paves the way for the police to move into the Negro community exercising gestapo tactics, stopping any Black man who is on the sidewalk, whether he is guilty or whether he is innocent. . . . They can go in and question, brutalize and murder. . . . This makes the Negro community a police state.[14]

Malcolm frequently referred to the Black community as being treated as if they were in a police state and continued to condemn the press for creating the imagery to back up the brutal policing of Blacks. In one of his last speeches, he echoed his NOI preaching about the "tricknology" or "science of tricks and lies" practiced by the White devils. He had stripped back the anti-White rhetoric while simultaneously training his sights on the whole structure of Whiteness when he argued that Whites deployed a "science that's called 'image making' . . . that they use, very skillfully, to make the criminal look like the victim, and to make the victim look like the criminal."[15] In outlining the media mythmaking that marked the dominant image of the Black community as a criminal one, Malcolm was describing a prelude to what would later be explained by Elijah Anderson's theory of the "iconic ghetto where the media paints the ghetto as 'where "the black people live,"' symbolizing an impoverished, crime-prone, drug-infested, and violent area of the city."[16] Anderson argues that the result of this is that all Black people, no matter where they are found, are considered as embodying the ghetto and therefore will always receive unjust treatment. Malcolm was making this exact argument when he spoke about America as a police state for Black people, pointing out that it did not matter if you were "educated" or "dumb," "well dressed" or "poorly dressed," the criminal image gave the police a green light to brutalize you.[17] He explored the influence of the iconic ghetto still more deeply, to explain to the community that it was so powerful that "some of our own Black people have eaten this image themselves and digested it."[18] It seems that as well as predicting the "iconic ghetto," Malcolm foresaw Farrakhan being fooled by the mirage of the savage urban jungle.

Malcolm also made it very clear that when he spoke about the problems facing Black people, he was not just referring to those trapped in the ghetto. He mocked the press for trying to discredit him for having spent time in prison, telling them, "That's not a stick you can beat me with, I don't feel that stick."[19] He told his audiences, "Don't be shocked when I say I was in prison. You're still in prison."[20] He declared that "if you are Black, you were born in jail" and that "America is a prison house for the Black man and woman."[21] Malcolm consistently reminded his audiences that they were catching "more hell today than your grandfather caught 100 years ago."[22] While in the Nation of Islam, Malcolm also described the direness of the situation in biblical terms: "Here in North America today Black people are in a worse condition than they were in the time of Moses, they're in a worse condition than they were when Jesus was looking for the last sheep, in worse condition than the last Hebrews were in the land of Babylon."[23]

A consistent theme in Malcolm's thought was how central racism was to the American system of government, and that it could never be reformed away. In the NOI, this meant separating from the wicked devils, and once he left, it meant creating global revolutionary change. He was clear that "you will never be accepted into the mainstream of American society . . . never be respected by the American White man as a human being."[24] He came to believe this was not because they were a race of devils but because the nation was built on a political and economic system "that can no more provide freedom, justice and equality for the Black man, than a chicken can lay a duck egg. It's just not meant to do it."[25] That metaphor perfectly encapsulates Malcolm's analysis that racism was and is so fundamental to the makeup of the West that you are asking it to do something impossible in treating Black people fairly. No amount of reform, protest, and legislation can make society work for those it was not built for. He went on to joke that "if a chicken ever did lay a duck egg, I'm sure you would say it was a revolutionary chicken."

Unfortunately, the knee-jerk reaction any time anyone suggests revolution is to immediately think about Communism. We've been trained to see Marxist thought as *the* radical agenda, meaning it is no surprise that there have been efforts by the Left to claim Malcolm as one of their own. One of Malcolm's weaknesses was that he accepted invitations everywhere, and he once acknowledged that he could "never resist a platform."[26] He spoke a number of times at the Militant Labor Forum, a White left-wing collective, some members of which took responsibility for putting together collections of Malcolm's speeches and publishing them after he died. The White Left has a long history of trying to insert itself into Black issues, trying to convince us that our real problem is capitalism, not racism, and that we should unite with working-class White folk.[27] Malcolm's appearances at the forum have been used to support the myth that he was embracing White people and even to suggest that he was coming around to a Marxist position. One of his comments, made at the forum, that he had been considering socialism because of the African independence movements, has been taken to mean that he was ready to man the ramparts of the proletarian struggle. Yes, he spoke to Fidel Castro and once said, "Show me a capitalist and I'll show you a bloodsucker."[28] There is also little doubt that he wanted to overturn the existing economic order in the coming revolution, but this did not make him a Marxist.

It is a delusion of Whiteness (that far too many Black thinkers share) to consider any anti-capitalist politics that wants to equalize the distribution of wealth as Marxist. Capitalism is only a few hundred years old. A collective conception of the economy as underpinning society was probably the dominant idea for the majority of the history of human civilization. Dead White men did not create all these ideas! Ironically, it was Cedric Robinson who most devastatingly captured the limits of Marxism when he explained that Marx "imagined that the industrial Proletariat was the hero of capitalism and invented a history whose narrative justified this."[29] Of course, in Marx's thinking, the proletariat (working-class White men) had to be the savior. Marx was one of a long line of White supremacist political thinkers. I called it ironic that Cedric Robinson defined the limitations of Marxist theory so clearly because Robinson named his history of the so-called Black radical tradition *Black Marxism*, once again centering the ideas of the White man (in this case, Marx). His mistake was one most Black academics make, trying to justify Black intellectual thought to the White academy.

Black radicalism is a centuries-long political movement that does not need to be shoehorned into the (alive or dead) White man's theory. Malcolm's understanding that "you can't have capitalism without racism" stands as a precursor to Robinson's concept of "racial capitalism" that has become a buzzword in Black movement circles.[30] The difference with Malcolm's position, however, is that it is part of the radical Black liberation movement rather than produced in the White academy. I have purposely not engaged with the White Left's flagrant misreading of Malcolm so we can have a serious discussion about his political ideas.[31] When the Socialist Workers Party turns up to Black meetings, we just ignore them, so I am going to use the same policy for Malcolm's theory.

Malcolm could never accept the underlying theme of Marxism: that the fundamental oppression of those poorer people in society (who formed its majority) was based on class, therefore uniting all of those oppressed by capitalism, regardless of the color of their skin. Responding to a question at the Militant Labor Forum about whether the senators who were blocking the civil rights bill had done just as much harm to poor Whites as to Black people, Malcolm responded, "I just can't quite go along with that. You see, it's the Black man who sits on the hot stove. You might stand near it, but you don't sit on it."[32] In testament to the absurdity of the conversations that can emerge from engaging in these dialogues, Malcolm was asked at the same meeting if there was any comparison between the troubles facing Black people and those of old White people on pensions. To give Malcolm credit, he answered with far more patience than I would have, outlining just how distinctive anti-Blackness was in its total oppression:

> Our people were outright slaves—outright slaves. We pulled plows like horses. We were bought and sold from one plantation to another like you sell chickens or like you sell a bag of potatoes. I read in one book where George Washington exchanged a Black man for a keg of molasses. Why, that Black man could have been my grandfather. . . . You can't compare someone on old age assistance with the plight of Black people in this country. No comparison whatsoever.[33]

He was far less forgiving when a White journalist asked for acknowledgment for the sacrifice of Reverend Bruce Klunder, who was killed by a bulldozer in 1964 when protesting racial housing discrimination in Cleveland. Malcolm rebuked him:

> We're not going to stand up and applaud any contribution made by some individual White person when 22 million Black people are dying every day. What he did—good, good, great. . . . Hooray, hooray, hooray. Now Lumumba was murdered, Medgar Evers was murdered, Mack Parker was murdered, Emmett Till was murdered, my own father was murdered. You tell that stuff to somebody else. It's time that some White people started dying in this thing.[34]

Malcolm's anger was palpable because he understood the violent condition that was (and often still is) part of the very nature of Black existence. Black people did not have the luxury of choosing to sacrifice their life for their cause; it could be taken from them at any moment.

Throughout his career, Malcolm was repeatedly questioned about why he was not happier with the progress that was being made. It might seem ludicrous looking back now, but with civil rights legislation being passed, and more Black people integrating into White schools, neighborhoods, and jobs, there was an illusion that the problems of Black people were being addressed. When asked in a 1964 interview on Boston radio if he acknowledged the successes of the civil rights movement, he responded that "they've been successful in going to jail . . . in becoming the victims of police dogs, police clubs and water hoses" and that "Martin Luther King has been successful in disarming the Negroes."[35]

TOKEN INTEGRATION

Critical race theory emerged in America at the end of the 1980s out of dissatisfaction with the results of the civil rights movement. Legislation had been changed, landmark court decisions won, and even affirmative programs installed to supposedly give Black people a push up the ladder. But little has improved in Black communities, and with the advent of mass incarceration they are arguably worse than in the pre–civil rights days. If the key metric was integration, then the movement has proved an abject failure, with schools more segregated than they were before *Brown v. Board of Education* and White people fleeing to the suburbs, leaving behind so-called chocolate cities. In the classic *Faces at the Bottom of the Well*, one of CRT's founders, Derrick Bell, issued a warning that I use so much I have memorized it: "What we designate as 'racial progress' is not a solution to that problem. It is a regeneration of the problem in a particularly perverse form."[36] CRT resonated with me because of the idea that the changes we have seen are not incremental steps on the long march to freedom but actually represent an illusion of progress. Once again, however, this was not a new idea to me. Malcolm predicted that we would find ourselves exactly where we are if we limited our dreams of freedom to those of civil rights.

One of Malcolm's earliest political warnings was of the dangers of what he called "token integration." In a speech at Harvard in 1961, he explained:

> When one uses a "token" on the bus or streetcar that "token" is a substitute for the real money. Token means "a substitute," that which takes the place of the real thing. . . . Two Black students at Georgia University is token integration. Four Black children in New Orleans White schools is token integration. A handful of Black students in the White schools in Little Rock is token integration. None of this is real integration; it is only a pacifier designed to keep these awakening Black babies from crying too loud.[37]

Rather than seeing the civil rights reforms as victories, Malcolm decried them as efforts to pacify the masses and not real change. The cunning Northern Fox didn't legislate against Black people but passed meaningless laws designed to keep us in our place while thanking the Fox for it. For Malcolm, "every maneuver that America has made, supposedly to solve this problem, has been nothing but political trickery and treachery of the worst order," and therefore we should have "no confidence in these so-called liberals."[38] He drew specific attention to the fact that "nine White liberals on the Supreme Court bench came up with this desegregation decision in 1954 . . . and the schools haven't been desegregated yet."[39] That was only nine years after the decision. Now, more than sixty years later, he can only be looking down on us, saying, "I told you so."

Malcolm saw through the limits of the civil rights movement because it "condemns the system and then asks the system that it has condemned to accept them into their system."[40] Integrating into a racist system made no sense to Malcolm, which is why he was opposed to the tactic of sit-ins in order to desegregate public spaces like diners. He did not want to "sit at your table and watch you eat, with nothing on my plate, and call myself a diner. Sitting at the table doesn't make you a diner."[41] Access to the facilities without the means to enjoy them would mean very little and was the definition of token integration. He almost mocked those seeking to racially integrate housing, laughing that "as soon as you move out of the Black community into their community, it's mixed for a period of time, but they're gone and you're right there all by yourself again."[42] Malcolm foresaw that White flight would mean more ghettoization and less power for Black people.

There were no edits that could be made to American society, and therefore the efforts to reform it were just dangerous window dressing. For Malcolm, the very people—the civil rights activists—who were trying to convince the Black community about change were the problem. He explained that if America was a prison for Black people, then "your warden is in Washington, DC. Your warden is in the White House." The president had no intention of letting you out of jail but was "offering you civil rights in the same way the warden offers you time off for good behavior."[43] It might feel like a reprieve, but you were still a prisoner. The branches of government and the Supreme Court were all just different faces of the same warden, and as long as Black people waited on them to the solve the problem, we would just be "going in circles for another thousand years."[44] The so-called changes were nothing more than a trick to lull the Black masses to sleep.

As to the futility of passing laws, Malcolm singled out the 1964 Civil Rights Act, pointing out that it "means nothing, because already now they are asking for new legislation, which shows in their aims, and the sheer hypocrisy on the part of the government as regards the rights of Black people."[45] The campaigns, legislation, and court victories were little more than a merry-go-round, keeping those on board entertained while staying stuck in the same place. We have already seen that Malcolm had no time for the 1963 March on Washington, and he stressed that rather than achieving substantive change, "it did nothing except give many of the bourgeois Negroes a chance to feel like they were doing something without really having to do anything. It became a status symbol just like going to the Kentucky Derby for those who know nothing about horses . . . a chance to say, 'I was there.'"[46]

Token integration was more about the performance than the substance, and that included the protests. Malcolm argued that the performative nature of the march actually worsened our condition by having you "thinking you're going somewhere, but you're going nowhere."[47] He went further to say that tokenism was not only a ruse but "a program that was designed to benefit only a handful of handpicked Negroes" who would gain access to the system. They could then be used to placate the masses, convincing them that change was coming: "These handpicked Negroes were given big positions and they were used to say, 'Look at how much progress we're making.' . . . The masses of the Black people in this country continue to live in the slum and in the ghetto . . . remain unemployed . . . continue to go to the worst schools and get the worst education."[48] The "status symbols don't take it out of the alleys and out of the slums," but that was never the point.[49] Malcolm was trying to tell us that even where we think there were some successes, like "better jobs and housing," they were "only temporary solutions. They are aspects of tokenism and don't go to the heart of the problem."[50]

This is the predicament that the CRT thinkers have found themselves in. Due to the struggles of those who had gone before, they found themselves in high-paying, prestigious jobs that otherwise would have been impossible to attain. But they also realized that this had not led to any progress for the majority of Black people in the country, in particular those catching hell in the ghettos. Unfortunately, although they grasped Malcolm's analysis that racism was a permanent feature of American society, they avoided his conclusion. As we will discuss later in this book, Malcolm was not resigned to racism being a never-ending cycle. Once he had diagnosed it as a hereditary condition of Western society, the solution was simple: revolution, destroying the old and bringing in the new. But Bell, likely blinded by what Malcolm would see as his bourgeois sensibilities, could not see past the current unjust social order. Instead, as he says in *Faces at the Bottom of the Well*, he became resigned to "*both* the recognition of the futility of action . . . *and* the unalterable conviction that something must be done, that action must be taken."[51] At least King and the activists marching between the "feet of a dead man named Lincoln, and another named Washington" thought they were going to change the world.[52] Bell would have seen the futility of the civil rights jamboree *and* led the choruses of "We Shall Overcome." All CRT scholars do not share Bell's ultimate pessimism, but I think Malcolm would probably have said that it was more dangerous than the misguided optimism of civil rights leaders. Resigning yourself to a system that you know full well is genetically opposed to your freedom is the exact mindset that token integration was meant to induce.

WE'RE NOT AMERICAN

Central to Malcolm's analysis was for Black people to wholeheartedly reject the trap of feeling a sense of belonging to America. I haven't come across Malcolm addressing Black American sociologist W. E. B. Du Bois's work directly, but Malcolm's theory stands in direct contradiction to one of the scholar's key ideas. Du Bois argued that Black Americans were afflicted with the double consciousness of being at once Black and American. He described the "peculiar sensation" of having to always feel this "twoness—an American, a Negro; two souls, two thoughts, two unreconciled strivings; two warring ideals in one dark body, whose dogged strength alone keeps it from being torn asunder."[53] This idea has been widely taken up to explain the identity crisis that can afflict Black subjects of racist countries. But Malcolm argued that there was no need for an identity crisis because "we're not American."[54] He thought that it was "sheer hypocrisy, insanity for our people to celebrate the 4th July."[55] He identified as "one of the 22 million Black victims of Americanism." To those waving the flag and embracing the Greatest Country in the World™, he reminded them that "we don't see any American dream. We've experienced only the American nightmare. We haven't benefited from America's democracy. We've only suffered from America's hypocrisy."[56] It was in rejecting America and the delusions of progress that he would make Black people whole.

Malcolm had difficulty comprehending how "a Negro can say America is his nation" when he was brought here in chains . . . put in slavery and worked like a mule for three hundred years . . . separated from his land, his culture, his God, his language! The Negro was taught to speak the White man's tongue, worship the White God, and accept the White man as his superior. This is a White man's country. And the Negro is nothing but an ex-slave who is now trying to get himself integrated into the slave master's house.[57]

Double consciousness was a delusion that Malcolm continually attempted to pierce in his speeches. He joked with his Black audiences that "some of you think you came here on the *Mayflower* with the White pilgrims who established the first of what became the United States."[58] He reminded them that they instead arrived "in chains, like a horse, or a cow, or a chicken," that the status of ex-slave was little better than being in bondage and therefore no allegiance should be pledged to the nation.[59] Malcolm also tried to undo the myths that kept Black people finding solace in the so-called American dream. In the deceptive "narrative of progress," the American Civil War has been framed as being waged by the North in order to end the Southern abomination of slavery. But Malcolm insisted that the "the Civil War was fought to preserve the union, this country for White people. It wasn't fought to set you free. It wasn't fought to make you a citizen."[60] Ending slavery became a necessity during the course of the war, largely to swell the ranks of the Union army so it could defeat the South.

In bursting this myth, Malcolm also had to take down Abraham Lincoln, who remains heralded for issuing the Emancipation Proclamation that was meant to free the enslaved. Malcolm charged that Lincoln "did more to trick Negroes than any other man in history."[61] He explained this was because "most Negroes have been tricked into thinking that Lincoln was a Negro lover" who "died because he freed them." This deceived Black people into thinking that victory in the Civil War gave them a stake in the nation and created the crisis of double consciousness. This is why Malcolm thought that "Lincoln did more to deceive Negroes and to make the race problem in this country worse than any man in history."[62] In reality, Lincoln could not conceive of the formerly enslaved as being a part of his White country and thought it was their duty to leave and go live in Africa or on a Caribbean island. Lincoln actually accused those leaders who demanded rights in the United States of possessing an "extremely selfish view" of the issue.[63] He was not alone in this conviction. Key abolitionists founded the American Colonization Society with the purpose of deporting the formerly enslaved and even founding a colony, Liberia, to do so. Malcolm could not have been more correct when he explained that "America's problem is us. We're her problem. The only reason she has a problem is she doesn't want us here. And every time you look at yourself, be you Black, Brown, Red, or Yellow—a so-called Negro—you represent a person who poses such a serious problem for America because you're not wanted."[64]

Black people were taken to America in chains, to do the labor that founded the nation. Once slavery was abolished, that left millions of unwanted Africans in the nation who could never be granted full citizenship. Malcolm saw clearly that you could trace all the problems facing Black Americans to the fundamental truth that they were ex-slaves who would never be truly integrated into the White man's country. The mass incarceration of Black people makes perfect sense once we understand that, rather than citizens, Black people remain ex-slaves. America spends hundreds of billions of dollars on the criminal injustice apparatus each year to keep almost six million Black Americans either in prison or on probation or parole. As the cycle of poverty and crime continues, the social cost of destroying entire communities is almost immeasurable. It would cost a fraction of this money to invest in communities and genuinely attempt to solve these problems. But prison abolitionist Ruth Wilson Gilmore has explained that, rather than being a failure of the American nation, mass incarceration was an essential "project of state-building."[65]

Malcolm was trying to warn the Black population that they were not citizens and therefore could never be included equally in the national project. Black people were enslaved when the nation was founded, and the first solution after emancipation was deportation. African Americans remained brutalized in the South, sharecropping the same fields they had formerly toiled on as the enslaved. At the turn of the century, there were genuine fears that the Black population would be eradicated in a genocide because they had become surplus to requirements. It is worth remembering that renowned scholar Carter G. Woodson founded Negro History Week in 1926 in large part because "if a race has no history, if it has no worth-while tradition, it becomes a negligible factor in the thought of the world, and it stands in danger of being exterminated."[66] American involvement in the First World War provided limited opportunities for Black Americans to flee the South, but there were real concerns that they would be erased similarly to those native to their land. The Great Depression only heightened those fears. It really was the Second World War that changed the fate of the Black population. With America so heavily involved in the conflict, this provided opportunities in the armed forces and also in the factories, railroads, etc. for Black people to flee north. Malcolm noted that it wasn't any civil rights legislation or White liberals who got Black people better jobs in the North; it was the war.[67] Once again they were needed, and the nation was reshaped by the Great Migration to the enlightened North. However, they were not treated as citizens but as ex-slaves, penned into the slums, the racial ghettos that still exist today. Malcolm reminded those fleeing the South that "America is Mississippi. There's no such thing as a Mason-Dixon Line—it's America. There's no such thing as the South—it's America."[68]

In the postwar settlement, a booming American economy meant there remained plenty of jobs for Black people to fill. But throughout this entire period America had been recruiting tens of millions more White immigrants from Europe to bolster its ranks. Malcolm offered a contrast of the treatment of those immigrants to that of African Americans. He pointed out that "those Honkies that just got off the boat, they're already Americans. . . . Everything that came out of Europe, every blue-eyed thing, is already an American."[69] He was incredulous as he reminded his audiences that even the "Germans, that they used to fight just a few years ago . . . the Russians, whom they're supposedly fighting right now . . . don't need legislation" in order to grant them civil rights.[70] If supposed enemies of the nation could step off a boat and have equal rights, then this should have told the Black population everything they needed to know about their status. Malcolm was clear that if the "twenty-two million Afro-Americans were actually citizens of this country it wouldn't be necessary to pass any additional legislation to be included in the constitution."[71] Token integration could only ever lead to "second-class citizenship" for the ex-slaves who would be forever locked out of the nation. Rather than seeing the passage of specific legislation for Black people as progress, Malcolm thought that "they're actually slapping you and me in the face when they pass a civil rights bill. It's not an honor; it's a slap in the face."[72] This was because the need for legislation meant it was *not* the intrinsic right of Black people to have full citizenship; if it were, there would be no need for new laws. If American so-called democracy was meant for Black people, then all you would need to do is enforce the Constitution. Malcolm strongly rejected the battle for civil rights and instead proclaimed that we must demand our human rights: "The civil rights struggle has failed to produce concrete results because it has kept us barking up the wrong tree. It has made us put the cart ahead of the horse. We must have human rights before we can secure civil rights."[73] He explained to his listeners that the American system was founded on the belief that our ancestors were "three-fifths of a man, subhuman." This justified enslaving us and trading us "like you sell a horse or a cow or a bag of wheat."

The fundamental problem was that Black people had never been accepted as full human beings and therefore were incapable of claiming civil rights. Malcolm was pointing out that there was no contradiction when slave owners declared that "all men are created equal," because we simply were not seen as people. He was arguing that neither emancipation nor the subsequent amendments altered the fact that Black Americans were not granted human rights, were not respected as human beings. Without first claiming human rights, they could therefore never achieve civil rights.

The response to the demands for Black freedom was not inclusion but greater exclusion. With intensification of the police state and mass incarceration, there are more Black American men in prison today than there were enslaved at the time of the Emancipation Proclamation.[74] If Malcolm thought that America was prison for Black people in the 1960s, it doesn't take too much imagination to know what he would say today. Importantly, this Black prison state is the inevitable consequence of a White supremacist society. Particularly now, with automation, artificial intelligence, and offshoring of jobs, Black American labor is largely redundant. Black people have been included into American so-called democracy in precisely the ways that Malcolm warned of: as ex-slaves who are fodder for the police state.

Malcolm was opposed to the civil rights movement because he knew that it had fundamentally misdiagnosed the problem. With their nonviolence and trying to keep influential White people onside, the civil rights activists were attempting to do the impossible. He argued against that "whole thing about appealing to the moral conscience of America," because "they don't know what morals are. They don't try and eliminate an evil because it's evil, or because it's illegal, or because it's immoral; they eliminate it only when it threatens their existence. So you're wasting your time appealing to the moral conscience of a bankrupt man like Uncle Sam."[75]

Here, Malcolm is once again predicting a key tenet of critical race theory, this time the idea of "interest convergence," which refers to the sad truth that the only way to get even token changes is when they converge with the interests of White society.[76] Malcolm was explaining how it was the threat of the powder keg exploding that had forced the president into action, rather than the nonviolent protests of civil rights. Legislation was introduced to pacify the angry masses who were threatening to burn down the whole plantation. As much as Malcolm railed against tricky individuals like Kennedy, he knew that they were symptomatic of the problem rather than the cause. Always one for a metaphor, Malcolm joked that "it is against the White man's nature to integrate you into his house. Even if he wanted to, he could no more do it than a Model T [Ford] can sprout wings and fly. It just isn't in him."[77] The White devil or Northern Fox was just a messenger for an entire society designed to oppress Black people. He explained, "We have a rotten system. It's a system of exploitation, a political and economic system of exploitation, of outright humiliation, degradation, discrimination—all of the negative things that you can run into, you have run into under this system that disguises itself as a democracy."[78] Trying to work within a system that was built in opposition to you was clearly nonsensical. No amount of protest or appeal could make the nation go against its founding principles of White supremacy. We therefore had to reject nonviolence and take up arms in self-defense because "you never will get protection from the Federal Government."[79]

Malcolm also called attention to the rigged electoral system, which ensured that Black people's rights would always be curtailed. His "Ballot or the Bullet" address was partly an education in how the Black vote had been abused by the political machinery. At this point, he was free from the Nation of Islam and working to build the Organization of Afro-American Unity, so he was thinking through how to bring his radical program into action. He drew attention to the process of racial "gerrymandering" and how it was used to "maneuver you out of power" so that "even though you can vote they fix it so you're voting for nobody."[80] Racial gerrymandering is the redrawing of the boundaries of electoral seats to purposefully disempower Black and racially minoritized voters. This can be done by packing Black voters into a handful of districts, so that they are the majority in a limited number of places and therefore cannot gain overall control of a city, county, or state. The other mechanism is to draw boundaries that disperse Black voters widely to make sure they are not the majority in any district and therefore cannot swing the balance of power. In America, with high levels of residential segregation, packing is a common tactic, but efforts to keep the Black vote contained leads to electoral maps drawn in such ridiculous shapes they look like a parody. The US Supreme Court has deliberated on a number of cases as to whether it is unconstitutional to gerrymander districts to get the electoral results you desire. In her book *One Person, No Vote*, historian Carol Anderson charts the history of voter disenfranchisement in America from emancipation to the present day.[81] Rather than such tactics being a problem only in the distant past, they represent an ever present danger. With the proportion of traditional White voters declining, the Republican Party is desperately trying to ensure Black people have as little voting power as possible. But Malcolm also warned Black people not to trust the Democrats, because the party only wanted to use the Black vote to get into power.

Malcolm delivered his "Ballot or the Bullet" address in 1964, four years after the Democrats gained power—with the help of millions of Black voters. They controlled all the levers of government but had not fully addressed the issue of civil rights. Malcolm told his audiences that this demonstrated that they could not be trusted and should not blindly receive the support of Black voters. He chastised them, "You put them first and they put you last. Because you're a chump! A political chump!"[82] The system was set up against Black voters, and they colluded in it by following the lead of the tricky Northern Democratic Fox. If ever there was a message that needed to be heard more today, I cannot think of one. In America, more than 90 percent of Black voters cast their ballot for a Democrat who has done nothing to erase the racism that afflicts society. We could all do with heeding Malcolm's declaration that "I'm not a Democrat or a Republican, not even an American and I've got sense enough to know it."[83]

Understanding that a chicken can never lay a duck egg opens up the radical imagination. If you believe in the impossible, that the system can be reformed through legislation and moral appeals, Malcolm has warned that "in your struggle it's like standing on a revolving wheel: you're running, but you're not going anywhere. You run faster and faster and the wheel just goes faster and faster. You don't ever leave the spot that you're standing in."[84] Once Black people give up the notion that America, Britain, or whichever nation-state we reside in can be redeemed, we can start to build a new future that will not permanently be defined by racism. But to do so, we need to comprehend the global nature of the system. Malcolm is one of the clearest voices telling us that we can never overcome the problem of racism without a global analysis and solution.

5

BENEVOLENT COLONIALISM

Malcolm captured my attention when I was a teenager because it felt like he was speaking directly to me. His words cut across time and space to narrate both my experiences and the conditions of the world around me. This was not incidental, but speaks to one of the most important dimensions of Malcolm's political thought. Although he lived in America and most frequently commented on his domestic situation, Malcolm insisted that the racism that he was struggling against was "not just an American problem" but one for the world.[1] He understood that we had to internationalize both the analysis and the solution, so in essence he *was* talking directly to me. This global understanding of racism is as necessary today as it ever has been, because Black people have been duped into having faith in our respective nation-states to deliver on their empty promises of freedom. One of the most chilling aspects of token integration is the extent to which Black populations have begun to identify with the nations that are oppressing them. We take pride in being Black British, African American, or even Jamaican or Nigerian, without comprehending just how much the nations themselves are a central mechanism of our oppression. Internationalizing the struggle was central to Malcolm's radical politics, connecting across the diaspora and the African continent to unite all those in the "same boat" facing the realities of anti-Black racism.

NOT JUST AN AMERICAN PROBLEM

Rather than seeing the problem of racism as a domestic creation, Malcolm frequently drew parallels between the experience of the so-called American Negro and Black people oppressed across the globe. He explained that racism "has become a problem that is so complex, and has so many implications in it, that you have to study it in the world context or in its international context, to really see it as it actually is. Otherwise you can't even follow the local issue, unless you know what part it plays in the entire international context."[2]

In doing so, Malcolm indicted the treatment of Black people in America as "colonial," arguing that "America is just as much a colonial power as England ever was" or "France ever was."[3] He was taking direct aim at the notion that America was the supposed leader of the free world, a nation that traded heavily on its revolutionary victory against the British Empire. Malcolm was reminding the world that Uncle Sam's treatment of Black people was no different from the European devilishness that had conquered the globe. America was not exceptional, and not a place where liberty could be won for the formerly enslaved. As limited as the Nation of Islam orthodoxy was in condemning all White people as devils, its analysis shared a global dimension: White people were a scourge across the entire world, and when judgment was brought down, it would free the globe from the evils of White society. Once free from the shackles of the NOI, Malcolm developed his international analysis fully. He charged that America had "colonized 22 million Afro-Americans by depriving us of first-class citizenship, by depriving us of civil rights, actually by depriving us of human rights. She has not only deprived us of the right to be a citizen, she has deprived us of the right to be human beings, the right to be recognized and respected as men and women."[4] The ghetto that locked Black Americans into "rat-infested . . . criminal conditions" was the same as the colonies that kept their populations caged and exploited.[5]

It is easy to limit Malcolm's philosophy to a narrow, American-centered nationalism focused around gaining economic and political control of segregated neighborhoods. This certainly was the extent of the Nation of Islam's political engagement as it built both mosques and businesses such as restaurants and laundries. The NOI was hugely successful in building up an economic base for its operations, not unlike many Black churches. While in the Nation of Islam, Malcolm preached the party line and tied the morally uplifting message to a responsibility to build community wealth. In 1959, he railed against the amount of money that Black people spent on whiskey in New York, quoting a figure of $60 million annually. He reasoned that "if you have 60 million dollars, you can build a factory that employed every Negro from here [Harlem] to the Hudson River."[6] He also referenced a book, *Fifteen Million Negroes and Fifteen Billion Dollars* by William Bell, that argued Black Americans had a buying power of $15 billion and therefore could reshape their destinies by wielding that economic power collectively. This is the kind of economic nationalism that W. E. B. Du Bois had in mind when he argued that Black people needed to develop an "economic nation within a nation, able to work through inner cooperation, to found its own institutions" as the only hope for Black America.[7] This romantic delusion that all we need to do is pool our economic resources still holds sway, with slogans like "Buy Black" and "Keep the Black pound circulating." Apparently, today Black buying power is more than $1.8 trillion in the United States, which is more than the average GDP of many so-called sub-Saharan African countries.[8] With such staggering wealth at our disposal, if we can just spend it more wisely, we will surely be all right. After leaving the NOI, Malcolm described his political and economic philosophy as Black nationalism and argued for the need to invest economically in the Black community to create businesses and other ventures. But this was an effort to gain some amount of control over conditions that faced the community rather than the solution itself. No matter what some social media influencers would have you believe, our route to freedom is not simply in pooling our economic resources.

The myth of Black buying power is as dangerous as any other because it fools us into believing that if we just spend more wisely then we could be free. Remember that Malcolm was also indicting the financial system itself; he would never have supported any Black nationalist program that made us better capitalists. In the diary he wrote during his travels to Africa and the Middle East, he questioned the validity of simple economic nationalism, writing, "Can the American Negro really become economically independent (control his economy) simply by controlling the retail stores in his community? Who would control the warehouses from which he would buy his goods?"[9] This is the crux of the problem for those advocating for Black capitalism. Black people in the West have purchasing power in a system that is founded on White supremacy. To take control of retail means still having to deal with the wholesalers, and even if you could control wholesale, the real money is in the production. Black Americans do not have anywhere near enough wealth to take control of production ($1.8 trillion may sound like a lot, but that is just two Jeff Bezoses). Even if they did have the wealth, they would find that the mechanisms of production are as racist and almost as violent as in the days when their ancestors were picking cotton on slave plantations. Sweatshop labor, agricultural exploitation, and children squeezing themselves into mines are essential to produce the commodities that African Americans consume.[10] The uncomfortable truth is that the $1.8 trillion is derived off the backs of Black and Brown labor and exploitation. In the narrow nationalism of American exceptionalism, it might be possible to blind your eyes to the worldwide blood on our hands, but Malcolm certainly could not. This is why the global view is so powerful, because it forces us to seek truly systemic solutions. For Malcolm, political and economic nationalism was necessary for survival and was drawn from his understanding of the colonial situation in America. Due to being hemmed into segregated communities, we were able to be economically exploited, so that "even when we try and spend our money on the block where we live or the area where we live, we're spending it with a man who, when the sun goes down, takes that basket full of money in another part of the town. . . . So we're trapped, double-trapped, triple-trapped. Any way we go, we find that we're trapped."[11]

The Black economic situation was mirrored on the political scene, where we were trapped between the Fox and the Wolf, neither of whom had our best intentions at heart. Malcolm therefore argued that we needed to organize the Black vote to ensure that the "time when White people can come in our community and get us to vote for them so that they can be our political leaders and tell us what to do and what not to do is long gone."[12] In drawing attention to this control and domination, Malcolm was part of an intellectual heritage that saw the Black American population not as a "nation within a nation" but rather as an internal colony. After all, he asked, "What is second-class citizenship if nothing but twentieth-century colonialism?"[13] Following Malcolm's reasoning, in 1968 Kwame Ture and academic Charles Hamilton documented that "the White power structure is as monolithic as Europe's colonial offices have been to African and Asian colonies" and that "colonial politics causes the subject to muffle his voice while participating in the councils of the White power structure."[14] Later on, scholars such as William K. Tabb fleshed out the internal colony argument, arguing that key institutions such as schools served to further embed exploitation by teaching Black people to remain in their place and affording opportunities for some to escape and bolster the ranks of the colonial elite.[15] Malcolm saw the impact of this colonial control on the Black population, arguing that "the Black man has been a beggar economically, a beggar politically, a beggar socially, a beggar even when it comes to trying to get some education. . . . This type of mentality was developed in this colonial system among our people."[16]

In order to overcome both the colonial mentality and the realities of indirect rule in the ghetto, Malcolm argued that nationalism was an essential first step to take back some power. Malcolm's nationalism must be seen in the same context as the nationalist movements that swept Africa, determined as the Black people there were to gain the political and economic levers of their societies. This was never meant to be the ultimate solution, but was seen as a necessary step toward connecting Africa together. Malcolm's untimely death has allowed those who want to embrace Black capitalism to use him as a standard-bearer, but it is a dangerous misinterpretation of his political program.

By highlighting the ghetto as an internal colony, Malcolm was trying to tie together the struggles facing Black Americans and those facing all Black people across the globe. When he visited Britain, he made it clear that he saw the people there facing the same realities of racism as those in the land of his birth. On his second visit to Britain in 1965, he went to the borough of Smethwick, now part of Birmingham. This was unplanned because he had left London to fly to Paris, but once he arrived in France he was told by the authorities that he was deemed an "undesirable person" and so was deported back to Britain. There is a lot of speculation about why the French government took this approach, considering that he had spoken in that country before. One of the theories I have heard in Black movement circles is that the French had forewarning that the US intelligence agencies were arranging for Malcolm's assassination to take place in their country, and France wanted nothing to do with it.[17] Malcolm was assassinated just nine days after he subsequently left Britain, so it is not hard to see why this theory persists.

Hearing of his unexpected return to Britain, the Indian Workers' Association in Birmingham seized the opportunity of the newfound gap in his diary to bring Malcolm to the city. They took him to Smethwick because it was a hotbed of racism at the time. In the 1964 general election, the Conservative Peter Griffiths had won the seat of Smethwick with the unofficial slogan "If you want a nigger for a neighbour, vote Labour," which was painted in huge letters on one of the walls in the area. The local council was refusing to rent housing to Black and Brown immigrants and the local KKK was burning crosses on people's doors.[18] Britain likes to pretend it did not (and does not) have the violent, ugly racism of America, but there were just as fearsome Wolves ready to draw the blood of the Black population. I interviewed a number of activists who were on the ground in the 1960s for *The Guardian*'s "Black Lives" series, which the newspaper launched following the Black Lives Matter summer of 2020. It featured profiles of lesser-known Black figures, including activists in Britain. Everyone I spoke to who was active from the 1960s to the 1980s told of the fear they had when walking the streets. Guy Reid-Bailey, of the Bristol bus boycott, explained how Black people, with absolutely no help from the police, had to go out in groups to avoid being beaten up by racists in the street. Malcolm was not surprised by the racism facing colonial immigrants in Smethwick and, always one to talk directly, remarked that he was visiting because "I have heard they are being treated as the Jews were under Hitler." He also warned that he "would not wait for the fascist elements in Smethwick to erect gas ovens."[19] There was little doubt that we were catching hell in Britain, and Malcolm was keen to point this out. But he also saw the nuances of racism in the country; Smethwick was not representative of the whole nation, and such ugly, direct racism was easy for White liberals to call out and condemn.

Griffiths's reign was very short-lived, as he was voted out seventeen months later after an early general election called by Labour's Harold Wilson. The prime minister decried the election of Griffiths and dubbed him a "parliamentary leper" because of his openly racist views and campaign.[20] Malcolm was wary of the tricky British Foxes, like Wilson, and described how "the West Indian in England faces a covered and subtle form of discrimination. In the USA at least he knows the KKK is just the town sheriff in disguise. At least in the USA the Black man knows his enemy."[21] Wilson's government passed the first race relations legislation, which Malcolm would no doubt have savaged just as harshly as he did the changes to American civil rights, and, given how ineffective these supposedly landmark steps have been on both sides of the Atlantic, he was right to be skeptical. Malcolm's message to all of us was to remember that "you're not of the West. You're in the West," and that therefore we should never expect equal treatment.[22] Perhaps this shouldn't have been a surprise to those migrating from colonies to their self-proclaimed mother countries in Europe. But the indoctrination in the colonies was so thorough that the first wave of migrants genuinely expected to be welcomed. Guy Reid-Bailey has described the disappointment of quickly learning that Britain was "a mother without any affection for Black people."[23] What Malcolm said has resonated so deeply with me because, by the time my generation came along, we had enough experiences of racist Britain to know better than to ever expect racial equality.

As much as the racism of America should have been indisputable, Malcolm challenged the image of itself that America projected abroad, arguing that "there is no system more corrupt than a system that represents itself as the example of freedom, the example of democracy, and can go all over this earth telling other people how to straighten out their house, when you have citizens of this country who have to use bullets if they want to cast a ballot."[24]

BENEVOLENT COLONIALISM

Just as Malcolm railed against the Foxes at home, so did he on the world stage. When he traveled in Africa, he was dismayed to see the propaganda being spread by the US Information Agency (USIA). The agency was founded in 1953 by President Dwight D. Eisenhower as a Cold War effort to "understand, inform and influence foreign publics in promotion of the national interest, and to broaden the dialogue between Americans and U.S. institutions, and their counterparts abroad."[25] The aim was to discredit the Soviets while boosting the reputation of the Land of the Free™. One of the initiatives the USIA created was the Fulbright scholarship that continues to fund American scholars to travel abroad. America spent millions of dollars on this initiative, in no small part because the civil rights troubles were a significant stain on the nation's global reputation. Malcolm dismissed the agency as one of the "most vicious organs that has ever been put together," declaring that it was so heinous it made "the propaganda machine that Goebbels had under Hitler look like child's play." This was because the USIA relentlessly used

the passage of the civil rights bill to make it appear that Negroes aren't being lynched anymore . . . voting rights aren't being trampled upon . . . police aren't busting Negroes' heads with clubs, nor are they using dogs and violence and water hoses to wash us down the drain. They make it appear that the civil rights bill created a paradise in the United States for 22 million Negroes.[26]

Such propaganda was essential to US foreign policy, to convince emerging independent nations to side with America against the growing Communist threat. Today, revolution sounds like some distant dream, but in the 1960s the threat from the East was an existential one for the West; there was no guarantee that capitalism would triumph. So, America engaged in typical colonial violence in wars in Korea and Vietnam, as well as aiding in the murder of more than a million Communist activists in the underdeveloped world.[27] But soft power was just as, if not more, important to project the image of the United States as the leader of a new, free world. Malcolm saw this hypocrisy firsthand when he traveled in Africa and when he spoke in Ghana in 1964. He warned his hosts of White American duplicity:

The fact is, these same Whites who in America spit in our faces, the same Whites who in America club us brutally, the same Whites who in America sic their dogs upon us, just because we want to be free human beings, the same Whites who turn their water hoses upon our women and our babies because we want to integrate with them, are over here in Africa smiling in your face trying to integrate with you.[28]

Such tactics were necessary because, following the devastation caused by the Second World War, European colonialism was no longer viable. The empires had bankrupted themselves in both economic and manpower and had needed to arm the natives, who were now eager for independence. This allowed America to step in and become the new seat of empire. In his typical style, Malcolm captured this shift perfectly:

When you're playing basketball and they get you trapped, you don't throw the ball away, you throw it to one of your teammates who's in the clear. And this is what the European powers did. They were trapped on the African continent, they couldn't stay there; they were looked upon as colonial, imperialist. So they had to pass the ball to someone whose image was different, and they passed the ball to Uncle Sam. . . . He was in the clear, he was not looked upon as one who had colonized the African continent. But at that time, the Africans couldn't see that though the United States hadn't colonized the African continent, he had colonized twenty-two million Blacks here on this continent.[29]

Uncle Sam, or the United States, used this opportunity to seize control, and it was an inevitable transition. The American nation is Europe on steroids, a place where White supremacy could flourish free from constraints after the genocide of the native people. I have described this moment as ushering in "the new age of empire."[30] Malcolm accused America of developing a system of seemingly "benevolent" or "philanthropic" colonialism, where foxy Uncle Sam posed as the friend of the underdeveloped countries of the world so that he could lure them into his den to devour them. This was solely out of necessity, because the old brutal forms were no longer fit for purpose. Returning to the CRT theme of interest convergence, this "helpful" international image was the trade-off for the limited civil rights gains that were achieved for Black people. As Malcolm explained, the USIA used the Civil Rights Act as a magic bullet to wipe away all the negative stories that were coming out of the United States concerning racism. The images of lynchings and police dogs brutalizing Black people signaled to the world that America was *not* the land of freedom, and made African people, in particular, wary of trusting the friendly approach. So, a bill had to be passed, something had to be done to arrest the negative headlines.

Prior to the passage of the Civil Rights Act in 1964, the American government's negative international image had been forcing its hand. After the Second World War, President Harry Truman had understood that "the United States is not so strong, the final triumph of the democratic ideal is not so inevitable that we can ignore what the world thinks of us or our record."[31] During the infamous *Brown v. Board of Education* case, which eventually ruled segregated schooling unconstitutional, the US State Department submitted a written statement to the court in favor of desegregation. The brief argued that "the undeniable existence of racial discrimination gives unfriendly governments the most effective kind of ammunition for their propaganda" wars, which were being waged in the press and via bodies like the United Nations (UN).[32] At the much-heralded 1955 Bandung Conference of African and Asian nations—those who were nonaligned with either the West or the Soviets—America's subjugation of African Americans was discussed as a reason to distrust the new imperial power. This was exactly the danger that the State Department was worried about: that if the United States did not clean up its global image, other important nations would choose the evil Communist side. In 1957, when nine Black students tried to join the all-White Central High School in Little Rock, Arkansas, and were unable to do so, receiving a huge onslaught of racist abuse from White opponents in the process, the fiasco caused international outrage.

Again for the "Black Lives" series published in *The Guardian* in 2020, I interviewed one of the students, Minnijean Brown-Trickey, who was a victim of the thousand-strong mob that greeted the students on the first day they tried to enter the school. She could only describe the mayhem as "crazy," with the crowd jeering, throwing objects, and spitting at the Black children.[33] On that first day, the mob was supported by the Arkansas National Guard, who refused to let the children enter. President Eisenhower was not an advocate of desegregation and would rather have left individual states to decide their response. He waited twenty days before intervening in the standoff, and only took action after seeing the international backlash against America that the scenes were causing. Across the world, America was being condemned, with the feeling best summed up by an official at the Dutch embassy who worried, "What is happening in Arkansas will weaken America, in her contest with Soviet communism over the uncommitted areas of Asia, Africa and the Middle East."[34] A Libyan newspaper questioned how America could present itself as the "mother of liberty and democracy while permitting sixteen million African Americans to be smashed under the soles of the whites and live a life of humiliation."[35] The president was inundated with letters from around the world and a report from US intelligence that warned of the severe damage to the reputation of the nation that Little Rock was causing. It was this pressure that led Eisenhower to mobilize the National Guard and escort the children into the school, to break the standoff almost three weeks after it had started. The president didn't authorize spending the equivalent of more than $37 million in today's money to provide nine children with a personal armed guard to go to school because he was dedicated to desegregation; it was to save face around the world.

Malcolm explained that whenever America engaged with the underdeveloped world, just as with the USIA, its actions were always nefarious. President Kennedy created the Peace Corps in 1961 to send "a pool of trained American men and women . . . overseas . . . to help foreign countries meet their urgent needs for skilled manpower." The president continued that this was necessary to bring "to man that decent way of life which is the foundation of freedom and a condition of peace."[36] The first three countries where volunteers were sent were Ghana, Tanzania, and Colombia, and it is no coincidence that all three were nations that America wanted to keep out of the clutches of the Communists. The paternalistic aims exemplified by the Peace Corps, to bring decency to the underdeveloped world, were part of the same PR offensive as that of the USIA, to show the good public face of the "promised land." Malcolm saw right through the ruse and rebuked that the "American Peace Corps men are but neo missionaries."[37] He knew that America did not offer a helping hand but pretended to do so while exploiting you. For Malcolm, the offers of help were so that the "Peace Corps could get a piece" of whatever country they were in by tricking the nation into accepting American support.[38] Malcolm was drawing attention to the devastating consequences of development aid that is presented as a leg up by the West, but in fact always ends up siphoning off resources from the underdeveloped world. The billions spent in aid have not shrunk the gap between the rich and poor countries but cemented it, by ensuring that those nations stay part of the wicked global economic system of White supremacy.[39] Today the Peace Corps has thousands of volunteers working in sixty countries and has explicitly retained the USIA-like aim of helping to "promote a better understanding of Americans on the part of the peoples served."[40] Malcolm would have been even more wary of the institution during the current state of affairs, when people have almost stopped questioning the motives of the American Fox on the world stage.

As much as Malcolm saw the supposedly benevolent side of America's leadership of the Western empire, he also understood the violence that underpinned its soft power. One of the reasons he was suspicious of the supposedly supportive hand America was holding out was because Uncle Sam was "sending the Peace Corps to Nigeria, while sending hired killers to the Congo."[41] The carnage in Congo was a frequent theme in Malcolm's speeches, and he connected the violence there with the fallacy of benevolent colonialism. Malcolm often indicted the press for perpetuating the lies that justified White supremacy, his criticism of the USIA being the perfect example. As we discussed in the last chapter, he argued that the press had spread the image of the iconic ghetto that seared the dangerous Negro into the minds of society. He similarly revealed how the press "create[d] images of Black people as criminals and help[ed] America colonize Africa."[42]

In the specific case of Congo, America sent mercenaries to support the counterrevolutionary Moise Tshombe, who had seized power by murdering the elected leader, Patrice Lumumba, in 1961. Lumumba's followers rose up in the Simba rebellion, and America supported Tshombe to put the rebellion down with money, weapons, and fighters. Malcolm accused the press of creating "hysteria . . . trying to get the sympathy of the White public" in favor of American aggression to quell the rebellion. In areas under their control, the rebels took hostages, and Malcolm castigated the press for its reporting: "Remember how they referred to the hostages as 'White hostages.' Not 'hostages.' They said these 'cannibals' in the Congo had 'White hostages.' Oh, and this got you all shook up. White nuns, White priests, White missionaries. What's the difference between a White hostage and a Black hostage? . . . You must think there's a difference, because your press specifies Whiteness. 'Nineteen White hostages' cause you to grieve in your heart."[43]

This was particularly galling to Malcolm, given the violence that American money and manpower was inflicting in bombing campaigns of Congo, but the Black lives lost were not seen as worthy as those of White hostages. When reporting on Cuban pilots in the country, Malcolm explained that the press "will call them anti-Castro Cubans, and that's supposed to add to their respectability, and eliminate that fact that they're dropping bombs" on defenseless African villages.[44] He was angered that the press would "give them the glorious name of mercenary" rather than explain that these were people not "killing for some kind of patriotism or some kind of ideal" but were "paid killers, hired killers."[45] America had supported the overthrow of the elected leader of Congo and sent money and soldiers to brutally crush the rebellion. But the press was framing America as on the side of the anti-Castro pilots, trying to free the saintly White hostages from the native savages. It is this kind of lunacy that led

Malcolm to reason that "if you're not careful, the newspapers will have you hating the people who are being oppressed, and loving the people who are doing the oppressing."[46] But this propaganda was necessary because, he argued, the "American image abroad is so bankrupt."[47] As much as you want to hide the dark side of colonialism, it is extremely difficult when the evidence is so abundant. Malcolm condemned White America's hypocrisy: "Here he is standing up in front of other people, Uncle Sam, with the blood of your and my mothers and fathers on his hands. With the blood dripping down his jaws like a bloody-jawed wolf. And still got the nerve to point his finger at other countries."[48]

Western propaganda was powerful: It could paint revolutionary leaders as being problematic at best and evil bad guys at worst. Malcolm explained that if a leader had the "mass support" of his people, "the West classifies him as a dictator." But the real reason that leaders such as Kwame Nkrumah in Ghana, Gamal Abdel Nasser in Egypt, Ahmed Ben Bella in Algeria, and Sékou Touré in Guinea were viewed as "anti-West" was "because the West can't tell them what to do."[49] This was such an important feature of so-called benevolent colonialism, because the "puppet" leaders of many of the countries populated by Black and Brown people around the world were a key mechanism for ensuring White supremacy. Lumumba was killed because he had mass support for a political and economic program that would have taken Congo's vast mineral wealth out of the control of the West. By installing Western-friendly leaders who were willing to do the bidding of their paymasters, the economic devastation being wrought upon these nations could look like there was a consensual partnership going on, one meant to lift the backward nations out of poverty. As a rule of thumb, when judging world leaders today, we should stick to

Malcolm's yardstick. If the West is praising them, we should be trying to bring them down.

Malcolm thought that the friendly seeming approach of the Fox was essential for America to retain its global dominance on the world stage. Capitalist economics depends on forever expanding, growing the economy and finding new markets. Malcolm reasoned that

> America has run out of markets. And it's impossible for her to find new markets anywhere, unless there's some customers on the moon or in some other planet. And as long as this situation exists, America's economy is going to continue to go down, and the dollar will continue to lose its value, and when it loses this value she's lost all of their friends. Because the only friends she has are those whom she has bought. . . . The nations of Africa and Asia would rather buy their manufactured or finished products from other than America.[50]

It is important to remember that Malcolm was working in a very different global political landscape than the one we inhabit today. The framework of benevolent colonialism was still being laid down. National liberation struggles were being waged, and the world was on the precipice of revolution. The threat from Communism was very real, and it was not clear that capitalism would survive. Malcolm foresaw a demise in the American economic machine because he had faith in the underdeveloped world to unite and fight back against imperialism. He was entirely correct to predict the end of American power if the country lost its markets, which is why Uncle Sam fought so hard with both foxy diplomacy and the brutal violence of the wolf.

Malcolm spoke from a place of optimism but didn't live long enough to see the domination of the globe by the American empire. The fall of the Soviets and the capitulation of China to capitalism heralded the end of any resistance to purportedly benevolent colonialism. In fact, the Chinese have embarked on a kind of diplomatic charm offensive in Africa that makes even the American Fox look like a Wolf in comparison. Trading on Maoist rhetoric and seeming support for revolutionary movements in Africa, China poses as a friend to the continent. But China's involvement in Africa only really increased after China had joined the World Trade Organization, and it is in actual fact based on the same resource-extraction model as the West.[51] China is perhaps the best example of benevolent colonialism nowadays because it has reaped the benefits of the Western violence that decimated Africa, pretended to be a friend while feasting on its corpse. Were Malcolm alive today, he might have dubbed China the Eastern Hyena, laughing all the way to its dinner.

Malcolm predicted the end of America's power prematurely because he didn't apply his domestic understanding of "token integration" to the world stage. In the same way that America opened up enough for a limited group of bourgeois Black people to gain second-class citizenship, this is exactly what has happened all around the globe. Seeming independence is nothing more than token integration, an illusion of power while you are still being controlled by global White supremacy. The elite are either directly handpicked or raised and trained in Western schools and unleashed to ensure that their nations stay permanently embedded close to the top of the wicked system of global oppression. Malcolm died before the International Monetary Fund (IMF) and World Bank became the biggest Foxes on the planet, handing out loans to underdeveloped countries that opened up their economies to West-ern imports. America cannot run out of markets because it has ensured that it has access to the entire world. No doubt, if Malcolm were still alive he would have understood and explained all of this, but in the early 1960s he was hopeful about the future because he believed in the ultimate success of the struggle that was taking place against White supremacy across the globe. This faith led to his only real misjudgment of analysis in the fight against racism.

THE WORLD COURT

Malcolm was keen to internationalize the struggle for freedom, argu-ing that "any kind of movement for freedom of Black people based solely within the confines of America is absolutely doomed to fail."[52] Racism was a global system and therefore required a global solution. The purpose of framing the situation in America as colonial was not just to help increase solidarity but also to concretely tie the African American struggle to that of Black people around the globe. He spe-cifically wanted to "internationalize" the civil rights struggle because "as long as you fight it on the level of civil rights, you're under Uncle Sam's jurisdiction. You're going to his court expecting him to correct the problem. He created the problem. He's the criminal! You don't take your case to the criminal, you take your criminal to court."[53]

In principle, it makes sense to elevate the domestic struggle to the world stage. American courts and the government were incapable of facilitating freedom, justice, and equality by their very nature, and therefore it was necessary to seek redress elsewhere. Malcolm argued that African Americans should take Uncle Sam "to court and charge him with genocide, the mass murder of millions of Black people in this country—political murder, economic murder, social murder, mental murder."[54] He specifically wanted to charge the nation with "violating the UN charter of human rights." In fact, his insistence on claiming our human rights was in large part a tactic to get the plight of Black Americans before the UN so that it could be considered by the Commission on Human Rights. He specifically stated that the American struggle needed to be elevated to the same level as that of problems such as apartheid in South Africa and the oppression in Angola, which were being considered under the human rights charter of the UN. Malcolm wanted to shift the discussion from civil to human rights so that the newly independent countries in the underdeveloped world could support the struggle of Black Americans. He admonished those who picketed outside the UN headquarters in New York demanding change by explaining that "you don't get anything on the agenda of the UN through picketing. . . . The best thing for you to do, who are liberals, is to go to the UN and get all of the books on human rights."[55]

Malcolm's faith in the UN was based on the idea that "each country has one vote . . . no matter how wealthy a nation" and also that since the end of colonialism, the former colonies within the organization far outnumbered the colonizers. This presented an opportunity because "the grouping together of the dark nations who formerly were colonized has given them enough political power to offset the military power and prestige of these mighty White nations of the West."[56] He considered that in the world court, we held the balance of power and could bring the weight of the dark nations to bear. Malcolm was once specifically asked about how he could have so much faith in the UN when America had shown it was always capable of wielding the greatest amount of power, whatever the setup of an institution was. He insisted on the fact that there was strength in numbers. But the problem with this argument is that democracy within the UN is limited to the General Assembly, the only place where there is one nation, one vote. Malcolm was correct that the General Assembly could potentially "side with us and indict Uncle Sam."[57] It was from the platform of the General Assembly that Fidel Castro denounced America and capitalism in New York, on his visit in 1960 when he met with Malcolm. In 2014, the UN launched the International Decade for People of African Descent, which declared that "people of African descent represent a distinct group whose human rights must be promoted and protected," almost fifty years after Malcolm's death.[58] The 2014 initiative suggested that member states should take action to address racism and consider reparatory justice, so it very clearly sided with Black people, at least rhetorically. However, the decade came with no funding and no legal requirements to do anything. In fact, I would guess that unless you have read one of my other books or were one of the lucky few invited to a conference, you have no idea that the decade even happened. Theoretically speaking, the General Assembly might have been a court in which we could have won a victory, but it would have been an entirely symbolic one or, as Malcolm himself would have put it, a token one.

In reality, the UN is just as devilish an institution as the IMF and World Bank, maybe more so, because it has tricked so many into having faith in it. The body was not designed to equalize power across the world but the opposite. The real political power lies in the Security Council, whose permanent members have the right of veto over any substantive decision. This means that America, Russia, Britain, France, and China can effectively prevent anything they do being declared illegal. There is a reason that America's atrocities in Korea, Vietnam, and, later on, Iraq did not come under the scrutiny of international law. Malcolm's "world court" was just as rigged as Uncle Sam's domestic arrangements. Petitioning the UN was not even a new move, let alone a radical one. In 1951, a group of activists, including W. E. B. Du Bois, submitted "We Charge Genocide," a paper highlighting the racism of the United States, to the UN.[59] Neither the General Assembly nor the Commission on Human Rights even took up the document for discussion because of American domination of their respective bodies. In 1951, there were very few so-called independent nations that had voting rights in the UN, so Malcolm probably reasoned that the approach would be more successful over a decade later, following the string of newly created countries in the dark world. But this logic demonstrates the other problem with Malcolm's faith in the UN: There was (and remains) little independent about the formerly colonized nations. Even if the UN *was* strictly one nation, one vote on important issues, the former colonies are so economically dependent on the West they would be unlikely to bite the hand that barely feeds them. Demonstrating the umbilical cord between the UN and bodies like the IMF and World Bank, there is evidence that countries that stick more closely to the US position (based on those countries' votes in the UN General Assembly) receive better terms on IMF loans.[60] Malcolm understood the nature of neocolonialism and the dangers of the nation-state yet still maintained a misguided faith in the UN. Just as the American Constitution, written by slave owners, was designed to oppress Black people, so was the Atlantic Charter, which founded the UN, created by the premier colonial and neocolonial powers of Britain and America. The UN is no more capable of providing freedom, justice, or equality for us than a chicken is able to lay a duck egg.

Malcolm's professed faith in the UN was most likely a "short-range" part of his political program. It seems unlikely that he actually thought that the UN would solve the problem of racism as he understood it. Malcolm knew that racism was an integral part of the White supremacist world order, so the UN could never deliver any ruling or create any law that would free Black people in America or anywhere else. This is where we must be very clear in distinguishing Malcolm's tactics from his solutions. The UN could be a place to connect with oppressed nations around the world, to internationalize the Black American struggle and forge the necessary alliances to build a revolution. But the UN itself was not going to be the body that ended White supremacy. This is why it is mistaken to portray Malcolm as "America's prosecuting attorney," as scholar Peniel E. Joseph does in his book contrasting Martin Luther King and Malcolm.[61] When Malcolm spoke about taking America to the world court, this was metaphorical. He knew that there was no body in front of which he could prosecute America. His condemnation of Uncle Sam was his analysis, not his solution. Malcolm was not simply making a case against White supremacy—he was intent on building the machinery to destroy the wicked system once and for all.

6

THE MOST DISRESPECTED PERSON IS THE BLACK WOMAN

It would be very easy to dismiss Malcolm as a sexist theorist who marginalized women in his analysis and activism. He frequently talked about the role of the Black man in liberation, and it is not difficult to find questionable quotations about his views on women. In his much maligned biography, Manning Marable argues that Malcolm did not trust or respect women, assuming them to be "inherently inferior and subordinate to males."[1] For all the transformation Marable informs us took place in Malcolm's life, the writer assures us that Malcolm's misogyny was deep-rooted and unshifting toward the end. Marable has taken this line from Malcolm's autobiography, where Malcolm states "that women, by their nature, are fragile and weak," as core to his being.[2] Black feminist icon, and my personal mentor, Patricia Hill Collins similarly critiques Malcolm over the descriptions of women in both his autobiography and the language of his speeches.[3] While describing his break from the Nation of Islam, Malcolm joked that if Elijah Muhammed had only admitted to his affairs with the women he impregnated, he would "shake his hand and call him a man. A good one too."[4] It is in this same speech that he challenged "these Uncle Tom Negro leaders [to] stand up and fight like men instead of running around here non-violently acting like women."

Malcolm was part of the NOI for eleven years, a group notorious for its patriarchal treatment of women, who were relegated to keeping the home while men carried out the business.[5] No one could deny that, on the issue of gender, his analysis was often deeply problematic. But it would also be a mistake to reject Malcolm's politics as a whole because of these issues. In this book, I have been at pains to stress there was no great transformation in Malcolm's ideas after leaving the NOI—but the only exception to this rule was his thinking about the role of women in the struggle. Free from Nation of Islam orthodoxy, he could, and did, build an organization where women were fully engaged in all activities. In reality, neither Malcolm's theory nor his practice is aimed at Black men *or* women; the fundamental theme running through his work is that *all* Black people must unite to rebel against White supremacy. Once he left the NOI, he was able to fully develop a political program that was applicable as equally to the lives of Black women as to Black men's. The nuances in Malcolm's outlook led to feminist scholar Angela Davis calling for a "feminist appreciation of Malcolm's political contributions."[6] I take up this mantle in this chapter to explore the important dimensions of gender in Malcolm's work.

PROTECT OUR WOMEN

When Malcolm spoke directly about women, it was usually to offer what Black feminist Farah Jasmine Griffin dubbed the "promise of protection."[7] In the teachings of the NOI, the role of the man was to be the provider in the home and to shield his wife from the dangers of the outside world. Beyoncé recently popularized a Malcolm quotation—"The most disrespected person in America is the Black woman"—but the rest of the passage is too lengthy to fit into a tweet or on a T-shirt. More importantly, the entire passage may well put off the myriad of people sharing the snippet. Malcolm fully embraced the promise of protection, making it the role of (strong) men to protect, but also to possess, "their women." The quotation is from one of the rare Malcolm speeches that was mostly recorded on video. It was delivered in 1962 in LA, where he was visiting after the police had shot and killed Nation of Islam member Ronald Stokes. Delivered in a church, the speech is vintage Malcolm, and if you have not watched it, I strongly recommend you do a quick search on YouTube. It includes the most extensive discussion of women that I have come across in a speech by him, so the excerpt is worth quoting here in full.

> The most disrespected person in America is the Black woman. The most unprotected person in America is the Black woman. The most neglected person in America is the Black woman. And as Muslims the Honorable Elijah Muhammad teaches us to respect our women and to protect our women. The only time a Muslim really gets real violent is when someone goes to molest his woman. We will kill you for our woman. I'm making it plain. We will kill you for our woman. We believe that

if the White man will do whatever is necessary to see that his women get respect and protection, then you and I will never be recognized as men until we stand up like men and place the same penalty over the head of anyone who puts his filthy hands out in the direction of our women.[8]

I have to be honest; I am surprised at how many Black women I know and respect find little wrong with the full quote. I had assumed that the possessive nature of "our women" would have been seen as problematic. But a common refrain I have heard at academic conferences is that Black men have not been there for Black women, so Malcolm's promise of protection at least pays attention to the struggles facing our sisters.

In *Blackness at the Intersection*, I shared the story of a coeditor of the collection, Kimberlé Crenshaw, telling us that many Black male activists shouted down the #SayHerName contingent of a Black Lives Matter rally because they saw police violence as a male issue.[9] I struggled to understand where the hostility came from: Surely Black women being killed by the police should evoke the same pain as when it is Black men who are murdered? In 1985, in Britain, the police shooting and paralyzing of Cherry Groce led to the Brixton rebellion, and when Cynthia Jarret died after a police search of her home, it was the spark that lit the racial powder keg on the Broadwater Farm estate in Tottenham.[10]

As far as I understand the view of the patriarchy, violence against Black women would always be seen as a more serious offense than violence done to men, and one that required a quick response from any decent Black man. I was brought up in the vein of Malcolm's incredulity that civil rights leaders would allow Black women to be brutalized in civil rights marches by the police:

They took this Black woman down in Selma, Alabama, and knocked her right down on the ground, dragging her down the street. It showed the sheriff and his henchmen throwing this Black woman on the ground. And Negro men standing around doing nothing about it, saying, "Well, let's overcome them with our capacity to love." What kind of phrase is that? . . . And then it disgraces the rest of us, because all over the world the picture is splashed showing a Black woman with some White brutes, with their knees on her holding her down, and full-grown Black men standing around watching it. Why, you are lucky they let you stay on earth, much less stay in the country.[11]

This quotation is taken from one of Malcolm's last speeches, indicating that his position on protection certainly hadn't changed by the time he died. In a time when Black men do not always stand up for Black women, it is easy to see why the promise of protection would be alluring: At least it is something, some recognition of the struggles facing Black women. Malcolm declared that if Black men went to prison for protecting Black women, they should do so proudly and state, "I came here because I defended our Black women from the filthy paw of that blue-eyed White man."[12] That idea of sacrifice may have a certain romantic appeal, but scratch the surface of the promise of protection and you see that it is underpinned by the principle of possession.

Malcolm's rationale for protecting Black women was that it was for their benefit but also for Black men to be "recognized as men." He made it plain that "you and I will never be respected until we get some respect for this Black woman."[13] In the "most disrespected person" quotation, he essentially uses the racist violence of Black men being lynched in the South as a justification for "taking the head" of any

White man who touched "our women." Lynchings were often carried out in retribution for perceived slights against the purity of White womanhood, as when fourteen-year-old Emmett Till was shot and dumped in a river for allegedly wolf whistling at a White woman. (She later admitted it never happened. Do we call her an ally for unburdening her conscience!?!) Racist violence often erupted over fragile White manhood, with the idea that we are coming after "their" women. If a White woman had sex with a Black man, it *must* have been rape; she could not have possibly desired the ape. The yearning to protect "our women" is also likely rooted in the fact that we could do little to prevent the industrial levels of sexual abuse suffered by Black women during slavery. But to reverse the logic used to justify lynchings is perverse and means that the purpose of protection is to prove ourselves *as men*. Women are simply objects to be possessed and defended to boost the male psyche.

It is statements like these that have led some to believe that the Black Power movement was a quest for Black manhood, or what author Michelle Wallace has called the "Black Macho."[14] Indeed, Malcolm talked about how the Black man had been "castrated" by White society, stripped of his power and dignity. When Malcolm spoke of the right to be respected as a human being, this was partly a call for men to be restored to full manhood, and one route toward this was to be the protector of Black women. The Black Macho embraces traditional gender roles, giving women a very specific place in the struggle. Malcolm explained that the reason Black female Nation of Islam members were not out at public protests was because they were worried that someone might molest them, and "when you put your hands on our sister, we are obligated by our religion to let your head roll in the street. . . . We are religiously obligated to take the life of a man who disrespects our women."[15] Protection meant to be hidden away; the fragile woman was to be kept indoors, to be protected from the hostile world.

White supremacy destroyed Black family relations, first through slavery, which tore families apart in the United States, and further still when it was commonplace for husbands, wives, and children to be sold off to different plantations. The harsh realities of life for the enslaved made it extremely difficult to maintain family relationships, especially when slave owners committed rape on an industrial scale and even studded out the best Black male specimens as though they were prize horses.[16] The conditions post-enslavement were only barely better, with enforced poverty making conditions for any stability highly difficult.

In Britain, we have given a name to the problems caused by migration from the Caribbean for the children left behind when their parents came to the UK for work. They are dubbed "barrel children" because they would be sent barrels of goods back from the mother country.[17] There is a whole generation of family trauma caused by parents moving and resettling, then having other children once in Britain. But less is said about the same impact on Black American families from the Great Migration (from South to North) because we are trapped in a nation-state analysis: Although family members might be migrating within the same country, the distance from the South to the North could be thousands of miles. When the migration started, after the First World War, travel was severely limited, so parents would be physically cut off from their children when migrating for work.[18] Malcolm often told his listeners about the slum conditions, overcrowding, and lack of privacy in the North that again put a strain on family life. Lynchings, police brutality, and incarceration also made it difficult for Black men to play the role of husband and father. Like everything else, the Black family has felt the negative impact of White supremacy, a fact Malcolm was keen to point out. The higher rate of single-parent households was a theme he would go back to, lamenting that there were "thousands of Black children who have no father to act as their protector or their provider" and instead looked to those working in the welfare system as their second parent.[19]

Racism has meant that the traditional gender split has largely not applied in Black communities. In the patriarchal structure, men are supposed to be in the public sphere, working to provide the money for the private sphere, the home, where women take their place. But capitalism is based on slavery, which took Black women and put them to work. After emancipation, Black women still had to work to help make ends meet, and nothing changed with the Great Migration to Northern cities. While White feminists were railing against the "housewife" role, Black women were laboring, often as domestics in White homes.[20] The only place we can see the differentiation between public and private spaces within Black communities is through experiences of violence.

In the early twentieth century, outside of the home, Black men were disproportionately subject to being lynched.[21] Now we are more likely to be killed by the police or incarcerated.[22] In her book *When They Call You a Terrorist*, Black Lives Matter cofounder Patrisse Khan-Cullors explains that it was witnessing her brothers and cousins being hassled by the police that raised her consciousness.[23] It was the murder of unarmed teenager Trayvon Martin that sparked the Black Lives Matter movement, just as it was Emmett Till's mutilated body that was the catalyst for the civil rights movement. The spectacle of Black men swinging from nooses or policemen kneeling on their necks for almost ten minutes causes outrage and sparks protest. But the violence against Black women has always tended to be behind closed doors: rape and sexual violence, or being forcibly evicted for not being able to provide for her family. We therefore see racial violence generally through a male lens, which to some extent explains, but does not justify, the rejection of the #SayHerName campaign by some Black male activists. Reading Crenshaw's book *#SayHerName*, which recounts the stories of Black women killed by the police, I couldn't understand why the stories of people like Michelle Cusseaux, Tanisha Anderson, and Kayla Moore in the United States did not receive more media and movement attention.[24] But it is clear that police violence is still largely seen as an attack on men, and to bring the experiences of women into the picture takes the focus off the assault on the endangered Black male.

This is a painful regression, one that moves away from Malcolm's view that violence against any of us is an attack on all of us. Malcolm's wife Betty Shabazz explained, in a piece for *Ebony* magazine after he died, that her husband "felt that Black men should be especially concerned about protecting their women collectively; by doing so they were protecting themselves collectively."[25] Ida B. Wells argued that her anti-lynching work was feminist because when Black men were killed, it shattered the lives of the women they left behind. When Malcolm rallied Black men to defend "their" women from abuse, no matter how problematic some of the rhetoric, it ultimately stemmed from the same position, viewing an attack on women as one on the whole community. I struggle to think how strongly Malcolm would condemn any attempt to ignore the violence against Black women to keep the light shining on the problems of men. It shows how far our politics have deteriorated that to be a real man for many means to ignore the pain of women.

In trying to protect women from public harm, however, Malcolm missed the reality that it was in the private sphere that Black women predominantly experienced violence. Not going to protests was not going to protect Black women from private violence. The uncomfortable truth about the violence facing Black women in Malcolm's time and today, too, is that it is more likely to come from Black men than White ones. But this is also the case for the more public violence facing Black men, who are significantly more likely to be murdered and assaulted than women, more often than not at the hands of other Black men.[26]

Malcolm indicted the conditions that Black people were forced to live in that produced higher levels of domestic and interpersonal violence, spaces where some of us have internalized the racist myth that our lives are worth less due to our Blackness. This is why moral reform was so important to Malcolm, both within and outside of the NOI. Not as individual uplift but as a necessary step for the community to combat the damage being done to us by White supremacy. In the Nation of Islam, there were strict prohibitions against being violent toward women, and the militant wing of the group, the Fruit of Islam, would punish those who broke the rules.[27] A real man was not one whom his wife needed protection from. For the NOI, the denial of the opportunity for the traditional nuclear family for Black people was an impact of racism that needed to be overcome. If the NOI could restore real Black men to the role of protectors and providers, this would allow women to take their rightful place in the home. This is why Farrakhan pledged to marry thousands of Black couples at the Million Man March: restore the family, restore community, and grow both together. Malcolm's own personal relationship with his wife, Betty Shabazz, certainly mirrored the traditional family role. While Malcolm was out building the Nation of Islam and then traveling the world, Betty was at home raising their six daughters. In her *Ebony* piece, she said that her husband thought "that the Black woman has the chief responsibility for passing along Black cultural traditions to the children" and that "if you educate a woman, you educate a family." This suggests the traditional role of women contributing to the revolution by rearing the children and caring for the family. But Shabazz also stressed that, contrary to popular belief, Malcolm "did not believe that a woman's role was just in the home and in the bed" and that "in the movement, he felt that a woman's role should be determined by her qualifications."[28] Once he left the Nation of Islam, Malcolm was able to put into practice this principle of organization.

GREATER CONTRIBUTION THAN MANY OF US MEN

After he left the NOI, there was a marked shift in the way that Malcolm spoke about women, moving away from solely the promise of protection. While traveling in Africa in 1964, he commented,

> The degree of progress can never be separated from the woman. If you are in a country that's progressive, the woman is progressive. If you are in a country that reflects the consciousness toward the importance of education, it is because the woman is aware of the importance of education. But in every backward country you'll find the women are backward . . . and I frankly am proud of the contributions that our women have made in the struggle for freedom . . . because they have made a greater contribution than many of us men.[29]

His acknowledgment of the role of women in the public sphere was novel, breaking the traditional boundaries that lay at the foundation of the NOI. This may have been partly because on his travels he met a number of Black women who were at the forefront of the struggle. In

Ghana, there was a contingent of expatriate African Americans who greeted him when he arrived. Shirley Graham Du Bois was a talented musician and composer who staged an opera with an all-Black cast and orchestra in Cleveland in 1932. In the 1940s, she joined the Sojourners for Truth and Justice, who were Black women working for global liberation, and became a key member of the Communist Party. This was all before she married her famous second husband, the scholar-activist W. E. B. Du Bois, who is credited as a leader in both the civil rights and Pan-African movements, in 1951. The couple settled in Ghana in 1961 and were friends of the first president of the so-called independent nation, Kwame Nkrumah. Shirley Graham Du Bois spoke at the All-African People's Conference and was key to Malcolm's efforts to link his Organization of Afro-American Unity to the Organization of African Unity on the continent itself.[30] Malcolm also met with and was inspired by a young Maya Angelou, who was living in Ghana with her son when he visited. Angelou was planning to become a part of the OAAU and the battle to indict America in the UN when she returned to the country. But Malcolm was killed before she had the chance.[31]

Malcolm was no stranger to strong Black women who were engaged in politics. His mother, born Louise Langdon in Grenada, had been an active member of Garvey's Universal Negro Improvement Association, which is where she met Malcolm's father.[32] The *Autobiography* opens with a story about Malcolm's mother, pregnant with him at the time, confronting a group of Ku Klux Klansmen on horseback "surrounding the house, brandishing their shotguns."[33] After Malcolm's father was killed, Louise tried hard to keep the family together, but she struggled with her mental health and ended up being committed to an institution. Seeing the deterioration in his mother was no doubt a great personal tragedy to Malcolm, which only strengthened his resolve to bring down the system of White supremacy that had hurt her. Malcolm's mother was a key influence on his politics, particularly in embracing his Blackness. Louise was light-skinned because she was the child of a White man who had raped her mother. Rather than trying to use the privilege that could come with light skin, she joined the UNIA, that most Black conscious of organizations. Malcolm was also light-skinned, and, contrary to the advice of the day, he remembers his mother "would tell me to get out of the house and 'let the sun shine on you so you can get some color.' She went out of her way never to let me become afflicted with a sense of color-superiority."[34]

One of Malcolm's other major influences growing up was his older half sister, Ella Collins. After Malcolm's mother was institutionalized, he went to live with Ella in Boston in 1940. He credits this as so important that no other "physical move in my life has been more pivotal or profound in its repercussions."[35] In Boston he learned from Ella, who was resourceful and helped him to find work on the trains. In Spike Lee's "epic," Ella was a peripheral figure, but in reality she was probably Malcolm's primary influence. It was actually Ella who was a key voice influencing Malcolm to join the Nation of Islam. He stayed extremely close to his sister throughout his life, and Ella was meant to join him on his hajj to Mecca that was so eye-opening for him. But they only had enough money for one of them to go, and Ella insisted that it be Malcolm. Ella was an organizer throughout her life, a model of Black womanhood that could not be forced to stay in the private sphere. When Malcolm died, it was Ella who took over leadership of both the Organization of Afro-American Unity and Muslim Mosque Inc., which he had founded after his split with the NOI.

According to Earl Grant, one of Malcolm's close friends, during his time both in and out of the NOI, he was keen for "women to be given a more defined role" in the organization.[36] Malcolm actively recruited women for leadership roles in the OAAU, like Lynn Shiflet, who ran the organization when he was on his travels, and Sara Mitchell, who crafted the aims and objectives.[37] Malcolm understood the importance of fully including women in the leadership of organization. The OAAU was the vehicle for his revolutionary politics, the most important legacy he was developing. Committing to a female chairperson shows that his commitment to Black women in the movement was not a tokenistic or solely symbolic gesture. Marable's dismissal of Malcolm as someone who "did not trust women" is ridiculous, given this reality. He would not facilitate stewardship of the OAAU to someone he distrusted. Malcolm did not put limits on women's involvement in the struggle based upon their gender. The clearest example of this is in his speeches on the question of violence.

NO MORE UNCLE TOMS IN CHINA

Malcolm's rhetorical embrace of violence has perhaps been the most important factor in connecting him to the caricature of the Black Macho. There certainly were cartoonish Black male figures in the Black Power movement, who were, in the words of Michelle Wallace, a popular Black feminist writer, intent on representing themselves as a "black man with an erect phallus . . . pushing it up into the face of America."[38] Eldrige Cleaver, who was once a prominent member of the Black Panther Party, stands out as the icon of the Black Macho idea. He rose to fame for his prison memoir *Soul on Ice*, where he justified the rape of White women as an anti-racist tactic to help Black men regain Black manhood, and he excused the rape of Black women as practice for this liberatory act.[39] The fact the Panthers welcomed him *after* this book tells you all you need to know about the problematic gender politics in the party. He came up with the concept of "pussy power," arguing that women had the ultimate control in the movement because they could withhold sex from their partners in order to get them to support the struggle.[40] Cleaver was constantly advocating direct acts of violence against the police and dubbed the group's survival programs, which fed and provided medical support to the community, a "sissy" approach. This grand revolutionary wanted to go out in a manly blaze of glory. Once he left the movement, he went into fashion, creating a pair of "penis pants," which, rather than forcing a man to hang to either the left or right when wearing trousers, allowed him to put his penis in a pouch that stuck straight out of his trousers in the middle. He explained that "we've been castrated in clothing," and that he was opening up "new vistas."[41] No, I am not joking; he literally wanted to "push his phallus in the face" of the world. Cleaver had been in exile after somehow escaping America while on bail for the attempted murder of police officers. Once he returned to the country in 1975, he denounced the Panthers, and after a spending a few months in prison, the charges against him were mysteriously dropped. He was supported by a wealthy Republican and made an unsuccessful run for a Senate seat with the party.[42] If you are gullible enough to believe that Cleaver was not a government stooge by this point, then I am happy to forward you an email I received from a Nigerian prince who wants to pay you to move his money into the country. There is no worse representative for the Black Power movement than Elridge "Stooge" Cleaver, and yet his Black Macho caricature dominates the reputation of Black revolutionaries on the issue of gender.

When we think about Malcolm and women, we need to dispel the caricature. As explored in Chapter 3, Malcolm embraced violence as a tactic of self-defense within America. There certainly are times when he invoked a patriarchal promise of protection, but it would be a critical error to confuse advocating violence with claiming masculinity. In his conception of revolutionary violence in the underdeveloped world, he gave a telling example of the kind of approach he thought was necessary:

> When I was in prison, I read an article in *Life* magazine show-ing a little Chinese girl, nine years old; her father was on his hands and knees and she was pulling the trigger 'cause he was an Uncle Tom Chinaman. When they had the revolution over there, they took a whole generation of Uncle Toms—just wiped them out. And within ten years that little girl become [*sic*] a full-grown woman. No more Toms in China.[43]

If a "little Chinese girl" is the image of the revolutionary that comes to mind for Malcolm, then it is clear that he is not gendering this category. This story was not told in the context of shaming men into action; it was just an example he gave for revolutionary violence. Here, the counterrevolutionary was male, the violent revolutionary female. In one of his last speeches, he received a question from a Black woman in the audience, asking, "Why couldn't we go over there and shoot up guys in Alabama?" in defense of the civil rights protesters. Malcolm encouraged her, "My! Good work, sister, you're talking my kind of talk." She went on to say of those Black men who wouldn't sup-port the effort, "If I'd been over there, I'd have shot brothers who didn't go out." Malcolm responded, "I know you would." The woman contin-ued to say she would "blow them away," to which Malcolm concurred, "I *know* you would."[44] He expressed certainty that this Black woman would pick up a gun for the revolutionary cause before the Black men in the South would do so.

It could be argued that Malcolm's use of the example of the Chinese girl and his encouragement of this Black female audience member demonstrated that he was embracing the masculine vision of a bloodthirsty revolution and just wanted women to join in. But that would be offensive to the countless women who have been involved in violent revolutionary struggles for freedom. I grew up revering women like Dahir Al-Kahina in Tunisia in the seventh century, Queen Nzinga in Angola in the sixteenth, Nanny of the Maroons in Jamaica in the eighteenth, Cécile Fatiman in Haiti in the nineteenth, and Yaa Asantewaa in Ghana in the twentieth, just to name a few. In fact, when Yaa Asantewaa was resisting the British attempts to seize the important Asante Golden Stool, she called out the men for their inaction, declaring: "If you, the men of Asante, will not go forward, then we will. We, the women, will. I shall call upon my fellow women. We will fight! We will fight till the last of us falls in the battlefields."[45] Violence is the fundamental underpinning of Western imperialism, and therefore Malcolm understood it would take violence to overturn it. He did not gender those who would have to fight and bleed for freedom. Ironically, it is the patriarchy that leads us to perceive violence as a supposedly male form of resistance, while women, by the same token, are assumed to look for more passive ways of political struggle.

THE BLACK MAN

Listen to any of Malcolm's speeches, and you will notice that he constantly talks in what I call the "royal he." Everything is addressed to or about "the Black man in America." His speeches are full of what "he" needs to do to bring about change. Taken at face value, we could view this as his words only being addressed to Black men. I have heard countless times that no Black social movement has ever responded to the needs of Black women, and no doubt the language used has a lot to do with this dangerous misconception. If Malcolm had only been talking to men, it would be surprising to see that so many Black women were at his talks, asking questions too. Black women have been equally moved and inspired by his words as men have. Undoubtedly, women *can* be swept up by the patriarchy; the NOI still has plenty of Black women in it who have submitted to conservative gender roles. That women were involved in the struggle by no means indicates that there was no patriarchy.

After Malcolm was assassinated, one of the pretenders to the throne who emerged to fill the void was Ron Karenga. He founded the US Organization (with "US" commonly thought to stand for "United Slaves"), along with a friend of Malcolm's, Hakim Jamal, in 1965. But Jamal quickly left US Organization behind, because he knew that Malcolm would have disapproved of Karenga's total focus on culture as the solution to the problem. Karenga anointed himself as "Maulana" (which means "master teacher" in Swahili) and insisted that his followers adopt a "complete acceptance of an alternative lifestyle . . . dress, mannerisms and an entire social life."[46] Karenga essentially started a cult based on adopting a so-called African lifestyle that would heal your broken soul and lead to liberation. A key ingredient of this supposedly liberatory way of life was installing patriarchal gender roles into Black relationships. He dictated that the role of the woman was to "inspire her man, educate her children and participate in social organization." He went further, insisting that "what makes a woman appealing is femininity and she can't be feminine without being submissive."[47] This is a clear articulation of the principle of possession. Women support men, raise the children, and look after the home, and in return, men provide for and protect them.

The NOI was a major influence on Karenga, and he mirrored their gender relations. Groups like the Nation of Islam and United Slaves were fundamentally patriarchal; to remove the patriarchy would be to radically transform them into something else. Patricia Hill Collins calls their brand of politics a "civic" religion because they depend on the same tools as any other faith. There is a belief in a divine will (Africanness), a prescription as to what to believe and how to behave. The congregation believes that if they follow those teachings they will be individually transformed and saved.[48] But there is potential to develop Malcolm's promise to one based on equality.

The difference between Malcolm and the NOI is that he did not limit the role of women simply to the helpmate of their men. From Malcolm's ideas of protection, it is possible to develop a position where, of course, we must protect Black women, because we should protect all Black people. Black women would not need special protection or to be kept off the front lines because of their fragility, and rather than protecting women as our property, we would offer protection to the entire community as part of redeeming all of our lives. This message is inherent in Malcolm's call to self-defense: that we collectively have to protect all of us from the violence of White supremacy. So far, I have tried not to speculate about Malcolm's views without showing the receipts. But given the changes in his thinking after he left the NOI, it is likely that he eventually ended up at this place. I would also stress that the patriarchal promise is still very clear in his final speeches.

I also wonder if the promise of protection (linked to manhood) goes some way to explaining the rejection by male protesters of the #SayHerName slogan. Remember, Malcolm argued that letting a Black woman be brutalized by the police "disgraces all of us," chiding that, for a man who did nothing, "you are lucky they let you stay on earth, much less stay in the country."[49] To internalize the message that state violence against women makes you less of a man would mean that seeing such brutality would cause an immense amount of shame. Perhaps it was that shame that led some to reject the names of Black women killed by the police being chanted, not because they didn't care, but because they had to shun the object of their impotence. Whatever the case, the promise of protection is ultimately unhelpful and needs to be replaced with a more equitable conception of community self-defense.

When offering the promise of protection, Malcolm was directly talking to men when he used "he." But, speaking more generally, that language choice was also due to him using the conventions of the time. My contention is that he was actually very rarely talking directly to either men or women. There are very few instances where he directly addressed the specific issues of either gender. Recall some of the key concepts we have discussed so far: token integration, the Fox and the Wolf, the permanence of racism. These may play out in gendered ways, but they are not about *either* men or women. Part of Malcolm's appeal is because he talked to and about Black people as a collective, and these ideas can then be applied in specific circumstances. A perfect example of this would be one of Malcolm's most important conceptual ideas, when he declared that there was a "new type of Negro on the scene, who calls *himself* Black. . . . He doesn't make any apology for his Black skin."[50] It would be easy to dismiss this as evidence of Malcolm's patriarchy, and it is possible that when he said it he really was only referring to men. But the meaning of this declaration remains true if we de-gender it: "There is a new type of Negro on the scene who calls *themself* Black. . . . Who makes no apology for *their* Black skin." The point Malcolm is making is that we should claim Blackness and use it as the basis of a radical politics.

It is also undeniably true that Black women were central to this process of self-definition. The Afro, one of the most recognizable and powerful symbols of the "Black is beautiful" age, was at first largely a statement by Black women. My mother told me about the impact of going into work one day and, rather than tying back her hair as usual, combing it out into a huge Afro. She described the jaws dropping so vividly to me, it is as though it is my own memory.

The same is true for the quotation that is the title of this book: "Nobody can give you freedom," which was delivered by Malcolm in a speech after he had left the NOI, in 1964. He continues in the same speech, "Nobody can give you equality or justice or anything. If you're a *man*, you take it."[51] Given the history of men being seen as the agents of history and women as the passengers, we could read this as a typically patriarchal formulation. But Malcolm delivered this line while he was introducing legendary civil rights activist Fannie Lou Hamer to the Organization of Afro-American Unity in New York. Hamer was speaking about her experiences as part of the Mississippi Freedom Democratic Party, which was trying to get seated at the political convention instead of the all-White delegation whom the state party had endorsed. Hamer was an activist on the ground trying to register Black voters in one of the most dangerous states for civil rights organizers. In 1963, she was arrested for trying to extend democracy and suffered such a severe beating in the jailhouse, from two inmates who were forced to administer it, that she suffered permanent kidney damage and from then on walked with a limp.[52] Hamer's speech at the Democratic convention in 1964 was so powerful and damaging that President Lyndon Johnson swiftly organized a press conference at the same time to try and block it from being televised. After detailing how, after her arrest—which was for her temerity to try to register Black people to vote—two Black prisoners were ordered to beat her in a prison cell, Hamer questioned, "Is this America, the land of the free and the home of the brave, where we have to sleep with our telephones off of the hooks because our lives be threatened daily, because we want to live as decent human beings, in America?"[53]

Malcolm's remarks in response did include some of the promise of protection, as he opined, "When I listen to Mrs. Hamer, a Black woman—could be my mother, my sister, my daughter—describe what they had done to her in Mississippi, I ask myself how in the world can we ever expect to be respected as men when we will allow something like that to be done to our women, and we do nothing about it?"[54] But Malcolm was not simply engaging in the problematic promise of protection, holding up Hamer as an object of possession to be protected by Black men. Malcolm acknowledged her as a leader of the movement, speaking in Harlem to drum up support for the struggle. Hamer considered Malcolm "one of the best friends I ever had. A remarkable man" and explained that he was due to join her in Mississippi (the week after he was assassinated).[55] When Malcolm spoke of those who would "take" their freedom, he certainly included Hamer and all the other Black women who he knew had contributed, and would continue to do so, to the movement. There is no reason to imagine that it is not possible to include women in Malcolm's vision because he did not exclude them.

The power of Malcolm's work is that it connects Black people across time and continents. The underlying promise is a unity that brings us together to create a radically different society. Malcolm understood that this was impossible without women, and once he left the confines of the Nation of Islam, he began to put into practice an approach to Black revolution that fully included them. He was by no means perfect in this regard, and when he died, he was still weighed down by the promise of protection. But his position was evolving, like most of his practice after finally leaving the NOI.

Malcolm died sixty years ago with an unfinished political program because of his assassination. If we are to continue his revolutionary work, that doesn't mean ignoring its problematic elements but evolving the ones that are essential and moving past those that are not. To do so means dispelling the Malcolm myth as a misogynist with nothing to offer Black women but a place in the home breeding revolutionaries. As we have discussed so far, the key features of Malcolm's analysis predate critical race theory, which has been a central site for developing Black feminist analysis. Dealing with the inconsistencies around gender is essential, given the potential power of a Blackness that could truly unite Africa and the diaspora. Anything that marks out hierarchies in that Blackness is disastrous because it undermines the unity necessary to deliver freedom. If people feel alienated and excluded from radical theory and practice because of gender, then we cannot build successful movements that can truly achieve liberation. We don't need to throw out Malcolm's work, just develop the necessary elements to use it today. One of Malcolm's most important contributions is his formulation of Blackness as the basis for revolution.

7

WHO TAUGHT YOU TO HATE YOURSELF?

When researching for this book, I took a trip to the Schomburg Center for Research in Black Culture in Harlem, Malcolm's old stomping ground. It was not the first time I had visited Harlem, but walking down Malcolm X Boulevard, formerly Lenox Avenue, took on even greater significance given the nature of the project. Gentrification is gobbling up the area, but the further across 110th Street you travel, the more you can feel the heartbeat of the community. Harlem was once the capital city for the African diaspora, and as Malcolm explained when he was alive, the neighborhood held the "largest concentration of people of African descent that exists anywhere on this earth." He declared that there were "more Africans in Harlem than exist in any city on the African continent," and when he visited the University of Ghana he told his audience that "in Harlem they call it Little Africa, and when you walk through Harlem, you're in Ibadan [in Nigeria], everyone there looks just like you."[1]

With mass urbanization taking place on the continent and gentrification in New York since the 1960s, it is certainly no longer the case that Harlem houses the most Africans, but even today you can understand why Malcolm described Harlem as a colony. Racial segregation in America remains something to behold. Gus Newport, who knew Malcolm, told me that they had tried to get Malcolm to run for Adam Clayton Powell's seat in the House of Representatives. As unlikely as it sounds that Malcolm could have won political office in America, given Harlem's demographics, he would have been a shoo-in.

I went to the Schomburg Center to read the missing chapter of the *Autobiography* that was donated in 2018. I was hoping it was the chapter on the Organization of Afro-American Unity that Haley chopped from his version of Malcolm's life story, but it turned out to be a different piece of the picture that was removed. The title of the chapter was "The Negro," and it outlined one of Malcolm's key theoretical contributions to understanding the plight of the ex-slaves fighting for freedom. In the missing pages, he captured just how completely the unmaking of the enslaved was to turn us into beasts of burden.

Malcolm explained how we internalized the hatred that was beaten into us and how undoing this damage was the first step toward being free. By locating the school system as a key site of reproducing "the Negro," he aimed to show Black people that we needed to educate our children to love ourselves. In this chapter, we explore the problem of the image of the Negro and the essential need to overcome it to gain freedom.

THE SO-CALLED NEGRO

In order to understand the scale of struggle necessary to liberate the Black masses, Malcolm argued that we must "realize that the White slave master severed every link with anything remotely resembling a past, to render his bastard creation 'the Negro' into a human blank, a human kind of putty."[2] To enslave us, we had to first be unmade, turned into the beasts of burden who could do the labor that built the modern world. To do so, the slave masters had to

> invent a system that would strip us of everything about us that we could use to prove we were somebody. And once he had stripped us of all human characteristics, stripped us of our language, stripped us of our history, stripped us of all cultural knowledge, and brought us down to the level of an animal—he then began to treat us like an animal, selling us from one plantation to another, selling us from one owner to another, breeding us like you breed cattle.[3]

Malcolm reminded his audiences that when we were brought over in chains, "you lost your name, you lost your language, you lost your mind, you lost your culture."[4] He explained that "Negro means a slave. Someone who has been left out of society politically, economically, and otherwise. . . . It's not an anthropological term. It's a slave term. It was invented by slave masters and attached to their property or chattel or merchandise."[5] The idea of "racialization" has become commonplace in academic discussions of racism today, whereby groups are put into racial categories so they can be oppressed, exploited, or excluded.[6] Malcolm was describing this process in relation to Black people being turned into Negroes so that we could be enslaved. He stressed that "we were made into Negroes" and that the whole concept is a product "of Western civilization, of Western crimes."[7] Malcolm was articulating that this creation was a central product of Western civilization. We were turned into the building blocks of Western society. In the missing chapter from the *Autobiography*, he explained that "when anyone invents something, it is something he needs to make his life easier, to make him richer, and meanwhile something he can control and command."[8] His understanding of the Negro explains why he knew that racism could never be separated from White society. Anti-Blackness is the foundation stone upon which America and the rest of the West is built, so of course trying to find freedom for Black people would be like asking a chicken to lay duck egg.

The Negro was as lucrative a creation as anything ever created by the devilish White man, who needed Black people "enslaved and contained" and therefore "supplied the Negro with the substitute culture."[9] This process began "simply by dividing us from our African brothers and sisters for 400 years" and then "converting us to his Christian religion, and then by teaching us to call ourselves 'Negroes' and telling us we were no longer African."[10] To create the Negro, therefore, the enslavers stripped us of our native languages, religions, customs, and even names. The most famous literary example is in Haley's other classic work of faction, *Roots*, where Kunta Kinte is mercilessly whipped in public on the plantation until he accepts his new name of Toby.[11]

X

The surname X was adopted by members of the Nation of Islam to replace the names passed down from slave owners. Adopting the X marked the unknown, the absence created by White supremacy. It might be a surprise to learn that Andrews is not actually the name of my ancestors in Africa but the surname of the last White man to own my family members. As a member of the NOI, Malcolm legally adopted the surname Shabazz, which is why his wife, Betty, carried that name. In the misguided effort to see Malcolm as a different person after he left the Nation of Islam, I have heard a number of people argue that we should call him el-Hajj Malik el-Shabazz to better represent him. This ignores the fact that Malcolm adopted Shabazz in the NOI but specifically embraced the X out in the world because it represented the conditions that needed to be overcome. He held his slave name in such disregard that he refused to utter it in a 1963 television interview, despite the presenter's repeated attempts to press him into revealing it. After initially asking Malcolm, "What is your real name?"—and following up with the ultimate Karen question, "Did you go to court to establish it?"—the presenter still refused to give in. After Malcolm told him the history of how slave names became attached to Black people, the presenter continued to plow ahead:

Presenter: Would you mind telling me what your father's last name was?

Malcolm: My father didn't know his last name. My father got his last name from his grandfather and his grandfather got it from his grandfather, who got it from the slave master. The real names of our people were destroyed during slavery.

Presenter: Was there any line, any point in the genealogy of your family when you did have to use a last name and if so, what was it?

Malcolm: The last name of my forefathers was taken from them when they were brought to America and made slaves. And then the name of the slave master was given, which we refuse; we reject that name today.

Presenter: You mean you won't even tell me what your father's supposed last name was? Or gifted last name was?

Malcolm: (*with a smile*) I never acknowledge it, whatsoever.

It is only at this point that the presenter gave in and looked down at his papers before moving on. The scene is funny, if only to witness Malcolm frustrating his opponent, so I would recommend watching the video clip online.[12] But Malcolm was also deathly serious and gave the presenter a look that made his resolve crystal clear: He would never acknowledge his slave name, which is why I have kept it out of this book entirely. There was one transformation in Malcolm's life, and it was joining the NOI and adopting the X. That name change was one he never abandoned, so it is an essential part of his politics.

For the Nation of Islam, those Black people who had not accepted the Muslim religion were lost and deemed to be mentally dead. To be stuck in the nonbeing of the Negro was a terminal fate that could only be treated by conversion to the NOI. For their recent biography of Malcolm X, Les and Tamara Payne explained how they took the title from a report: When Malcolm was successfully recruiting to the Nation of Islam, he would tell Elijah Muhammad that "the dead . . . are arising."[13] The Negro was the ex-slave, the second-class citizen, the jungle savage brought to America to be saved and civilized. It was the ultimate degradation, the label of the nonperson, who had "never been accepted as a human being," much less a citizen. Malcolm often put "so-called" in front of Negro because he was so disgusted with the label. He once almost apologized to an audience, saying, "Excuse me if I say 'so-called' because it is hard for me to just outright say Negro when I know what that word Negro really means."[14] When Frantz Fanon talked about the zone of "nonbeing," he was talking about being the Negro, a state of "social death" hallmarked by the absence of humanity.[15] Once we were seen in such terms, we could be traded like cattle and bred like horses to be forced to labor on the plantations. We can now be shot dead in the street or forced down makeshift mines to retrieve the minerals necessary for so-called progress.

The term "Negro" was dangerous not only because it allowed White people to oppress us, but we also internalized the messages that were given to us. Malcolm explained that "when you have no knowledge of your history, you're just another animal; in fact, you're a Negro; something that's nothing."[16] He warned that "usually, when you find a man who calls himself a Negro, he can't tell you what language that he spoke before he came to this country. It's of no consequence, no interest. He believes that prior to coming here, he was a savage in the jungle, and therefore he had no language, and this justifies his lack of knowledge concerning that mother tongue today."[17]

Malcolm tied this delusion into the desire for integration, arguing that "they actually think that the White man is the personification of perfection. And whenever they're allowed to go live in his neighborhood or sit in his restaurant or mingle or socialize with him . . . that they have made progress."[18] Malcolm's rejection of integration was partly a rejection of the idea that there was a privilege in being able to join White people—that was for the Negro, those who had been cowed into believing the lies they had been fed about themselves.

We had to be subdued to be controlled, and we became stuck in the image that the devilish White man created. Malcolm was the one who pointed out that to maintain the lie of the Negro, we had to be taught how to hate ourselves, and he argued that anti-Blackness remained deeply ingrained in Black culture. While he was a street hustler, he would "conk" his hair, meaning to perm it, to remove all the African kinks. To do so, he applied lye to his hair and essentially burned it straight. In one speech, he joked about people who continued to try to look the smooth-haired White part, saying, "Lye would put a hole in steel, and you know your head is not that hard."[19] This self-hatred was conditioned into us, and Malcolm responded to accusations that the NOI preached hate by rebuking his audience,

Who taught you to hate the texture of your hair? Who taught you to hate the color of your skin to such an extent that you bleach to get like the White man? Who taught you to hate the shape of your nose and the shape of your lips? Who taught you to hate yourself from the top of your head to the soles of your feet? Who taught you to hate your own kind? Who taught you to hate the race that you belong to so much so that you don't want to be around each other? No, before you come asking Mr. Mohammed does he teach hate, you should ask yourself who taught you to hate being what God gave you.[20]

ONLY A FOOL WOULD LET THE ENEMY TEACH HIS CHILDREN

Malcolm knew exactly who it was that had ingrained self-hatred into the so-called Negro. The slave master whipped submission into us, but the school system picked up from where he left off. Malcolm condemned the "textbooks of the American educational system" because they "try and make it appear that we were nothing but animals or savages before we were brought here, to hide the criminal acts that they had to perpetuate upon us in order to bring us down to the level of animals that we're on today."[21]

.   Malcolm quipped that this rewriting of history was so thorough that "by the time the Negro in America was receiving education, the White man's books had so 'Whitened' history that even the White man was being self-brainwashed."[22] Here Malcolm was again leading the way on Black critical theory, challenging the institutions of schooling, which became a central feature of civil rights activism. Malcolm explained that the very nature of the school system taught inferiority to Black children:

> The White man teaches you that Columbus discovered America, George Washington founded it, Patrick Henry said, "Give me liberty or give me death," and Abraham Lincoln was the one who was responsible for the emancipation of the slaves. From the cradle to the grave you and I are taught to look up to White people. He refers to himself as the great White father of all of the great deeds. He claims that he's the one who did them.[23]

This propaganda in schools was central to maintaining the delusion of the Negro, because if White people did all the great things in history, then Black people did nothing and were the savages waiting to be saved. The "cradle to the grave" nature of Whitewashed schooling is important because it indicates that Malcolm extended his critique of the system to universities too. Malcolm was alive when Black students were first entering predominantly White institutions in increasing numbers, gaining access to the elite education that would supposedly propel them forward. But we must always remember that the racist knowledge that masquerades as a curriculum in schools is directly drawn from the universities that produce it. Bizarrely, I have found myself in the position of having to justify the role of research to senior management at the university where I teach, when it is the fact that universities produce knowledge that separates them from the school system. Students are not paying tens of thousands of dollars to be taught by teachers who are repeating what they have read. The very definition of the university is that these are the people at the cutting edge, making knowledge that filters down to the common people from their lofty positions in the ivory tower. Teachers are graduates from universities, trained in universities with books written in universities. It is utterly impossible to decolonize the school curriculum without taking a sledgehammer to the racist knowledge produced in the esteemed halls of learning.

Given the nature of what is taught in the universities, Malcolm explained the dilemma facing Black graduates: "Today you're coming out of college, you're coming out of the leading universities, you are trying to go in a good direction but you don't know which direction to go in."[24] Malcolm reminds us that no matter how high the prestige of the White education system, it was not meant to liberate Black people. It could never be a solution to our problems. This leaves the Black graduate trapped, never to be accepted by White society but with no knowledge that could help Black people.

These ideas followed from the work of Black American scholar Carter G. Woodson, who wrote the classic *The Mis-education of the Negro* in 1933.[25] Woodson, who was born to formerly enslaved parents in 1875, took advantage of the racially integrated Berea College in Kentucky to receive his higher education. He then went on to study at the University of Chicago and complete a PhD at Harvard. He was therefore very well acquainted with the Whitewashed instruction he had received throughout his career. In the *Mis-education*, he savagely critiqued the lessons he was taught as providing nothing useful for Black graduates, leaving them devoid of any skills to uplift the community. Worse still, due to its Whitewashed nature, schooling taught Black people the inferiority necessary to keep us in our place. He wrote that

> when you determine what a man shall think you do not have to concern yourself about what he will do. If you make a man feel that he is inferior, you do not have to compel him to accept an inferior status, for he will seek it himself. . . . You do not have to order him to the back door. He will go without being told; and if there is no back door, his very nature will demand one.[26]

There is no better description to capture the essence of Malcolm's understanding of how the Negro is created and maintained in contemporary society. By breeding the inferiority into us, we become the image that the racist society requires us to be. Woodson founded Negro History Week in America in 1926 as an antidote, which later became Black History Month and spread to Britain in 1987.

The legacy of the Negro in the school system was just as prevalent in Britain. In Bernard Coard's classic *How the West Indian Child Is Made Educationally Sub-normal in the British School System*, he argued that "when Black children are saturated with images of great White men and racist stereotypes of Black people they cannot help but develop a deep inferiority complex. He soon loses motivation to succeed academically since, at best, the learning experience in the classroom is an elaborate irrelevance to his personal life, and at worst it is a racially humiliating experience."[27] At the time Coard wrote the book, up to 70 percent of Black boys in parts of London were being labeled as "subnormal" and removed from mainstream schools.[28] Coard wrote the book with community support to put pressure on the schools to stop this racist practice. Schools have been a site of resistance and continue to be so because they continue to teach the inferiority that is essential to maintaining the image of the Negro. I have purposefully not used the word "education" here because the propaganda being pumped into children is schooling in racism rather than a genuine attempt at a broad education. It may not be as overt today as it was in the past, but the reality is that schools continue to teach White supremacy, and its ideas are pumped into most of their students, which is why there is not much activism to transform the curriculum.

One of the first landmark civil rights legal victories was *Brown v. Board of Education* in 1954, which started the process of desegregating the schools in America. We have already discussed the case of the Little Rock Nine and their perilous struggle to attend the White high school in Arkansas. These scenes were repeated across the South and even in the North, where Black children were put on buses to attend predominantly White schools. The primary solution to the problem in America was to desegregate and open up opportunities for Black children. But Malcolm questioned not only whether such acts were genuine or token efforts at integration but also the strategy itself. In reality, desegregation of schooling meant Black students going to learn in White schools, as though there was something inherently better about the education that they would receive there. But Malcolm was scathing about the propaganda that masqueraded as an enlightened education and the damage that it could do to Black children. He bristled at the suggestion of fighting to send his children to White-controlled schools: "Send my children to a school where their brains are being crippled? No."[29] Importantly, though, Malcolm didn't limit his understanding of a White school to those that had White teachers and students. There were plenty of schools, then and now, with predominantly Black students and even some Black teachers that act on the same principles as any White school.

In New York, Malcolm supported the campaign of Reverend Milton Galamison, who was attempting to desegregate schools in the city. Malcolm was adamant that "this does not make me an integrationist," but he did agree that a segregated school system is "detrimental to the academic diet of the children who go to that school" and decried the "crippled minds that are produced" by segregation.[30] The problem was that a segregated school was controlled from the outside by White decision-makers. The bind that the civil rights activists found themselves in when arguing for desegregation was that the majority of Black children went to Black schools with Black teachers, but they were underfunded and under-resourced and therefore struggled to adequately teach the children. This made it seem as though the Black schools were inferior by nature, and *Brown v. Board of Education* was predicated on the belief that Black students were disadvantaged by being stuck in Black schools. Black psychologists Kenneth and Mamie Clark argued that segregation built a sense of inferiority in the Black children who were denied access to White schools. They used results from their famous doll-tests study (where Black children preferred White dolls over Black ones) to demonstrate this learned inferiority.[31]

Kenneth Clark was apparently described by his peers as an "incorrigible integrationist," so you can imagine that his view did not exactly chime with Malcolm's.[32] Rest assured that Malcolm was not making the case that Black students needed access to White schools to feel secure in themselves. Instead, he understood that the underfunded schools that Black teachers and children were forced to engage with were a detriment to the community. In fact, he did not see them as "Black" schools. They were segregated schools, controlled by White society in order to reproduce a "crippling" form of schooling that would trap Black people into the vicious cycle of racism. Rather than trying to integrate Black children into White schools, Malcolm advocated for "an all-Black school, that we can control, staff it ourselves with the type of teachers that have our good at heart, with the type of books that have in them many of the missing ingredients that have produced this inferiority complex in our people, then we don't feel that an all-Black school is necessarily a segregated school. It's only segregated when it's controlled by someone from outside."[33]

This notion of a "segregated school" as being one controlled from the outside remains important today in struggles for racial justice in education. We started the first Black studies degree in Europe in 2017. (Yes, it took until seventeen years into the twenty-first century!) One of the most common questions that I get from people is if we will ever get institutions in Britain like the Historically Black Colleges and Universities (HBCUs) in America. The problem is that HBCUs have traditionally been segregated, rather than being Black places of learning. They were mostly set up specifically to keep Black students separate from White ones and usually offered vocational and technical training rather than academic study (remember that Negroes can't think, but they can work). Many were set up by White philanthropists to help pull up the poor Black masses. They have a reputation for being extremely traditional and conservative in their politics and curriculum. Black studies emerged in America when Black students went to predominantly White institutions and were appalled at the overt racism they were experiencing in the classroom and on campus.[34] Although Black studies quickly established itself on the most prestigious university campuses, most HBCUs do not teach Black studies today. They are not bastions of radical Black thought; in fact quite the opposite is true. The first time Trump was president, one of his first photo ops was with the heads of the HBCUs, who, despite his openly racist rhetoric, felt the need to bend the knee to Agent Orange to protect their funding. When Malcolm was railing against the Black intelligentsia, those who were members would mostly have been employed at HBCUs. Just to be clear, I am not saying there is not excellent work taking place in HBCUs: All the evidence suggests that Black students are much more likely to succeed if they attend an HBCU than if they go to a predominantly White institution, and Xavier University in Louisiana graduates more Black trained doctors than any other university, even though it is relatively small. But even training Black doctors is an integrationist goal, not a radical one, and this is the purpose of HBCUs.

We may not have similar institutions in Britain (and never will) but we do have the equivalent in the former colonies. Remember that most of the descendants of Black people enslaved and colonized by Britain still live in the offshore locations of the empire. Institutions like the University of Ibadan in Nigeria and the University of the West Indies (UWI) in Jamaica are our HBCUs, and their reputations are just as conservative as their American counterparts'. In 1968, the Jamaican government decided that Guianese scholar-activist Walter Rodney (who was based at UWI and wrote the anti-imperialist classic *How Europe Underdeveloped Africa* in 1972) was a persona non grata. They refused to allow him to return to the country after he left for a conference, an act that sparked a student riot in protest. The government response was to detain the students until they agreed to go back to classes. In fairness to UWI, the university has immortalized this event in its official museum, although it does feature on a timeline of "student protest" that includes anti-apartheid activism, as though it were a history of resistance the university can somehow be proud of instead of a rebellion it insisted on quelling.[35] As Malcolm has warned us, just having Black people in an institution doesn't change its nature. When we think about the battle for Black education, it has to be about much more than just representation. Some of the Whitest schools are those in the inner city, with mostly Black children and many Black staff, but if they are just parroting the rest of the mainstream curriculum, they are doing harm to Black students.

Malcolm argued that it was impossible for Black children to get a positive sense of self from a White-controlled school. He explained that it "is better for us to go to our own schools and after we have a thorough knowledge of ourselves. . . . [Once] our own racial dignity has been instilled within us then we can go to any school and still retain our racial pride." This was the only way to avoid the "subservient inferiority complex . . . that is instilled within most Negroes who have received the sort of integrated education."[36] The Nation of Islam established the University of Islam to educate the children of its members, and Malcolm was proud that "in our schools you never have any delinquency problems, you never have any dropouts."[37] In the mainstream imagination of the Negro, Black children were incapable of learning; they were delinquents or predators who were not worth trying to teach. It is true that the NOI's racial uplift program can be accused of "respectability politics," given its efforts to turn ghetto dwellers into upstanding members of society. Malcolm's focus on the supposed delinquency of Black children certainly fits into that pattern. But that focus was a direct response to the construction of the Negro child. The Nation of Islam aimed to prove that we were not inferior and could be taught, if given the proper opportunities.

This again chimes with our experiences in Britain. The designation of "educationally subnormal" given to so many Black children was a label that meant we were inferior, had special needs, and were incapable of being taught. When Caribbean children first found themselves in British schools, they were told that patois was not a legitimate language but broken English, which was evidence they were backward.[38] This mirrored the experience of how Ebonics is used to label deficiencies in Black Americans. In Britain we started supplementary schools that ran after school or on weekends in order to teach our young people.[39] These schools were a major part of the Black Power movement, embracing the spirit of Malcolm to teach those whom the schools would not.

In the present context, it is dismaying the extent to which the image of the Negro has infected our communities. Rather than seeing the schools as sites of racism, we can often see ourselves as the problem. The most extreme example is of someone like the now disgraced Bill Cosby, who used the NAACP's fifty-year celebration of the *Brown v. Board of Education* decision to desegregate schools in order to lambaste the failings of the Black community. The problem was no longer racism; it was apparently the Black youth on the corner: "It can't speak English. . . . Everybody knows it's important to speak English except these knuckleheads. You can't land a plane with 'Why you ain't. . .' You can't be a doctor with that kind of crap coming out of your mouth."[40] He went on to essentially excuse the shopkeeper who shot an unarmed teen in the back of the head for stealing some pound cake, because the child should have known better. I can't even imagine what Malcolm would have had to say about Cosby. Rest assured he would have realized long before the rape allegations came out that Cosby was no one the Black community should have been defending. But this sentiment is present even when it is not as extreme. The Congressional Black Caucus supported President Bill Clinton's infamous 1994 crime bill that accelerated mass incarceration because of the fears of Negro "super predators." Far too many of us justify police stop-and-search protocols on the grounds of so-called safety, and the same is true of police in schools. When I was researching the supplementary school movement, it was jarring to discover the extent to which contemporary activists blame the parents and community for the supposed failures of the children rather than the schools. This is where the rejection of the dreaded "respectability politics" comes in. We shouldn't need to present our most supposedly respectable selves in order to succeed in life.

BE VERY CAREFUL AND CONSCIOUS OF HOW YOU LOOK

Anyone who has spent any time on Black Twitter (or Black X, I guess now, although given the political ideas we have been talking about, I would strongly suggest refraining from using such a term to describe Elon Musk's kingdom) will have come across the sordid notion of respectability politics. I have lost count of how many times I have seen a picture of suited and booted Black men in the 1960s contrasted with Black men today, with their trousers hanging below their waists, with some version of the tagline "When they took us seriously" and "Why they don't now." Uncle Obama advised that "brothers should pull up their pants," and when Jefferson Parish, Louisiana, banned the wearing of sagging trousers, the local chapter of the National Association for the Advancement of Some Colored People applauded the move.[41] In 2010, then New York State Senator (and now mayor of New York City) Eric Adams started a billboard campaign that read, "Stop the Sag! Raise

Your Pants!" He explained that it was "part of a larger campaign . . . to tell our young people and our community as a whole, we are better than this."[42] He argued that the clothes young people were wearing were the biggest indicator of criminal behavior.

The Nation of Islam remains famous for this kind of respectability politics. Members are always seen in public with their well-pressed suits and bow ties. They aimed to pull the brothers and sisters out of the slums and prisons and freshen them up to face the world anew. Malcolm was heavily influenced by these values. The only time I have ever seen a picture of Malcolm in anything other than a suit is when he was wearing Islamic dress or the African clothes he was gifted when he visited the continent. He was so committed to wearing a suit in public that when his house burned down the day before he spoke in Detroit in 1965, he actually apologized for his attire because his suits were all smoke damaged: "So I just ask you to excuse my appearance. I don't normally come out in front of people without a shirt and a tie. I guess that's somewhat a holdover from the Black Muslim movement, which I was in. That's one of the good aspects of that movement. It teaches you to be very careful and conscious of how you look, which is a positive contribution on their part."[43]

This commitment to the "good aspect" of the Nation of Islam could be seen as an embrace of respectability politics. But the problem with the respectability idea is not the notion that you should take care of your appearance; it is when we act as though all we need to do is project a supposedly better image to uplift ourselves. It is an even more perverse logic than Booker T. Washington's notion of pulling ourselves up by our bootstraps, meaning to work tirelessly to ensure we get freedom. In the respectability myth, pulling up our trousers is supposed to be the solution itself. If only we looked "better," we would be treated better. This is clearly nonsense, and Malcolm did point out that whether you are "well dressed" or "poorly dressed," the police will still crack your head open.[44] No matter what the present-day self-help gurus are telling you, there is no way to manifest yourself out of racism with positive affirmations.

Respectability politics dramatically misses the point that when cultures develop that are unhelpful to us, this is because of the conditions that produced them. For example, there is no agreement as to where the saggy-trousers style originated, but it is often labeled as from prison culture and is now associated with gangs. It may well be the case that a negative gang culture has developed that is symbolized by the wearing of saggy pants, but the problem isn't the trousers; it's the conditions that disproportionately lock up Black people and push us into crime to survive. Attacking the trousers is trying to cure a disease by treating the most minor of its symptoms. Malcolm was not advocating that you put on a suit to conquer the world. The value of the NOI was that it offered a whole new approach to living, along with a religion, and most importantly to work and opportunity. The suits were part and parcel of a plan to build a separate (and ultimately problematic) Black community. Even when Malcolm was in the Nation of Islam, he was not blaming the problems facing Black people on the community. The reason the NOI began the University of Islam was to provide an education where young Black people could fulfill their potential; once they were in a nurturing environment with a relevant curriculum, the students could excel. This is a critique of the White schools, laying the blame for delinquency and high dropout rates of Black children directly at their feet. It was always a problem with the social structure for Malcolm, not some internal failing of Black people.

Malcolm's insistence on a suit and tie led scholar Robin Kelley to describe him as the "epitome of bourgeois respectability." This was also apparently because he was "always exquisitely dressed, polite, and well-mannered. . . . He never sucked on chicken bones or licked his fingers at the table, and no matter how much of a hurry he was in, he never spoke with his mouth full."[45] This is a lighthearted commentary, but it reveals the problem with the respectability critique that Malcolm would have railed against. The idea that being "polite" and "well-mannered" is a bourgeois (and by definition White) trait is deeply problematic. Table manners were imported into Europe from the Arab-African Moorish empire, so the notion that these are the mark of civilized (White) people is a racist idea. The notion that Black people suck loudly on chicken bones is one created in the image of the Negro, the racist caricature of the minstrel show. You don't prove your Blackness by playing up to racial stereotypes. But Malcolm's embrace of the shirt and tie does bear exploring within his broader political ideas.

As a hustler, Malcolm also took great pride in his appearance. He went to lengths to conk his hair, burning the African kinks out so he could have that smooth, horsehair look. He also delighted in the extravagant zoot suits of his era with the oversize trousers (a nod to where we are today) and wide-brimmed hats. That package was part of the role, embodying the idea that to play the part you have to dress for it. When he went to prison, he was unmade and he began to rebuild himself. I can't overstate enough how to change your politics is to fundamentally transform yourself. Shifts in your entire worldview are imprinted on every aspect of your life, including your taste in fashion. Once Malcolm embraced his Blackness and committed to working to build the Black community, he could no more wear his old zoot suit than he could marry a White woman. Not because he rejected those people donning his former attire, but because he was on a different mission, had taken up a new role. In that role, he projected a different image, the upstanding preacher who abided by a different moral ethic.

It is correct to question the standard of the suit as the respectable way to present yourself. When my dad first saw a picture of Black American professor Cornel West, with his huge Afro and black suit, he laughed and said he looked "confused." I have to admit that, as much as I love Malcolm, I have one suit, and I picked it to be versatile enough that you will see me in it at funerals, weddings, and (some) job interviews. I have very much rejected formal clothes as the standard and wear Jordans to as many events as I can get away with (I am aware of the complicated politics of the shoes). Particularly as a recovering academic, suits for me go hand in hand with the dreaded management positions. If you're in a university and someone has a shirt and tie on, my advice is to be wary of them. Clothing has also been a key site of anxiety for me over the years, feeling the pressure to turn up to work in more "formal" clothes, lest I be mistaken for a Black male student and subject to racist scrutiny.

To embrace suits as the standard is problematic, but we live in very different times today and I have a very different role from Malcolm. What you wear is as much defined by the expectations of your audience as it is by your beliefs. Preachers still wear suits today, as do Nation of Islam ministers. There remains a very large element of emulating Whiteness in this choice of clothes. Malcolm was also frequently on television, and in those days, you had to don the shirt and tie as a convention of the times. The suit was largely a holdover from the NOI, and the image of Malcolm in a suit became almost as iconic as the X itself. Malcolm was also dedicated to *not* reveling in the culture of the elite. Several years ago, I accepted an invitation to speak at the Oxford Union, mostly because Malcolm had done so in 1964. The place is so stiff and stuffy it could moonlight as a mausoleum. All the other speakers and the majority of the old guard who came to the reception were dressed in their penguin suits, replete with bow tie. I decided to emulate Malcolm and defy convention by going with the suit with a straight black tie. It felt very countercultural in 2016, so Malcolm deciding to dress down (he did not wear a bow tie) for the Oxford Union fifty years earlier was certainly a statement. The suit became part of the role, Malcolm's projection of himself; it was not a plea for bourgeois respectability.

After Malcolm's exit from the NOI and travels on the African continent, it may seem strange that he did not dispense with the Western suit and embrace African formal wear. But this goes back to the reason he never publicly used his adopted Muslim name of Shabazz. For Malcolm, there was essential work to be done among Black Americans first to connect them to the revolutionary struggles on the continent. Malcolm resonated and connected with their experience, as did the image of the suit-wearing leader. He would not have reached the broad cross section of Black people in the West as Malik Shabazz wearing a dashiki. More importantly, changing his name and his dress wouldn't have elevated his politics. We also have to put his suit wearing in context with his language. Malcolm's pledge to "make it plain" was his statement of commitment to the masses over and above bourgeois respectability. He didn't indulge in fancy suits or language, promising that there would be "no flim-flam, no compromise, no sell out, no controlled show."[46] This was Malcolm's appeal and why (no matter what he was wearing) he captured the hearts and minds of the Black masses in a way that few other leaders could.

Malcolm understood the damage that had been done to Black people through centuries of Whitewashing through miseducation. We were not just enslaved, but broken in, turned into the Negro by the oppression of White society. Malcolm knew that when the physical chains were broken on the plantation, we still had not been liberated from mental slavery. Central to Malcolm's politics of resistance is that, unlike academics who embrace radical analyses but get squeamish about the revolutionary solution, he was deeply optimistic. Racism could never be removed from Western society, but we could overturn the system and build a world where we were free. The key was to unlock the power of the Black communities that had been oppressed by the system. The secret that those in power don't want us to know is that we have been fed these lies about Black inferiority to ensure that we can be exploited. The West does not exist without us; we have always had the power to revolt, which is why so much effort has been put into keeping us down through physical and symbolic violence. Malcolm's revolutionary solution was to unite Africa and the diaspora in order to unlock that radical potential. Rejecting any identification with the so-called Negro was the first, revolutionary step. As we will see in the next chapter, Malcolm prioritized a truly political Black education because "you are Negro because you don't know who you are, you don't know what you are, you don't know where you are, and you don't know how you got here. But as soon as you wake up and find out the positive answer to all these things, you cease being a Negro. You become somebody."[47]

8

THINKING BLACK

White society has broken down Black people, brutally oppressing us and unmaking our very selves. For Malcolm, the starting point for finding freedom was not just to reclaim ourselves but to rebuild, rejecting the racist molds handed to us and recreating ourselves in a revolutionary image. In practice, Blackness was perhaps the most important part of Malcolm's theory. Malcolm was one of the first to declare that we are "Black," and it was not just a description for those of African descent. It was a political identity, rooted in a resistance to the condition of White supremacy. He argued that we needed to become Black, to unite as a people in order to truly break our chains. Like most aspects of Malcolm's approach, even this most fundamental one has been misunderstood. If I hear anyone else smugly announce that "Blackness is not a monolith" as though they have had some great revelation that we are not all the same, I will be violently sick. I've heard very few people ever argue that we all need to be identical, and Malcolm certainly never did. The radical foundation of Malcolm's Blackness is that it is the glue that ties those of African descent together. Blackness is radical because it means committing to a political unity, with those in Africa *and* the diaspora, in order to transform our conditions.

DARK MANKIND

Malcolm's embrace of Blackness is a political identity, but it strongly differs from "political blackness." In the British context, cultural studies icon Stuart Hall argued that all immigrant groups from Asia, Africa, and the Caribbean "identified themselves politically as black. What they said was, 'We may be different [in terms of] actual colour of skins but vis-á-vis the social system, vis-á-vis the political system of racism, there is more that unites us than what divides us.'"[1] This idea of political blackness was also the basis of Steve Biko's Black Consciousness movement, which sought to bring together all those who were against the White rulers of the apartheid system in South Africa.[2] There is a practical utility in uniting all non-White groups against their common oppressor, but Malcolm's vision of Blackness is rooted in African ancestry rather than in non-White solidarity. Further confusing the issue is the fact that he made many an appeal to a non-White blackness, for instance explicitly declaring that the

> black revolution has been taking place in Africa and Asia and Latin America; when I say black, I mean non-White—Black, Brown, Red or Yellow. Our brothers and sisters in Asia, who were colonized by the Europeans, our brothers and sisters in Africa, who were colonized by the Europeans, and in Latin America, the peasants, who were colonized by the Europeans, have been involved in a struggle since 1945 to get the

colonialists, or the colonizing powers, the Europeans, off their land, out of their country.[3]

It is extremely easy to find a quotation in which Malcolm talks about the importance of "dark mankind" waking up and uniting to defeat the common enemy.[4] He talked very fondly of the Bandung Conference that took place in Indonesia in 1955, which brought together the leaders of twenty-nine Asian and African independent nations. He praised the organizers because "the number-one thing that was not allowed to attend the Bandung Conference was the White man. Once they excluded the White man, they found that they could get together. Once they kept him out, everybody else fell right in and fell in line."[5] The point was they understood in Zimbabwe, Burma, and Pakistan that White people were colonizing their countries, and they should organize together to resist. This was the sentiment of the Third World movement, which saw itself as separate from the White industrialized world and the equally White Soviet sphere of influence. Malcolm appreciated that at Bandung they realized that they had "in common a dark skin" and wanted to remain nonaligned from either of the White poles of influence.[6] For him, Bandung captured the feeling of the "dark masses of Africa and Asia and Latin America," which were "seething with bitterness, animosity, hostility and unrest, and impatience with the racial intolerance that they themselves have experienced at the hands of the White West."[7] Malcolm certainly expressed the solidarity at the heart of political blackness and at times invoked the term, but he did not ultimately embrace the non-White definition.

Almost all of the quotations from Malcolm that directly use "politically black" language were made while he was a member of the Nation of Islam and, in the case of the "Black Revolution" speech he made in 1964, just after he had left. He explained the source of his political blackness very clearly when he said, "By 'black man,' as we are taught by Elijah Muhammad, we include all those who are nonwhite."[8] In the NOI beliefs, there are only Black people and White people, and "Black is a basic color. . . . Black is foundation for all colors." The Nation of Islam referred to the "Asiatic Black man" as the true inheritor of the world until wicked Yacub created the White devils. There were no other human beings, and Islam was said to be the true religion that the devils could never accept, because of their evil nature. On the global scene, this was essential, because, as Malcolm explained, "as Muslims, we identify ourselves with the dark world. So, we're not any minority. We're a part of the majority and the White man is the minority. . . . We don't fight a battle like the odds are against us."[9] It was when he was within the Nation of Islam that Macolm first invoked the call to drag America in front of the UN. This was because "the whole dark world today is in unity" and they outnumbered the White nations in that global institution.[10] Malcolm was then expressing the political blackness of the NOI, which drew very clear battle lines between the White devils and the rest of the world.

It should come as little surprise that the Nation of Islam's view of Blackness is as one-dimensional as White and non-White. As we discussed in Chapter 2, the contradiction of the NOI is that although it professed hatred for the White devils, its entire worldview was shaped by them. The problem with being anti-White is that you become defined in relation to Whiteness. White becomes the standard, the norm by which everything is held in contrast. This is the most disempowering way to understand ourselves, always in relation to the oppressor. In practice, the Nation of Islam was actually Black, defined in African ancestry, reaching out to the so-called Negroes to build its membership. But on the theoretical world stage, it embraced a politically black identity to claim superiority over the White man. This is an idea that has long held influence, embodied in such terms as "people of color" and "global majority." There is a certain romance to believing that we are in the majority against the devilish White man, but it is simply not the case.

For all of Malcolm's praise of Bandung, in reality it was not a revolutionary meeting of the minds of dark mankind. America initially feared the potential outcome of the meeting but quickly realized that any radical rhetoric about Third World unity would stay solely at the level of critique. But it worked out even better for the United States, which found that pro-Western allies at the conference ensured that a strong free market capitalist sentiment was heard at Bandung and that when nations did condemn the evils of Western colonialism they also railed against the newer Communist totalitarianism.[11] Rather than being a revolutionary congress, Bandung was a victory for what Malcolm called "benevolent colonialism." But the allure of the event in the activist collective memory still holds sway. I have to admit, until I started looking more closely at the Bandung Conference for this book I had the misguided impression that it was a moment of Third World revolutionary solidarity, and no doubt 2025 will provoke teary-eyed reminiscences of the seventieth anniversary of the gathering.

The danger of the White/non-White binary is that we lump together the majority of the world because they do not have White skin. While it is true that Europeans colonized (and also ensured the underdevelopment of) large parts of the world, it is also the case that this was not an even process. Anti-Blackness was a key feature of White supremacy, and it is no coincidence that the world today places Black people at the bottom, White at the top, and a hierarchy in between.

It is entirely consistent with White supremacy that underdeveloped nations like China have utilized some of the same tools of benevolent colonialism to boost themselves up at the expense of Africa.[12] This was definitely a blind spot for Malcolm, who strongly believed in the revolutionary potential of dark mankind. Once released from the grip of the NOI, he evolved his position away from the disempowering definition of Blackness as not being White. But he never gave up his optimism about Third World solidarity. Malcolm's faith in the UN was predicated in his belief that "our African brothers and our Asian brothers and our Latin-American brothers" would rally to support Black people in America.[13]

To be clear, I am not criticizing Malcolm's insistence on solidarity with Black and Brown people across the globe or on the domestic scene. He understood that racism was a global system that impacted billions of people who were not Black, and therefore held out hope that we would all unite to overturn Western imperialism. My criticism of nations in the underdeveloped world who have embraced White supremacy in order to succeed, like China, is aimed at the governments of those countries. There are hundreds of millions of Chinese people kept in abject poverty so that the state can succeed in its benevolent colonialism. There is no doubt that the masses of Black and Brown people need a revolution and should work together to bring this about. On the national level, there has always been a connection between struggles of different racialized groups who are fighting against racism in our respective nation-states, and of course this should continue. But that solidarity should never be on the simple metric that we are all not White. It should be centered on our shared struggles. For example, in Britain, Black people are significantly more likely to be stopped by the police, incarcerated, and excluded from schooling than our Asian neighbors. It is misguided to believe there is a shared struggle on these issues because we all have darker skin. But racist immigration policy in Britain is predicated on trying to "keep Britain White." Here is an issue where there is clearly a shared struggle we can unite over. Unity based on shared struggle is a much more secure route to solidarity, rather than pretending that not being White means we have everything in common.

Malcolm was entirely against a narrow Black nationalism that pitted us against different groups and was insistent on solidarity in his world travels. He was clear that "division between Afro-Asians should never be. The press is responsible for division in places like British Guiana," and he accused those who peddled in anti-Asian rhetoric as imitating and succumbing to "White propaganda."[14] He also suggested "an organized effort to bring Africans and Asians together" over the struggle in Zanzibar.[15] This solidarity was necessary, given the colonial situation on both continents and the possibility of uniting to expel the British to bring an end to colonial rule. On his 1965 visit to Britain, he argued that "when the Afro and West Indian community . . . in England reach out and get the Asian community, it's trouble for old John Bull."[16] In the British context, this was especially the case, given our small numbers in the mother country. Black people only make up 3 percent of the population today. In 1965, we were even fewer in number and had little power to pressure the government by ourselves. Fighting against other oppressed groups is clearly counterproductive, and Malcolm denounced those who spent their efforts attacking other racialized people. He always advocated for the power of strategic unity, for instance, pointing out the power of the anti-racist coalition he had witnessed on his visit to France in 1964. He explained that "just by advocating a coalition of Africans, Afro-Americans, Arabs, and Asians who live within the structure, it automatically has upset France, which is supposed to be one of the most liberal countries on earth."[17]

But Malcolm was also very clear that the basis of that solidarity had to evolve from the simple Nation of Islam arithmetic. This was particularly the case when, after leaving the NOI, Malcolm revealed that Elijah Muhammad was as "anti-African as he was anti-White."[18] His claim to be an "Asiatic Black man" was necessary to avoid rooting his followers to the African continent. A common complaint about political blackness is that by homogenizing all groups, we lose specific attention on the dynamics of anti-Black racism.[19] Malcolm was accusing Muhammad of going further than simply ignoring Africa and actually perpetuating anti-Black racism. For Malcolm, it was impossible to breathe life back into the so-called Negro without linking us back to Africa. Once he had left the NOI, he developed a global definition of Blackness based on the need to "establish contacts with our African brothers, we must begin from this day forward to work in unity and harmony as Afro-Americans along with our African brothers . . . to show our brothers the necessity of us forming a coalition, a working community with our brothers on the African continent."[20]

A NEW TYPE OF NEGRO

An essential element to Malcolm's politics was the reformation of the Negro. He explained that "we are all Black people, so-called Negroes, second-class citizens, ex-slaves."[21] His starting point for organizing political activity was the "lost Negro," who needed to be brought back to life. Perhaps the most important feature of his work was the aim to create a "political program of reeducation to open our people's eyes" and bring us into a new consciousness.[22] According to Malcolm, the so-called Negro was so thoroughly brainwashed by White society that he diagnosed the Black community with "White disease," chiding, "You think you can't get along without the White man. . . . You're worse than the man who's hooked on heroin. The junkie only has the junk on his back. . . . You walking around here with a big old White Uncle Sam on your back."[23]

The process of breaking in and conditioning us into the Negro meant that, while we were taken in chains to America "Black minded . . . now you're White minded. You've been brainwashed. . . . The color has been taken out of your heart and out of your mind. . . . You're a White Black man. Black on the outside, White on the inside."[24] So complete was the indoctrination that Malcolm constantly lambasted the "Black people who are more White than White people."[25] This was not just a problem in America but something he identified when he traveled. He joked that when he was in Ghana he was quizzed about his politics by a doctor whom he described as a "Nigerian who has spent too much time in Europe."[26] In Britain he was critical of Caribbeans who were "running around here in search of an identity and instead of trying to be what they are, they want to be Englishmen."[27] When Malcolm critiqued the civil rights movement for being too influenced by White people, it was because of this brainwashing. The White influence was watering down the militancy of the masses, trying to keep us in the deferential, cap-in-hand Negro mindset.

For Malcolm, the first step in the revolutionary process was to wholly reject the Negro and to become Black. He argued that "there is a new type of Negro on the scene. This type doesn't call himself a Negro. He calls himself a Black man. He doesn't make any apology for his Black skin."[28] In contrast to the so-called Negro, "this new type of Black man wants to think for himself, speak for himself, stand on his own feet, and walk for himself."[29] Blackness was something that

Malcolm claimed for us as a radical identity. Prior to this we were referred to and called ourselves Negroes, colored, or, in Britain, West Indian. Malcolm embraced Blackness as a choice, to connect us back to our African roots and to reclaim ourselves as human beings. This is why Blackness linked to African ancestry is so important: It is a political identity, and one tied to a revolutionary political practice. For all of Malcolm's use of the non-White definition, it was his embrace of Blackness produced by our link to Africa that was the building block for his philosophy. He outlined how choosing to be Black "eliminates the necessity for division and argument, 'cause if you're Black, you should be thinking Black. And if you're Black and you're not thinking Black at this late date, well, I'm sorry for you."[30]

Academics who criticize Malcolm's position may point out the limits of what we like to call "essentialism," which reduces people to their skin color or some other identity. The idea goes this way: To say there is a Black way to think is to limit us and force us all to conform to some mistaken, probably colonial, idea of Blackness. To imagine that there is an essence that makes us Black is racist logic that says there is something fundamentally different about us due to our genetic makeup. Racism is built on the notion of essentialism, that our DNA separates us into a different race. It is for this reason that many famous Black scholars, including Paul Gilroy, Stuart Hall, Kwame Anthony Appiah, and Michelle Wright, have argued that we ultimately need to free ourselves from racial categories and seek a hybrid identity, one that is fluid and not rooted in absolutes.[31] The reasoning goes that if we free ourselves from race, we liberate ourselves from racism. Embracing Blackness is also critiqued because it is seen as something imposed on us by Europeans. I have come across this illogic so many times—that "Africans are not black"—that now I just roll my eyes when I encounter it.[32]

In British academia, it has become common to say we are "racialized as Black," as though we have to apologize for using the term. This is the perfect example of academics being out of touch with the community. We spend so much time in White spaces, reading White authors, that we assume White ways of understanding the world are all that exist: that because Europeans divided the world by skin color and imagined the Negro in order to oppress us, therefore Western notions of race are the only way to understand difference. What these arguments spectacularly miss is that while an attempt was made to racialize us into the "Negro" in order to control us, we resisted in large part by claiming our Blackness. "Negro" was the racial category imposed upon us; we *chose* to embrace being Black in order to destroy it. To reject Blackness is, therefore, to simply not understand it.

It would have come as little shock to Malcolm, either, that Black people who toil away in the Whiteness of academia have such a hard time accepting Blackness in all of its revolutionary potential. In the missing chapter on the Negro from his autobiography, Malcolm argued that the "educated Negro never thinks from the point of view of his own kind, or for the good of his own kind. If he did, his thinking would be intellectually focused on Black."[33] Trust me, to succeed in the university means you have to have spent years centering your thinking on White theory and ideas. The starting point of most Black academics is as far removed from community mobilization as is the sun from the earth. In his usual style, Malcolm did not hold back in his critique of those with education who rejected Blackness:

> The educated Negro, the professional Negro, is the worst offender of all. . . . This is the one who is drowning and when you are throwing a life preserver to him, he acts like you are

throwing it at him. Being a Negro is his profession. In his "intellect," his "thinking," he is White. Anything that he hears criticizing the White man is criticizing him, a Black man, he wants so badly to be White.[34]

Malcolm's scorn was not reserved for those of us in academia, but it might as well have been. We may have gotten more used to criticizing massa, but we still do it on *his* terms. In the jargon, journals, and the academic bubble, we have learned to ape White so-called intellectualism, and too many of us validate ourselves by being able to use the oppressor's language and tools. This has led a large proportion of Black academics not only to essentially reject Blackness but to do so in a way that no one (perhaps not even themselves) can understand. I guess the only blessing is that some of the most notable Negro academics in the bubble write in such unintelligible ways that no one, other than the already deluded, will read them. I wasn't going to name names, but it seems wrong in a book about Malcolm to duck the smoke. When I am on the bus reading a book and a Black person takes an interest in the text, I usually give it to them. But I was reading the twentieth-anniversary edition of *There Ain't No Black in the Union Jack* by perhaps Black Britain's most esteemed so-called Negro professor, Paul Gilroy, and a young Black woman asked me about the book. The work is a fascinating testament to the damaging effects of the academic industrial complex. This was Gilroy's doctoral thesis, and the book itself is readable enough, but the newer introduction he wrote for the anniversary edition showed the extent to which the White academy had apparently addled his brain. This was a good few years ago now, but I have to admit that I honestly had absolutely no idea what he was writing! It was like I had forgotten how to read, and it was a truly alienating experience. Reading Gilroy reminds me of stories of people suffering with a type of speech impairment called aphasia, where they think they are speaking normally but all that comes out is a nonsensical series of words.[35] I was reading the introduction when she asked me about the book, and I struggled to say what it was about and of course never gave her my copy. The last thing I wanted to do was to put her off reading for life after encountering Gilroy's academic aphasia, given how much other excellent work is out there.

Unlike scholars like Gilroy, Malcolm understood that Blackness was a political, not a genetic or cultural, essentialism. He never said that we should all eat, dance, or speak the same way. To begin with, Malcolm preached the NOI orthodoxy that Black people were superior to the inherently evil White devils who were bred to conquer the world. But he evolved from that position to locate the problem in White society rather than in White people. For Malcolm, Blackness was a political essentialism that meant understanding the racist nature of society and that all Black people were in the same boat and therefore should unite to row toward freedom. "Thinking Black" meant embracing this political challenge as the necessary first step to building the revolution. Malcolm never saw it as inevitable that we would think Black, but he spent his life trying to convince us to do so.

Thinking Black was purposefully meant to be inclusive of the variety of differences within our communities. The point was to bring us together across identity barriers that would otherwise keep us apart. The one area where Malcolm had a complete break from his public position in the Nation of Islam was on the role of religion. For the NOI, the only solution to the problem of racism was for Black people to convert to Islam, separate from the evil devils, and wait for God to bring forth Armageddon. In his 1960 debate with civil rights icon Bayard Rustin, Malcolm took the party line, describing how "Mr. Muhammad does not believe in a political solution. . . . Our entire approach is a religious approach."[36]

Once he had left the group, he completely changed his tune, declaring that

Islam is my religion but . . . my religious philosophy is personal between me and the God in whom I believe. . . . If we bring up religion, we'll have differences, we'll have arguments, and we'll never be able to get together. But if we keep our religion at home, keep our religion in the closet, keep our religion between ourselves and our God, but when we come out here we have a fight that's common to all of us, against an enemy who is common to all of us.[37]

Malcolm put these words into practice when he founded the Organization of Afro-American Unity for his political program and Muslim Mosque Inc. for his religious beliefs. It may sound ironic, but as he became a more devout, orthodox Muslim, he separated his politics from his religion. Even his travels followed this pattern; he visited Mecca and the Islamic world for his own spiritual journey and to secure funding for Islamic scholarships for those in America, but he visited Africa to connect the political struggle of the continent to those in the diaspora. He outlined how politically "Black nationalism will link us to Africa and Islam will link up spiritually with Arabia and Asia."[38] I once explained this to a White academic at an event, who then dismissed my position as secular and therefore "Western." Apparently, the idea of separating religious beliefs from political action is a uniquely

White idea (I am picturing the eye-roll emoji). This is delusional, given that the dominance of the Abrahamic religions is relatively recent and people managed for thousands of years without them. It also misses the point that there is something deeply spiritual about Malcolm's articulation of Blackness. He was calling for us to embrace a connection to our ancestors in Africa and have faith in each other to uplift ourselves. This is secular only in the Western (non)sense of the word.

In testament to the inclusivity of Malcolm's Blackness, he specifically called out to Christians to join the movement, arguing that "we're not brutalized because we are Baptists. We are not brutalized because we're Methodists, we're not brutalized because we're Muslims, we're not brutalized because we're Catholic. We are brutalized because we are Black people in America."[39] He was appealing to Christians to think Black—not to become Muslims but to realize that "all of us catch hell from the same enemy. We're all in the same bag, in the same boat."[40] He specifically warned Christians that "when you walk in a Negro church and see a White Jesus and a White Mary and some White angels, that Negro church is preaching White nationalism." But he was not dissuading them from the religion, urging that if they saw a "pastor of that church with a philosophy and a program that's designed to bring Black people together and elevate Black people, join that church."[41] He even extended his urging to join groups that he had previously lambasted, including the NAACP, as long as they were preaching his brand of revolutionary Black nationalism (this may have been damning them with faint praise, given Malcolm likely knew this was extremely unlikely to ever occur). But his commitment to a hybrid Blackness was epitomized in his call for Black people to "join any kind of organization—civic, religious, fraternal, political or otherwise that's based on lifting the Black man up and making him master of his own community.["]42 The new type of Negro was not limited to any particular church, group, or designation.

LOVE TEACHING

It is all too easy to believe that being pro-Black is the same as being anti-White. Malcolm defended his pro-Blackness by explaining that it was necessary to speak positively about Black people to undo all the brainwashing we had received over the centuries, so that

> when you hear us often refer to Black in almost a boastful way, actually we're not boasting, we're speaking of it in a factual sense. All we're doing is telling the truth about our people. When you exalt Black, that's not propaganda; when you exalt White, that's propaganda. Yet no one can give biological evidence to show the Black actually is the stronger or superior of the two if you want to make that kind of comparison.[43]

Loving our Blackness was the central ingredient in overcoming the damage done by the imposition of the Negro identity. Malcolm never apologized for this unconditional commitment, even though "we love our own people so much, they think we hate the ones who are inflicting injustice against them."[44] He rejected the idea that he was teaching hate by declaring, "This isn't hate teaching. This is love teaching. If I didn't love you, I wouldn't be telling you what I'm telling you."[45] Love as a political metaphor is often assigned to Malcolm's opposite, Martin Luther King, who argued we needed to meet the physical force of White racism with a "soul force" that made clear to the oppressor that no matter what they say or do, "we will still love you."[46] Malcolm poured scorn on the notion that we should love those who hate us and mobilized love for ourselves and each other. As discussed in the last chapter, we were taught to hate ourselves and therefore we had to learn to love everything about our Blackness.

It would be easy to read Malcolm's contempt for mixed-race relationships as expressing hatred toward White people, but his position was about loving Black people and not hatred for anyone else. In his 1961 debate with James Baldwin, the iconic author said he dreamed of a "world in which there are no Blacks, there are no Whites, where it does not matter." Malcolm retorted,

> As a Black man and proud of being Black I can't conceive of myself as having any desire whatsoever to lose my identity. I wouldn't wanna live in a world where none of my kind existed. Intermarriage and intermixing would take place on such a vast scale that it would produce a chocolate colored race. . . . I think it's disastrous when the racial pride is disappeared and they don't care if their blood is mixed up.[47]

According to Malcolm, Blackness was not imposed on us from above, but something we needed to reclaim from within. Genetic integration was therefore no solution to the problem, and for him would mean erasing the Blackness that lay at the foundation of the identity necessary for revolution. Instead, we had to love our Blackness, which for Malcolm naturally meant to love Black women and to raise a Black family. This is not anything like the racism where White people want to keep their families pure from the polluting genes of the ex-slaves. Malcolm was not saying that White blood was inferior, but he was worried about the loss of racial pride and pointing out that if we were all a chocolate-colored race we would cease to recognize our Blackness and be lost forever in this wicked system. To escape Negroness, Malcolm argued that "we must recapture our heritage and our identity if we are ever to liberate ourselves from the bonds of White supremacy."[48]

Connecting back to Africa was central to this love teaching, because the Negro could only ever have been created by unlinking us from a past of civilization and greatness. Malcolm explained how a hatred of Africa was instilled in us.

> They projected Africa always in a negative light: jungles, savages, cannibals, nothing civilized. Why then naturally it was so negative [that] it was negative to you and me, and you and I began to hate it. We didn't want anybody telling us anything about Africa, much less calling us Africans. In hating Africa and in hating the Africans, we ended up hating ourselves, without even realizing it. Because you can't hate the roots of a tree and not hate the tree. You can't hate your origin and not end up hating yourself. . . . You can't have a positive attitude toward yourself and a negative attitude toward Africa at the same time.[49]

Malcolm was intent on reversing these negative ideas of Africa, telling his audience that, rather than the racist images they had previously received, "Africa is the root of civilization, Africa is the home of civilization. They learned civilization from you. They learned to wear clothes from you. They learned science from you."[50]

He was critical of Negro History Week activities for "only showing you down home, not back home. They'll praise Washington Carver, but he only made money for the White man."[51] (George Washington Carver was a renowned African American scientist who pioneered agricultural research.) But for Malcolm, it was not possible to counteract the Negro solely by highlighting Black excellence in America. I can't explain how exasperated I get when we reduce the teaching of Black history to a parade of Black scientists, investors, and capitalists, as though all we need to do is to show that there are models of greatness that can inspire us to overcome our low self-esteem. Malcolm was warning against such simplistic notions. They may inspire us, but only do so in order to feed into a system of White supremacy that is ultimately against us. His warning here is that we don't want to replace the subservient, savage Negro with the talented one who is allowed to be successful to further enrich the oppressor. I doubt Malcolm had anything against Carver personally, but he was critiquing the way the man, or rather the myth created around him, was being misused. We had to restore our connection to Africa, to rebuild ourselves—and the myth of Black excellence often does completely the opposite by reveling in our amazing, so-called successes in White society. Malcolm stressed that we needed to embrace our

> African blood, African origin, African culture, African ties. And you'd be surprised, we discovered that deep within the subconscious of the Black man in this country, he's still more African than he is American. He thinks that he's more American than African, because the man is jiving him, the man is brainwashing him every day. He's telling him, "You're an American, you're an American." Man, how could you think you're an American and you haven't ever had any kind of American treat over here?[52]

Malcolm's travels to the continent were personally and politically affirming. In Nigeria he was given the title Omowale, which means "the son who has returned." On his visit to the neighboring country, he declared, "I don't feel that I am a visitor in Ghana or in any part of Africa. I feel that I am at home. I've been away for four hundred years, but not of my own volition, not of my own will."[53] Malcolm could have stayed on the continent, and seriously contemplated doing so. But he felt it was his duty to return to the land of his birth to continue his revolutionary love teaching that could restore us from our Negro status. He saw the potential power of Africanness at work when those from the continent were served in places that Black Americans never would be. He pointed out that "there are Africans who come here, Black as night, who can go into those cracker hotels." This phenomenon was noted in the South; in her autobiography, scholar and activist Angela Davis admitted that she and a friend who could speak French would wrap up their heads, pretend to be from an African country, and get service in the very same restaurants that would usually reject them.[54] For Malcolm, the reason that Africans could get service and legendary civil rights activist Ralph Bunche could not was that "Bunche doesn't know his history, and they, the Africans, do know their history."[55] This was clearly an oversimplification, given that even those Black Americans, like Malcolm, who were fully versed in their glorious history would be lynched before they were served in an all-White restaurant in the South. But it shows the importance that he placed on restoring the Negroes to embracing their African roots. It meant being whole, strong, no longer an ex-slave but a human being.

AFRICANISM

When Malcolm created his revolutionary organization, the reclamation of the so-called Negro was the priority. The best way to understand Malcolm's theory is to explore his practice, and he was adamant that "we are going to build an organization that will be run exclusively by Negroes and only for Negroes."[56] There can be no doubt how he defined and mobilized Blackness, given this nature of the Organization of Afro-American Unity. Also important to understanding how Malcolm conceived Blackness, he refused to limit his scope to the national stage:

> Many of us fool ourselves into thinking of Afro-Americans as those only who are here in the United States. . . . Anybody of African ancestry in South America is an Afro-American. Anybody in Central America of African blood is an Afro-American. Anybody here in North America, including Canada, is an Afro-American if he has African ancestry—even down in the Caribbean, he's an Afro-American. . . . The Afro-American is that large number of people in the Western Hemisphere, from the southernmost tip of South America to the northernmost tip of North America, all of whom have a common heritage and have a common origin when you go back to the roots of these people.[57]

Blackness was the shared connection to the continent for all those who had been forced or displaced from it. His aim for the OAAU was to break down the artificial, colonial nation-state boundaries and to unite all Black people in the Western Hemisphere. At the time, relatively few people had migrated from the colonies to their respective European mother countries, and those who had largely identified with their colonial homelands. So, the ex-slaves still lived in the Americas, for the most part, and Malcolm saw their revolutionary potential if they were awakened.

Africa was central to fusing together the struggles in the diaspora with a radical edge. This is why he traveled extensively across Africa, to connect the struggles for freedom together. A note he wrote in his diary during his travels is revealing as to how he viewed the political place of Blackness: "Europeanism has been such a strong poison for centuries it now becomes essential to emphasize Africanism to counteract it and Arabism to counteract Zionism, socialism to counteract capitalism etc. Orientalism to counterbalance Occidentalism or Whitism. . . . This is the present escalating world struggle."[58]

Africanism is the Black thinking that Malcolm was arguing was essential for freedom. The revolutions across the African continent changed how we in the diaspora saw Africa; we could not help but take note and feel pride. Malcolm argued that it became easier to organize Black people in the West once African nations started to become independent. He felt that the "African revolution . . . African independence that has been going on for the past ten or twelve years, has absolutely affected the mood of the Black people in the Western Hemisphere" to the point that "when they migrate to England, they pose a problem for the English. And when they migrate to France, they pose a problem for the French."[59] That lack of pride in Blackness was such an important ingredient in the creation of the Negro that it was just as present everywhere else that the ex-slave resided. By the turn of the twentieth century, almost the entire African continent was controlled by Europe, reinforcing the myth of our inferiority. But Malcolm's program was intended to create progress for all Black people, in the diaspora and in Africa. One of the central tenets of the constitution of the OAAU is that "Africa will go no further than we will, and we will go no further than Africa."[60] We were all, no matter where we resided, "in the same boat."

This expansive vision of Blackness was very much in the vein of perhaps Malcolm's biggest influence, Marcus Garvey. The Universal Negro Improvement Association styled itself as bringing together the Black world. As its founder and first president-general, Garvey had declared, "Africa for the Africans, at home and abroad," and aimed to bring together the "400,000,000 men and women with warm blood coursing through their veins" from the global Black nation.[61] The UNIA was the most successful Black organization to have ever existed, boasting a membership of between two and eight million across dozens of countries in the 1920s.[62] The UNIA took its role of representing the global Black nation so seriously that it appointed ambassadors to different countries and was so successful that it received observer status at the League of Nations. It should not be a revelation that Malcolm was so heavily influenced by the UNIA because, as activist Kwame Ture once argued, Malcolm's "basic ideology was Garveyism."[63] (Remember that both his parents were active in the UNIA and he attended meetings as a child.) Garveyism did more than any other movement to make us love ourselves, with Garvey's words, "The Black skin is not a badge of shame but rather a glorious symbol of greatness," providing the foundation for the Black Power movement.[64] Malcolm resuscitated these important messages from Garveyism, radicalizing Blackness to inspire us to overturn the wicked system that we are trapped in.

The major difference between Malcolm's political thought and Garveyism was that Malcolm saw the movement emerging from Africa as the central point through which to organize. It was the African revolution that inspired the diaspora to wake up and connect to the liberation struggles emerging from the continent. Malcolm named his organization after the Organization of African Unity, which was founded by so-called independent African states in 1963. By contrast, the most fundamental critique of Garvey is that his vision was steeped in the colonization movement that sought to raise Africa to the level of the White world, with the enlightened diaspora returning there with the skills to rebuild the continent. Garvey was operating at a time when the liberation movements in Africa were heavily suppressed and Ethiopia was the only truly independent nation, so the idea of connecting up African movements across the continent probably seemed impossible—but this shouldn't prevent us from criticizing the problematic elements of Garvey's program. I have very little doubt that, had the UNIA been able to succeed on the African continent, it would have had a radically different practice than some of the more bombastic rhetoric of Garvey would imply. It was a mass organization that wanted to bring the Black nation together to completely liberate Africa from colonialism, and staying true to this mission would have meant organically developing a more radical framework. Malcolm picked up the mantle from the Universal Negro Improvement Association and completed its unfinished project, creating a revolutionary platform for Black people worldwide.

Thinking Black was the starting point for Malcolm's revolutionary politics. The street hustler who ended up drug addicted and in prison for burglary was the result of White thinking, embodying the Negro that White society put so much effort into creating. It was at his lowest point, in prison, that he began to read as many books as he could get his hands on. Diving into Black literature transformed his life, because he began to think Black and therefore everything changed. He could never go back to being the Negro, that figment of the White imagination that haunted from within the ghetto. Malcolm articulated a

Blackness that connected the diaspora to the African continent on the political basis that we are all in the same boat and need each other to achieve our freedom. He understood that the conditions to open our eyes to that necessary unity would always be present in this wicked system and that all the masses needed was "someone to start the ball rolling."[65] Malcolm pushed the ball down the hill, but it has stalled, as we have found every possible excuse to avoid thinking Black. If we want to fulfill Malcolm's vision, we have to be unapologetic in our Blackness.

9

HOUSE AND FIELD NEGRO

Thinking Black was the essential starting point for Malcolm, but we should never confuse this idea with the "weak Black nationalism" that has been the pitfall of so many of our politics.[1] To think Black does not mean to support every Black person no matter what, out of some deluded sense of melanin loyalty. I can promise you that Malcolm would have muted disgraced R&B singer R. Kelly long ago, and, as for Michael "I turned myself White" Jackson, I don't think it's difficult to know where Malcolm would have stood. He spent more time firing shots at misguided Black folk than he did at the wicked devils. A central tenet of thinking Black is to stop focusing on White people. Once you accept that a chicken can never lay a duck egg, it becomes tiresome calling out White racism. The White people Malcolm targeted the most were the Foxes like JFK who he thought were luring Black people into the doghouse. Malcolm would have had far more to say about Joe Biden than he would have about Donald Trump, not because he would have supported Agent Orange but because Trump's teeth are so glaring that no (sensible) Black person could believe he was anything but a bloody-jawed Wolf. Most of Malcolm's scorn was poured on the Black people he felt were leading others astray, because they were even more dangerous than the tricky Foxes. Malcolm saw the nuances in Blackness. To think Black was to embrace the politics of revolution that could set you free. Therefore, there *is* an authenticity to Blackness; you can't just pose and fake it for the cameras. But for Malcolm, to be authentically Black is related purely to your political position. Complicating our understanding of this, Malcolm frequently connected politics to the Black individual's place in the economic hierarchy.

In the Malcolm myth, he was a racial firebrand who avoided exploring other dimensions of oppression. For instance, the indispensable Patricia Hill Collins argued that "missing from Malcolm X's analysis is a structural analysis of social class that addresses those features of capitalist political economies that profoundly shape both black and white social class dynamics."[2] The last part of the charge is certainly true. Malcolm did not spend any time exploring class or any other dynamics in White society. Even after leaving the Nation of Islam, he wrote off White society as fundamentally evil and something that Black people needed to escape from. He no doubt recognized that there were hierarchies within the wicked system, but he simply had no interest in exploring them. Thinking Black meant looking through the lens of Black people, and Malcolm understood that no matter how marginalized some White people might be, they were dependent on the system of White supremacy for any potential uplift. Malcolm concentrated his efforts on Black communities, and here he developed a very clear class analysis, deeply rooted in our relationship to racial capitalism. One of his most iconic, and perhaps misunderstood, distinctions is between the House and Field Negro. Understanding this dynamic is vital to unlocking the potential of thinking Black.

HOUSE AND FIELD NEGRO

Malcolm's 1963 "Message to the Grassroots" speech, delivered to young activists in Detroit, is where he most clearly outlined the difference between the House and Field Negro. He described how during slavery some of the enslaved "lived in the attic or the basement, but still they lived near the master." Due to being in the house, they dressed and ate better than the rest of the enslaved, and because of this Malcolm described how "they loved their master more than the master loved himself. They would give their life to save the master's house quicker than the master would. The House Negro, if the master said, 'We got a good house here,' the House Negro would say, 'Yeah, we got a good house here.' Whenever the master said 'we,' he said 'we.' That's how you can tell a House Negro."[3] Their slightly better treatment made them think White and see the plantation as the only place to be. Malcolm joked that "if the master got sick, the House Negro would say, 'What's the matter, boss, we sick?' We sick! He identified himself with his master more than his master identified with himself." The House Negroes were bleached all the way down to the soul and were inauthentically Black because they were blinded by their slightly elevated position.

Malcolm applied this metaphor to his contemporary America, outlining how

> this modern House Negro loves his master. He wants to live near him. He'll pay three times as much as the house is worth just to live near his master, and then brag about "I'm the only

Negro out here." "I'm the only one on my job." "I'm the only one in this school." You're nothing but a House Negro. And if someone comes to you right now and says, "Let's separate," you say the same thing that the House Negro said on the plantation. "What you mean, separate? From America? This good White man? Where you going to get a better job than you get here?"

Malcolm's position here was a clearly a class argument, that those with more access to wealth were more likely to buy into the American nightmare and could therefore not be trusted to support the politics of Black liberation. He articulated the position of the House Negro in relation to the middle-class, bourgeois Negroes, who had the wealth necessary to live in White neighborhoods or to hold professional jobs in offices where they were one of the few Black faces. At times, he used this critique in a cultural way, to highlight some deficiency in middle-class Black folk. For example, Malcolm once lampooned that the "real bourgeois Black American never wants to move out of his seat" when Black music was playing. He joked that "you can have some real soul music and he'll pretend it doesn't move him."[4] The buttoned-up House Negro did not want to be seen to be tempted by unruly Black culture. You'll notice, though, that Malcolm said, "*Pretend* it doesn't move him." Rejecting Blackness was seen as a conscious choice that went against the House Negro's real instincts. There is an inauthenticity to the rejection. In the same way, the desire to integrate into a racist society is also a pointless imitation. Malcolm's strong distaste for the House Negro led Robin Kelley to declare that "Malcolm saw the black bourgeoisie as both enemies and misguided souls, sell-outs and brainwashed Negroes who simply need a wake-up call from the Motherland."[5] In some respects this is true, but for Malcolm the House Negro is equally about mindset as it is about economics.

In contrast to the House Negro were those on the plantation who represented the masses. Malcolm explained that the Field Negro "was beaten from morning to night. He lived in a shack, in a hut; he wore old, cast-off clothes." Due to the harshness of the conditions facing those toiling away on the plantation, the Field Negro "hated his master," which for Malcolm meant "he was intelligent." Unlike the House Negro, "when the house caught on fire, he didn't try and put it out; that Field Negro prayed for a wind, for a breeze. When the master got sick, the Field Negro prayed that he'd die. If someone come to the Field Negro and said, 'Let's separate, let's run,' he didn't say 'Where we going?' He'd say, 'Any place is better than here.'"[6]

Malcolm marked out the position of the Field Negroes as authentic because they could never forget that they were enslaved. They were at the bottom; there was no way to rationalize that they were being treated well. Underpinning Malcolm's concept here is that the House Negroes are just as exploited and dehumanized as those toiling in the fields, but they have been deceived into believing that they have a good deal. Just as with the House Negro, Malcolm argued that he could see the same dynamics playing out in his time:

You've got Field Negroes in America today. I'm a Field Negro. The masses are the Field Negroes. When they see this man's house on fire, you don't hear these little Negroes talking about "our government is in trouble." They say, "*The* government is in trouble." Imagine a Negro: "Our government!" I even heard one say "our astronauts." They won't even let him near the plant—and "our astronauts!" "Our Navy"—that's a Negro that's out of his mind. That's a Negro that's out of his mind.

Malcolm's argument here is reminiscent of Patricia Hill Collins's Black feminist standpoint on epistemology, where racial and gender oppression gives the Black woman a unique insight into the nature of society.[7] Malcolm was saying that it is the view from below that allowed the Field Negro to see clearly in a way that those who were more comfortable could not. The House Negro was clouded by White thinking because of his class location. Malcolm's declaration that he was a Field Negro made it clear where he drew his authenticity from. Importantly, Malcolm was not saying that just by nature of his place at the bottom the Field Negro was perfect. Remember that Malcolm firmly rejected his hustler self, the classic Field Negro. He was wading as deeply in White thinking when he was a Field Negro on the streets as the House Negro flying an American flag in his otherwise White suburban neighborhood. Being excluded from society made it easier for the masses to hate the nation and instinctively feel the need for revolution, but it by no means meant that they would embrace a radical politics. The Field Negroes provided revolutionary energy because they had nothing to lose. They were impatient and could not be bought off with false promises. Malcolm pointed out that "if a person is sitting on a warm stove, he has patience to wait to get up because it's only warm, but for the masses of Black people who are sitting in a hot stove, they're impatient and no matter how much you tell them progress is being made it's not fast enough for them."[8]

Malcolm wanted to harness the power of the Field Negro, to turn that energy into a revolutionary force. He also saw the potential to ignite a different powder keg for the House Negro because of the false promises being made: "Once the slave has his master's education, the slave wants to be like his master, wants to share his master's property, and wants to exercise the same privileges as his master. . . . America has not given us equal education, but she has given us enough to make us want more and to make us demand equality of opportunity, which is causing great unrest."[9] Malcolm foresaw that the inability of a chicken to lay a duck egg would ultimately lead to even the House Negro being let down. A racist society can only produce racist outcomes. Once you raise the expectations for equality, when these are not met there will be unrest. Again, Malcolm was prophetic here: The generation that has been trying to make Black Lives Matter for more than a decade are the very people who are supposed to have been integrated into society.

Malcolm died before he could see the extent to which benevolent colonialism delivered the illusion of freedom at home and abroad. He was assassinated before the first Black studies degrees transformed higher education in America at the end of the 1960s and prior to affirmative action. Malcolm watched from the ancestral sidelines as a generation of Black people became elected officials, sat on the boards of top companies, and made billions of dollars from entertainment and sports. It took me more than a decade to dub Barack Obama the White House Negro, but Malcolm was likely chuckling to himself in 2008. With the forces of neocolonialism pacifying the African continent through so-called independence, and the Washington consensus of debt propping up puppet leaders, the revolutionary zeal that had sparked radical politics worldwide was doused. Malcolm warned that the dangers of token integration created a class of "handpicked Negroes" who were used as the examples of how we should all make it. The problem was, there were enough of these examples to delude far too many of us that we were on the right track. If Malcolm were alive today, he would be chiding us for choosing the wrong path. Rather than fighting to overturn the system, we marched down the path to token integration and second-class citizenship. In Britain, that looks like Black students being overrepresented in higher education because we have swallowed the propaganda that gaining qualifications will increase our opportunities. But having done everything that we are supposed to do, we still find ourselves less likely to be employed after graduation and have an even more remote chance of getting a well-paid professional job.[10]

Malcolm's warning that access to schooling would make us impatient has eventually come to pass. The Black Lives Matter protests, ignited by high-profile public killings of Black people, splashed cold water on the idea that society is any less racist than it was in the past. It is not a coincidence that the fuse for Black Lives Matter was lit during the White House Negro's presidency. Obama was meant to be a sign that times had changed, yet unarmed teenager Trayvon Martin was still pursued and killed by George Zimmerman in 2012. Just as with lynchings in the past, the police refused to arrest the White man (yes, Latinx can be White), and even when the protests meant he was eventually charged, he was acquitted because he had the right to "stand his ground" against the menacing Black threat.[11] Subsequent high-profile killings have only exacerbated the protests, culminating with the murder of George Floyd, captured on camera in 2020. The violence was the reminder that people needed of the racism that still exists, and the younger generation once again seems awake to the truth that we have been trying to make a chicken lay a duck egg. We are certainly at a moment where the timing may be perfect to reengage with Malcolm's politics. But to do so effectively, we will need to confront an uncomfortable reality.

Due to the efforts of token integration, it is no longer the case that the people who are "catching hell" at the harshest end of racism are in the diaspora. During slavery, there was no dispute that anything could rival the depravity of experience on the plantations. After emancipation, conditions got a little better, and there would have been only slight differences between the lives of those in the West and in the former colonies. Recently, I found a picture of my grandmother's house in Jamaica when she was a child, and it easily could have been mistaken for one of the tin shacks that made up the village I stayed in when I was doing volunteer work in South Africa. Even in Malcolm's time, Black people in America were having to march for basic dignity, and African nations were just gaining their independence. In Britain, racial discrimination in housing and employment didn't start to be outlawed until 1968. We might have been in the West, but no one could make a credible argument that we were part of it, least of all citizens of it.

In the last sixty years, we have been integrated into the West, unfairly and on racist terms, but the vast majority of us are now living in the plantation house. We have free education, varying levels of access to the welfare state, and at least some opportunity to live relatively comfortably. The contrast between the conditions that Black people in the West face today versus those in the underdeveloped world has never been starker. Here, we have struggles to get more Black professors, but on the African continent the fights are life or death. Consider that nine million people die of hunger every year, with a vastly disproportionate number of those people in Africa. We may go hungry in the West, but we are incredibly unlikely to starve to death. In the underdeveloped world, a child dies every ten seconds because of poverty, while in the West we rightly mourn every death of a minor as a rare and terrible tragedy.[12] For the most part, we are protected from the harshest abuses of the system. The Field Negro is on the African continent, in the Brazilian favela, or on a small boat desperately trying to get into the West. The fact that people risk their children's lives to try to get into the plantation house should tell you about the key dividing line in the world. Now that we are part of the house, far too many of us want to maintain the limited privileges that we have at the expense of the rest.

Malcolm was alive at a time when we were migrating from Caribbean colonies to Europe and African nations were gaining their so-called independence. He had too much faith in these national liberation projects and did not predict their almost total capitulation to the global system of White supremacy. In fairness to Malcolm, he planned to be actively involved in revolutionizing the struggle, both in the diaspora and on the continent. One of the primary reasons for the failure of revolution was the assassination of people like him who had the influence to build a truly revolutionary politics. He would have been deeply troubled by the current pattern of migration, which is seeing Africans try to flee the field-like conditions that face most people on the continent. A solution for those who have resources is to escape into the house. They may face racism and inequality, but they will have a basic standard of living that is not guaranteed everywhere in Africa. Believe me, I am fully aware that not everyone in Africa is poor, that you can find plenty of places that are far nicer and more beautifully built than in miserable England. This was the case in Malcolm's day, when he visited Ghana and reported that it was the "most beautiful continent" he had ever seen, and that it was teeming with White people "trying to integrate" with Africans.[13] When I visited Addis Ababa in 2021, it was breathtaking. Luxury hotels are popping up everywhere, and the place has a real-life Wakanda feel. But Ethiopia is still one of the poorest countries in the world, with an average life expectancy more than sixteen years less than that of Britain. Token integration has been taken to another level on the continent, with those who can afford Western education either leaving entirely or returning to manage the affairs of their supposedly independent countries, like colonial administrators of old. Malcolm would be devastated to see the extent to which neocolonialism has led many of us to run into the house rather than trying to burn down the plantation and start anew.

The reality is that no matter how much we try to make it into the house, there will always be limits attached to our progress. In America, the Great Migration from the South was in many ways similar to the global dynamics at play today. The former slaveholding states had created conditions so appalling that, between the 1910s and 1970s, Black people fled to the North seeking shelter in the house. But Malcolm warned that "there is no difference between the plantation boss in Mississippi and the plantation boss in Washington, D.C. . . . What you experience in this country is one huge plantation system, the only difference now being that the President is the plantation boss."[14] Now the whole world is "one huge plantation," where people in the underdeveloped world are fleeing the field hoping to find better treatment in the house of the West. Malcolm was trying to warn us that this is a strategy that would only bring more harm to Black people. The point of the House and Field Negro for Malcolm was not to disparage those with slightly more privilege than others. The purpose was to remind us that no matter how much progress we think we have made, we are still "ex-slaves" operating on the modern-day plantation. House Negroes were out of their minds because they had blinded themselves to the reality of their conditions.

This is an essential reminder to those of us who think we are special because we were born in the West. We do not deserve more because we were born in Britain, America, or any other bastion of empire. We should not be trying to pull up the drawbridge against those who look like us and who are still trapped in the field. Malcolm was using the metaphor to attempt to bring us together across our class differences, not to castigate those of us with slightly more money. He welcomed migration from the Caribbean colonies into Europe because it meant that we could use our numbers to create unrest in the centers of power. The migration from Africa would have troubled him because, as we have already noted, Malcolm was a Garveyite who saw an eventual physical return there as fundamental to his long-range program. Moving from the former slave colonies to cause trouble in the mother country is a project of a different nature than fleeing the continent for the relative luxuries of the house. Africa was the solution, not a place to escape from but the land where the revolutionary alternative could be built.

For Malcolm, the House Negro was as much a mentality as a fixed class location. To be a House Negro you have to "love your master," and Malcolm explained that this is more likely if you are receiving somewhat better treatment. But he did not see it as inevitable, and Malcolm was trying to convince us not to fall into the delusions that create the House Negro mindset. He never wrote off the House Negro, which is crucial in today's society, where the West has morphed into the house. Yes, we benefit from White supremacy simply because we live here, but that does not mean we have to be seduced by that relative privilege. We can see past our economic interest only if we unify around our Blackness, which is why the concept is so revolutionary. Once we see ourselves as one, then we automatically have to turn our focus away from how to improve conditions in the house to how to liberate those in the field. There are not enough positions in the house for the masses; if we want to liberate everybody, then we must build a radical alternative.

Malcolm never argued that the Field Negroes were in a morally superior place, that they were better people. He simply pointed out that the material condition of the masses meant they understood the stakes better than the bourgeois Black folk trying to make it in White society. Malcolm learned this approach in the NOI, turning ex-convicts and drug addicts into active brothers and sisters. Following Malcolm's example, the Black Panther Party recruited heavily from the streets, from the people who had nothing to lose in the battle for liberation.[15] Given the marginalization that goes hand in hand with being an ex-convict, it is certainly possible to argue that this is the one group who is firmly locked out of society. Mobilizing the masses was the key ingredient for Malcolm's political program because it meant that radical demands could not be watered down by those with a stake in White society. Hopefully, the younger generation has seen the cul-de-sac we have gone down in fighting for token integration and will now seek to overturn the wicked system.

UNCLE TOM

Malcolm used the figure of the House Negro as analysis, critique, and sometimes as interchangeable with another one of his important contributions: that of Uncle Tom. In his "Message to the Grassroots," Malcolm described the creation of the Uncle Tom:

> The slavemaster took Tom and dressed him well, and fed him well, and even gave him a little education . . . gave him a long coat and a top hat and made all the other slaves look up to him. Then he used Tom to control them. The same strategy that was used in those days is used today, by the same White man. He takes a Negro, a so-called Negro, and make him prominent,

build him up, publicize him, make him a celebrity. And then he becomes a spokesman for Negroes—and a Negro leader.

In this speech he called Tom a House Negro, which is not the only time he conflated the two. In one of his last speeches, he described how "back during slavery when Black people like me talked to the slaves they didn't kill them. They sent some old House Negro along behind him to undo what he said."[16] He even equated Black middle-class professionals with Uncle Toms at times, for instance, saying, "You might be a doctor, a lawyer, a preacher, or some other kind of Uncle Tom."[17]

But I am going to take a liberty here, using Malcolm's work to argue that the House Negro and Uncle Tom are significantly different. The classic example of the House Negro is someone hallmarked by White thinking, but they can be passive in their delirium. They live in a White neighborhood, send their kids to White schools, and passionately pledge allegiance to whichever terrible nation-state they reside in. They are not going to join the revolution, but they are mostly focused on trying to do their best inside the house. Malcolm described something very different with the Uncle Tom. They were actively sent out of the house to do the master's bidding, to quash any unrest emanating from the field. Not all House Negroes were of this type, just a select few, and for Malcolm these were the most dangerous people for Black radical ambitions. Reflecting on the downfall of the United Negro Improvement Association and its leader, Malcolm argued, "The White man never defeated Marcus Garvey, he got stool pigeons, he got Uncle Toms who, posing as educators, posing as preachers, posing as spokesmen for Negroes to infiltrate, to get in and create tensions and divisions and then accuse the man of doing that which he didn't do."[18]

Uncle Toms had power because, like the Northern Foxes, they posed as friends, but unlike the tricky White liberals, they had credibility with Black people. On the plantation it was the slave owner, and in Malcolm's contemporary America it was those Whites with power who supported the "White press" that boosted the image and esteem of the Uncle Tom.[19] Think back to our discussion of the Farce on Washington in Chapter 3: Malcolm was angry because the civil rights leaders had been paid by JFK and his backers to dull the revolutionary ambitions of the original march. The target of most of Malcolm's ire was the civil rights movement precisely because it was popular with Black people who didn't realize they were being sold very short. The key to being an Uncle Tom is having enough respect within the community so that you can lead the masses to their doom like the Pied Piper.

Never one to mince his words, Malcolm's favorite target for the label "modern day Uncle Tom" was Martin Luther King, but he spread the "Uncle" label liberally across the other civil rights leaders, including "Uncle Roy [Wilkins], Uncle Whitney [Young] and Uncle A. Philip [Randolph]." He quipped that "you've got a whole lot of uncles in there. I can't remember their names, they're all older than I, so I call them 'uncle.' Plus, if you use the word 'Uncle Tom' nowadays, I heard they'll sue you for libel, you know. So I don't call any of them Uncle Tom anymore. I call them Uncle Roy."[20]

This quotation is taken from one of his very last speeches. It shows that Malcolm never relented from publicly chastising those Negro leaders who he thought were marching us astray. He likewise never stopped attacking his nemesis, King, referring to him as "Uncle Martin" just a few days before he died.[21] Terms like "House Negro" and "Uncle Tom" are of vital use today, but we need to make sure we allocate these targets correctly.

Obama is an interesting figure to consider because his election fitted perfectly into Malcolm's warnings about the problem of supporting politicians. He cautioned about the dangers of supporting White Democratic presidential candidates who make empty promises, but it is uncanny how much his words apply to Obama as well: "Yet when the Negro helps that person get in office the Negro gets nothing in return. All he gets is a few appointments, a few handpicked, Uncle Tom, handkerchief head Negroes are given big jobs in Washington D.C. and then those Negroes come back and try and make us think that the administration is going to lead us to the promised land of integration."[22] Obama was both the elected president and the Negro with the big job who was meant to lead us to the promised land. Millions of Black Americans bought his snake oil, and many still defend the first so-called Negro president, even though he did less than nothing for Black communities. But he doesn't qualify for the title of Uncle Tom. Black people followed him belatedly, only when it seemed like he might win, and I am not sure we really expected much of him except his presence as the first Black president. He was the high point, the gold medal of token integration whose symbolic value was all we ever really expected. This is the only way I can explain the support for him, even though he never promised to do anything for Black people and then delivered on his non–campaign plan. You can't sell out if you make no promises. He is the first of a kind: the White House Negro, sent to soothe White America's conscience.

Every time I criticize Obama, I have to apologize to my mom, who is still holding out a candle of hope even though it is so burned down the flame will soon reach her fingers. But the fact that so many Black people are still clinging to the White House Negro is precisely why the critique is necessary. Malcolm was not just throwing around names to be mean—it was a central plank of his political thinking. Black people needed to be warned about those Black folk doing the White master's bidding. This is as true today as it ever was, which is why using these terms must be a part of radical Black politics going forward. All your skinfolk are not your kinfolk, and we shouldn't be afraid of calling out the Uncle Toms and House Negroes who are either actively or passively trying to hoodwink us, or who are used as examples to prevent us from seeing the reality of this wicked system.

"Coon" is not a term that I have come across Malcolm using, but it is definitely one that he would have added to his arsenal. The coon show was a racist performance where White actors would black up their faces and perform grotesque racial stereotypes. Black performers would sometimes be included in these shows, which were meant to titillate White audiences. The modern-day coon show occurs when a Black person goes on TV to say racist things about Black people to win likes from the anti-woke mob or to soothe the White public with the reassurance that racism is an evil that we have left in the past.[23] Malcolm condemned the "modern-day 'magicians, scribes, and Pharisees,'" alongside the Uncle Tom leaders who are sent out to pretend that they and we are together on a march for freedom.[24] He warned of the dangers of this approach, explaining that "you're the ones who are making it hard on yourselves because the White man believes you when you go with that sweet talk to him because you've been sweet talking him ever since you got here."[25] But Malcolm was warning us that this sweet-talking is not on our own account; it is very much a performance to keep White people happy. Malcolm never put any eggs in the basket of expecting White society to change and focused his energies on how Black communities could build the revolutionary alternative.

"Cooning" is so egregious that no self-respecting Black person can ever be drawn in by it. To coon is an activity that House Negroes engage in, tap-dancing to the tune of White supremacy to please the White crowd. To coon means that a House Negro has stopped passively accepting the benefits of White supremacy and has taken on a PR role in promoting them instead, but they are not necessarily intending to be deceptive in their cooning. From my time on the TV circuit, I've had the misfortune to interact with a number of those who coon, and at first I was genuinely surprised by how deeply they believed the anti-Black nonsense they spewed when the camera was turned on. I have it from a credible source that British Conservative Member of Parliament Kemi Badenoch, who is such a cartoonish right-wing figure that British fascists supported her bid to be prime minister, genuinely does not understand why Black people do not support her. It is apparently lost on her that declaring that the school curriculum "does not need to be decolonized, because it is not colonized" and calling for more focus on the "history of Black slave traders who existed before and after the transatlantic slave trade" could never play well with Black audiences.[26] Telling your children that Britain "is the best country in the world to be Black—because it's a country that sees people, not labels" may get the overwhelmingly White members of the Conservative Party gushing, but it is only going to turn off any Black people with sense.[27]

Worryingly, this kind of rhetoric may well be enough to make her the first Black prime minister in British history, but I guarantee it won't be because we voted her in. Our wake-up call, or Obama moment, will ironically be the same one that explodes the myth that Black people have any true voting power in Britain. We make up only 3 percent of the population and are highly concentrated in a handful of inner-city areas. Given the absence of guns, neither the ballot nor the bullet could apply in their literal sense in Britain. Badenoch cannot be accused of being an Uncle Tom because we wouldn't follow her to a chicken shop, let alone on a march to token integration. She undoubtedly fits into the House Negro category, someone who basks in the reflected glow from her proximity to massa and is now cooning her way into the highest political office. Uncle Toms, on the other hand, rely on their credibility in Black communities, so cannot be seen to be so openly pandering to White supremacy.

In Britain, the use of terms like "Uncle Tom" or "House Negro" is becoming increasingly criminalized. I have been hauled into a police station for a "voluntary" interview for calling GB News commentator Calvin Robinson a House Negro. I have also been asked to appear as an expert witness on cases where people have been questioned by the police or charged for carrying signs accusing Conservative politicians Rishi Sunak and Suella Braverman of being "coconuts," calling Black conservatives "coons," or even just posting a raccoon emoji on Twitter. "Coconut" is a term that is essentially the same as "House Negro": someone who is Black or Brown on the outside but White on the inside because they have so fully internalized the tenets of White supremacy. It is disturbing but by no means surprising that this language is being policed in such a draconian manner. The very first conviction under British race relations legislation passed in 1965 was of the activist Roy Sawh, who represented the Universal Coloured People's Association, for supposedly inciting racial hatred.[28] None of the mechanisms that we think are meant to protect us were made to serve that purpose, a fact that Malcolm was consistently reminding us about. If you are squeamish about the use of such terms, then you are rejecting the intellectual heritage of our activism. Malcolm "made it plain" and insisted at all times on "no skulduggery, no flim-flam, no compromise, no sell out, no controlled show."[29] The police, courts, and press might not appreciate our language or tone, but we have to embrace the Field Negro mentality of "we don't care who likes it or not, as long as we know it's the truth."[30]

BLACK UNITY

As contradictory as it may sound, the purpose of theorizing the House and Field Negro, and even the Uncle Tom, was to bring us together. Class differences were encouraging us to see ourselves as a fragmented community, pitted against each other. Malcolm wanted us to see that we were all "ex-slaves" and collectively embrace a Field Negro mentality. By all accounts, after his first visit to Africa in 1964, he came back genuinely wanting to engage in the civil rights struggle he had spent more than a decade skewering. He explained that "we have injected ourselves into the civil rights struggle" and was willing to work with any Black organization that wanted genuine freedom.[31] According to veteran civil rights activist Dorothy Height, Malcolm convened a meeting of civil rights leaders, including inviting the Big Six (Martin Luther King, James Farmer, John Lewis, A. Philip Randolph, Roy Wilkins, and Whitney Young), through actor and friend Ossie Davis. Malcolm had just returned from Mecca and wanted the group to know that he wanted to work with them. Height recalls that he told those at the meeting, "We need to get together and always be together. . . . We have to be in unity. . . . We have to now focus on our people."

Playwright Lorraine Hansberry was at the meeting and demanded an apology from Malcolm for publicly calling her a "traitor to her race" for marrying a White man. Apparently, Malcolm replied, "Sister, you're right. We all must work together and talk to each other before we talk about each other."[32] I would stress that it doesn't sound like a very complete apology, and that in one of his last interviews before he was murdered he called Black people marrying White people "Toms."[33] But there is no doubt that he reached out and in fact did so before he left the Nation of Islam, organizing unity rallies and calling for a "common front, a united front."[34] At his 1962 speech delivered in LA to rally support in the wake of the police killing of NOI member Ronald Stokes, he spoke in a church and praised the community for not falling for the police lies about the shooting, telling the crowd, "We don't care what your religion is. We don't care what organization you belong to. We don't care how far you went or didn't go in school. We don't care what job you have. We have to give you credit to not letting the White man divide you and use you one against the other."[35]

Black unity was always a vital ingredient in Malcolm's political program. He called his revolutionary vehicle the Organization of Afro-American Unity precisely because he understood that building a mass movement was essential. We had to come together in order to move forward. This is one area where we can find an important contradiction in Malcolm's stance that does need to be worked out. The OAAU was named after the Organization of African Unity, which brought together the newly independent African states. Malcolm praised this unity despite the political diversity of its members:

They represent probably every segment, every type of thinking. You have some leaders that are considered Uncle Toms, some leaders who are considered very militant. But even the militant African leaders were able to sit down at the same table with African leaders whom they considered to be Toms, or Tshombes, or that type of character. They forgot their differences for the sole purpose of bringing benefits to the whole. And whenever you find people who can't forget their differences, then they're more interested in their personal aims and objectives than they are in the conditions of the whole. Well, the African leaders showed their maturity by doing what the American White man said couldn't be done.[36]

However, he despised the Western-backed leader of Congo, Moise Tshombe, so much for murdering Lumumba that he used his name interchangeably with that of Uncle Tom. Just a few weeks later, Malcolm was again so incensed by Tshombe that he declared that the Congolese leader was so reviled he "can't go to any country where there are true Black men, and walk the street in safety. This is the worst African that was ever born."[37]

Malcolm's commitment to "thinking Black" simply cannot be squared with this desire for total unity. Weak Black nationalism, which rallies solely around shared Blackness, ends up being so watered down that it is worse than putting too much milk into your coffee. The OAU ultimately ended up becoming a tool of White supremacy in Africa because of the compromise it made with Uncle Tom leaders. A settlement that the Toms were happy with could never be a truly revolutionary one. The sovereignty of each nation-state was enshrined in the constitution of the OAU, and it could not be interfered with. This might sound reasonable—until you remember that all of the so-called nations in Africa were originally the creations of European colonizers or, in the case of Ethiopia, had the extent of their borders dictated to them by the colonial powers.

In 1963, at the founding of the OAU, there was a group of revolutionary countries, spearheaded by Ghana's first president, Kwame Nkrumah, who wanted to unify the continent as a whole, and another group, including the reactionary Tshombe, that was intent on maintaining their nation-states. In order to have unity, the leaders showed their "maturity" by ceding to the demands of the Toms. The result was a continent carved up and easily controlled from the outside by the West, and now increasingly the East as well. No individual so-called independent nation can stand up to the West (or the rest). But a unified Africa would have had the potential to be the most powerful place on earth, given the continent's mineral resources. A unified Africa has always been the only logical end point of Black radical politics, Malcolm's long-range program. Agreeing to noninterference among nation-states essentially erased any revolutionary potential from the OAU and made its eventual transition into the current, toothless African Union (AU) inevitable. It is nothing more than a lapdog running around between West and East for whatever scraps it can get. The nation-state compromise was made when Malcolm was still alive, so he should really have seen its shortcomings. But, just as with the UN, he was holding out hope for the revolutionary promise of the new African nation-states. From his comments on Tshombe and the Big Six Uncles, it is clear that Malcolm was reaching out for unity—but only on radical terms.

In 1963, Malcolm had written letters to the Big Six civil rights leaders, inviting them to speak at the Nation of Islam Harlem unity rally. None of them turned up, but they did send responses regretting that they were busy. Malcolm started his remarks by reading out the various apology notes, and he couldn't resist prodding at these Uncles' collective self-importance, saying,

> It makes me feel like that man Jesus was talking about who set
> a dinner and invited all the big shots, the doctors, the lawyers

and what have you. . . . They were all too busy to attend that feast, so Jesus told the man to go out in the alley, in the highway and in the byway and get those people, they're not too busy. They don't have any jobs, they don't have too many homes and they're not hooked up to the White man, so they don't have to ask his permission if he can come. They always come out.[38]

He went on to lambaste the attempts by the Big Six to take over and sell out the original aims of the March on Washington. So we have to take Malcolm's pleas for unity at all costs with a strong pinch of salt. There was never really any compromise with him, and although he invited everyone to collaborate, there is no evidence to suggest he would do so on anything other than his own, revolutionary terms.

The House and Field Negro is the prime example of Malcolm's uncompromising concept of Black radical unity. He was always trying to bring us together, at the same time as educating us to the nature of the wicked system. Malcolm aimed to build a mass movement, but he understood that not everyone was ready (and might never be) to row the boat to freedom. This lesson is vital. We need to support each other, but never at the expense of our politics. Thinking Black is a requirement of Black radical thought, and that means to embrace a Field Negro mentality. Importantly, no matter what your class position, you can embrace this mindset. This is a politics we have to choose to engage in. There is also a potentially gendered critique of the "house" and "field" positions, given that women were far more likely to be in the house than men. And that proximity to the master didn't often mean better treatment for Black women, who were frequently raped. But Malcolm never made the case that women were more likely to embrace a House Negro mentality than men were, nor was he saying that there was no suffering in the house. The purpose of the metaphor was a reminder that we were *all* suffering as slaves (and still suffering as ex-slaves), who needed (and still need) to come together to be fully free. That is a message vitally important to all of us, across all the intersections.

A BETTER WORD IS INDEPENDENCE

So far we have explored Malcolm's vision and touched on some of the principles of his solution. In this chapter, we will focus on Malcolm's concrete political program, which was extremely well thought-out—and he even left behind a constitution. The Organization of Afro-American Unity was the revolutionary vehicle that Malcolm was building when he died. Yet, although Malcolm is an icon, relatively few people have ever heard of the organization. Its almost total absence from the *Autobiography* goes some way to explaining this, but the speeches and documents have been there for anyone interested for the past sixty years. The uncomfortable truth is that many are happy for Malcolm to remain an elusive figure that can bend to fit whatever aims suit them. That way, his rhetoric can be evoked without having to get involved in the messy and uncomfortable work of revolution. My aim here is to put an end to all of that. Malcolm laid out a radical political program, and if we are not following it, then we should keep his name out of our mouths.

The OAAU was led by Malcolm but included what he called a "brain trust" of people, including the esteemed historian John Henrik Clarke, Black nationalist preacher Albert Cleage, and civil rights activist Gloria Richardson Dandridge.[1] While Malcolm was overseas, Lynn Shiflet effectively ran the organization, and Malcolm was clear that it was a collective effort, clarifying that "the OAAU is not me. . . . We take matters collectively."[2] At its second founding rally, Malcolm shared the charter of the organization, which set out a clear vision of how to build the revolution. The overarching goal of the OAAU was to "unite everyone in the Western hemisphere of African descent into one united force" and to connect this group to the African continent.[3] The revolutionary conception of Blackness was the foundation of Malcolm's radical politics and was at the heart of the OAAU. Harnessing the power of Black people worldwide was the long-range program of the organization. In this chapter, we will hopefully put an end to the idea that Malcolm had no solution to make plain his radical program for Black liberation.

"THIS WORD SEPARATION HAS BEEN MISUSED"

Any time you talk about uniting Black people, the issue of segregation rears its head. The Nation of Islam was a separatist organization. It wanted to save Black people from the coming racial Armageddon, which would wipe away the wicked race of White devils. When he was a spokesman for the NOI, Malcolm advocated for "complete separation on some land that we can call our own." In what was a kind of reparatory justice plea, he demanded that the "government should give us everything we need in the form of machinery, material, and finance, enough to last for twenty to twenty-five years until we can become an independent people and an independent nation in our own land."[4] He would have preferred this to be some land in Africa, but he was happy for a portion of land in the South of the United States to be given over for the Black nation. Such appeals go back at least as far as the 1920s, with the "Black belt thesis" from the Communist Party USA, which argued that since there was an area in the South that held a majority of Black people, due to the large presence of ex-slaves there, this should be turned over to the Black population to make their own independent nation.[5] The appeal of the NOI was, and remains, that it argued for Black self-sufficiency from White society, and the idea of a separate Black nation has long had currency in Black America.

On leaving the sect, Malcolm again evolved his views rather than completely breaking with his old way of thinking. For a start, he understood the basic pragmatics of the issue and realized that no government was ever going to allow Black Americans to form their own nation, let alone assist them in the endeavor. In 1964, he noted to Robert Penn Warren that "advocating a separate section of America for Afro-Americans is similar to waiting for a heaven after you die."[6] In one of his last interviews, he explained that he believed in the separate nation while in the NOI because he had faith in the teachings of Elijah Muhammad. But when he began to doubt that his leader "thought that feasible and I saw no kind of action designed to bring it into existence or bring it about, then I turned in a different direction," toward his OAAU program.[7] But Malcolm also saw the limitations of the Black belt idea, highlighting that having separate land did not necessarily mean being independent.

The OAAU was to be an independent Black organization, not a segregated one like the NOI. This is an important distinction that is often lost, as people lazily lump together every Black organization seeking nationalism, even though they include radically different views and agendas. In the Nation of Islam, Malcolm developed an analysis of the difference between segregation and separation, explaining that "we don't want to be segregated by the White man. We don't want to be integrated with the White man. We want to be separated from the White man."[8] At no point did Malcolm see segregation as a positive. To be segregated meant to be controlled by White power, given less resources and therefore guaranteed inequality. But Malcolm eventually argued that "this word separation has been misused. . . . A better word than separation is independence."[9]

Just being apart is no solution; we need to be able to be independent of the racism that will otherwise define our existence. Haiti is probably the best example of the problem of separateness. The world's first Black republic is widely celebrated as the only place in history to succeed in a slave rebellion, when it declared independence in 1804.[10] The Haitians kicked out the French, fought off the British and the Spanish, and stood alone. The problem was they were surrounded by slave colonies and the emerging seat of empire in America. Therefore, they were entirely subject to the racist world order, and in 1825 France forced them to pay a staggering amount in reparations for having had the audacity to free themselves from bondage. The crippling debt (which was only paid off in 1948), plus global isolation, explains why Haiti is currently one of the poorest countries in the world, with some of the most internal turmoil.[11] If separate but unequal were a nation, it would be Haiti.

To combat the limitations of revolution when restricted to one nation-state, the OAAU was intended to be all-encompassing of the African diaspora: those in Latin America, the Caribbean, Europe, and wherever we might be. Malcolm joked at the second founding rally that "if they're in Alaska, though they might call themselves Eskimos, if they have African blood, they're Afro Americans."[12] This reference to "blood" is a nod to Garveyism, with Garvey having once stated, "How dare anyone tell us that Africa cannot be redeemed when we have 400,000,000 men and women with warm blood coursing through their veins."[13] Following on from the UNIA, Malcolm understood the commitment to the global Black nation as extending well beyond the imagined borders of Western nation-states. The Nation of Islam vision of Black nationalism is a very limited one within America, and, even to the extent the NOI was arguing for land in Africa, it was only intended for America's ex-slaves. Malcolm abandoned narrow nationalism for the global Black nation, where we are just as responsible for those in the neighborhood that we live in as we are to those we are separated from by an ocean.

Central to the OAAU was its status as a grassroots membership organization that was trying to get the masses to join and pay membership dues. Malcolm regularly criticized the NAACP, as he felt it was a major civil rights organization that was only marching arm in arm with King for token integration. He had particular scorn for its funding model, which set the membership fee at $2.50 a year, and insisted that the OAAU would charge a $2 joining fee and $1 every week for each member. Malcolm argued that the NAACP was broken because it had to seek funding from White sources in order to maintain its operations. Relying on White funding would always limit the scope of any Black organization because you cannot bite the hand that feeds you. Malcolm invoked Garvey when explaining the much higher charge for OAAU membership: "This is why Garvey was able to be more militant. Garvey didn't ask them for help. He asked our people for help. And this is what we're going to do." Essentially, the model of the OAAU is to link the Black population together worldwide, collect taxes (in the form of membership fees), and use those to improve the lives of all of those of African descent. This is the practical application of the idea of the global Black nation.

The OAAU was specifically a Black organization, open only to those of African descent. Malcolm made it plain that "Whites can't join us. . . . They end up outjoining Negroes. The Whites control all Negro organizations."[14] All-Black membership was key to the independence to make decisions and, importantly, to take actions that might not gain White approval. Malcolm did say that they would "accept financial help but will never let them join us." This acceptance of money may sound contradictory, given the above stated aims around funding, but Malcolm was open to taking White financial support as long as it didn't impact the independence of the organization. By building a mass membership base that was contributing regular funds, the organization would be able to function independently. This didn't mean they could not take outside money in; they just couldn't rely on it. This is an important model for the future, especially in light of calls for reparatory justice. A debt is owed, and if White people, the government, or anyone else wants to donate, we shouldn't turn down the money. We just need to make sure that we can do without it so that the funding doesn't control us.

In creating the OAAU, Malcolm wanted to build an organization that meant its spokespeople were entirely free of being controlled from the outside. His main critique of the civil rights movement was that its leaders were puppets for the White hands that pulled their financial strings: "Any Negro who occupies a position that was given to him by the White man, his function never allows him to take a firm uncompromising militant stand on the problems that confront our people. He opens up his mouth only to the degree that the political atmosphere at the time will allow him to do so without rocking the boat."[15]

Malcolm was able to be outspoken because the Nation of Islam relied on funds from members and the businesses it built in the community. But he also felt hamstrung by the lack of political ambition of the NOI, which sought to distance itself from getting its hands dirty in the real world. For all the talk of White devils, Muhammad was also keen not to rock the boat too hard. The OAAU was to be free from all those constraints, allowing Malcolm and any other members to make plain whatever was necessary for us to gain freedom. This message of independence is particularly important, especially now that token integration has allowed more of us to become established in the plantation house.

Black politicians are no longer a rarity, and, following the White House Negro, we have seen the first Black female vice president in the United States in Kamala Harris. In Britain, there has been a host of Black and non-White members of the government. But the mainstream political parties are no place to take an uncompromising position on any topic, because they are ultimately funded and accountable to White supporters. It is painful to watch Black politicians have to bend whichever way the political wind is blowing. Following Israel's attack on Gaza in response to the Hamas terror attack in October 2023, there was dismay in the Black community in Britain when Black Labour MP David Lammy revealed his stance on Israel's war crimes. He initially refused to call for an immediate ceasefire and somehow managed to come to the conclusion that "it's wrong to bomb a refugee camp but clearly if there is a military objective it can be legally justifiable."[16] But we shouldn't criticize Lammy too much for the despicable positions he might take. Just like with the White House Negro, these are a necessary part of the job. While Lammy was refusing to condemn Israel for indiscriminately killing civilians, he explained that he was "hoping one day to be foreign secretary" (which he eventually became in 2024). So it seems in pursuit of high office Lammy was prepared to defend White supremacy. The problem is that *we* expected better from him because he was a Black person within a party of liberal Foxes. We can't blame him for what Malcolm would call *our* political immaturity. If you want to succeed in mainstream politics in the West, you have to serve the needs of a White, devilish society.

In America, there are areas that are overwhelmingly Black, where you could actually get elected on a Black agenda. This is what makes plausible the idea that Malcolm was considering running for a congressional seat in Harlem. We also know that he was asked to run on the left-wing, third-party Freedom Party ticket as a senator for Michigan, but Malcolm "wouldn't say yes or no."[17] As a congressman, he would have been limited by the job, even if he tried to elevate his role beyond it. More problematically, even if he could have kept his revolutionary rhetoric, he could not have put any of it into practice in a political party. At best, Congressman Malcolm X would have become an empty symbol, the firebrand with no political program. Independence means not only being free to say what you like but also being in a position to put it into action.

Malcolm's independence did not rule out either coalition or so-called allyship but set ground rules for both. Rather than flatly rejecting the White devils, he set out clearly the potential relationship of White people to the radical struggle, explaining that "they can form the White Friends of the Organization of Afro-American Unity and work in the White community on White people and change their attitude toward us."[18] Malcolm did hold out a limited degree of hope that

White society could change; he was just not *relying* on it to happen. For those who have deluded themselves into believing that Malcolm was becoming a Marxist, he was crystal clear about that: "There can be no worker solidarity until there's first some Black solidarity. There can be no White-Black solidarity until there's first some Black solidarity."[19] In the spirit of Garveyism, he retained his "race first" mentality. Malcolm was solidly committed to global revolution and working with oppressed people worldwide, but he did this while still rooting his politics in Blackness. There is absolutely no contradiction in seeing racism as a system that oppresses all racialized groups *and* understanding anti-Blackness as a specific feature of the system that other groups can benefit from. White supremacy has created a world with White on the top and Black at the bottom and various rungs in between. Chinese elites may have used this ladder to step up a rung or two higher than Africa, to gain a slightly more elevated position, but this does not change the nature of the system. It is notable that for all his travels to the Middle East and calls for Third World solidarity, Malcolm founded an organization "that will be run exclusively by Negroes and only for Negroes."[20] He set about building an organization that could be the revolutionary vehicle for Black independence and freedom.

POLITICAL, ECONOMIC, AND SOCIAL INDEPENDENCE

The OAAU recognized the impact of mainstream politics on people's lives. Therefore, Malcolm announced a "voter registration drive to make every unregistered voter in the Afro-American community an independent voter."[21] He argued that you could not trust either the Republican Wolf or the Democratic Fox, because "both have sold us out." By registering as independents, no party could take the Black vote for granted, as the Democrats currently do. Importantly, he was not making the zero-sum calculation that because the Democrats had sold us out, then we should run to the Republicans. To accept the rules of a game that oppresses you is more than just insanity; it is political suicide. This lesson is something that we desperately need to learn today, as rightful disillusionment sets in with supposedly left-ish political parties worldwide. There are more alternatives than simply switching to the other, more problematic side of the aisle. The OAAU proposed to "run independent candidates for office, and to support any Afro-American already in office who answers to and is responsible to the Afro-American community." By doing so, the organization hoped to be able to wield as much influence as possible in the political machinery. Alongside voter registration, Malcolm also proposed voter education to make people aware of their power over their elected representatives. He never held out hope that this strategy would win us freedom, but it was part of his "short-range program" to alleviate some of the worst conditions in Black communities.

Malcolm tied the political and economic together organically, with those who held the finances controlling those who were elected to office. He called the economic exploitation of Black Americans "the most vicious practiced on any people on this earth" and declared that the OAAU would "wage an unrelenting struggle against these evils in our community." Malcolm drew attention to the fact that we "do the hardest work for the lowest pay" and "we pay the most money for the worst kind of food and the most money for the worst kind of place to live."[22] He shone a light on the steep economic inequality that still persists today and tied it directly back to the political situation, reminding us that "all of the negative things that you can run into, you have run into under this system that disguises itself as a democracy." The system was "rotten" and would always fail us. The

OAAU's two-pronged approach to the issue of housing is a perfect example of how its political agenda worked. Malcolm outlined a plan to "support rent strikes," but only mass movements, "not little, small rent strikes in one block. We'll make Harlem a rent strike. . . . The Organization of Afro-American Unity won't stop until there's not a Black man in the city not on strike. Nobody will pay any rent. The whole city will come to a halt. And they can't put all of us in jail because they've already got the jails full of us."

A rent strike might sound like a relatively mainstream mobilization, but the scale on which he envisioned it elevated it to a more militant action. To get everyone to strike would lead to much more fundamental change. Malcolm was reminding us of our power as a collective. If a handful of people don't pay their rent, nothing happens, but if we unite together, we have significant power. The agency, the power, is within us, if only we seize it. It was vitally important that the OAAU was "not responsible to anybody but us. . . . We don't have to ask the man downtown what tactics we can use to demonstrate our resentment against his criminal abuse. We don't have to ask his consent; we don't have to ask his endorsement; we don't have to ask his permission."

As well as rent strikes, Malcolm proposed a "housing self-improvement program. Instead of waiting for the White man to come and straighten out our neighborhood, we'll straighten it out ourselves." The necessity for self-help should tell you everything you need to know about how he understood the relationship of Black communities to the state. We simply could not rely on the state, so we would have to solve our own problems. Any concessions gained would only come about through large-scale collective action that shut down the city. The government would have to be forced into giving us even the crumbs off the table. If ever there was a message we need today, it is this one: We cannot win gains through moral or principled appeals. We have to force change, giving the powers that be no choice but to meet our demands.

Perhaps the most controversial aspect of the OAAU's program from today's standpoint is the focus on the social ills that plagued Black communities. Malcolm declared that we "must accept the responsibility for regaining our people who have lost their place in society" and so rid the communities of drug addiction, prostitution, gambling, and crime. Included in this agenda was a call to fight back against police brutality and corruption, a far more popular arena of current politics. As much as we would like it not to be true, as a result of White supremacy, poor Black communities have been ghettoized, in the same way that we were turned into Negroes. We managed to retain our humanity, just as the ghetto has, but we cannot neglect the addiction and criminality that has become an escape for far too many. Malcolm did not see this as a result of individual failings of those people who fell into crime. After all, he had once been a hustler and ended up in jail. He understood that the system laid a trap for Black people to fall into disproportionately. On the subject of addiction, he explained that

> when a person is a drug addict, he's not the criminal; he's a victim of the criminal. The criminal is the man downtown who brings drug into the country. Negroes can't bring drugs into this country. You don't have any boats. You don't have any airplanes. You don't have any diplomatic immunity. It is not you who is responsible for bringing in drugs. You're just a little tool that is used by the man downtown.

Almost as if he were foreseeing the crack epidemic that sparked the mass incarceration of Black Americans two decades after his death, in the 1960s Malcolm saw how drugs were being used to victimize the whole community. But, although we did not create the problem, it was still our responsibility to solve it. Malcolm knew that the police were not there to stop crime; in fact, he noted that "the more cops we have, the more crime we have. We begin to think that they bring some of the crime with them."[23] Self-help extended to reaching out to all of those in the community to "create meaningful, creative, useful activities for those who were led astray down the avenues of vice." The hope was to build the OAAU into an independent organization with enough support to be able to transform the lives of all of those in the Black community, so that it wasn't necessary to rely on support from the hostile world outside. Malcolm stressed the need to create activities that pulled people out of addiction, gave them work and a stake in society, rather than trying to moralize them out of their seemingly purely individual plight.

EDUCATION IS THE PASSPORT TO OUR FUTURE

Just like a government, the OAAU was split into several departments that focused on the pressing issues for Black communities. It should come as no surprise that education was one of the original departments created, given that Malcolm had earlier declared that we "need a program of political reeducation to open our people's eyes."[24] He had been turned off the formal schooling route when his teacher mocked him as a child for declaring that he wanted to be a lawyer.[25] In the OAAU, education became the "passport to our future," perhaps the key mechanism to building the revolution. Since he had belonged to the NOI, Malcolm knew that the greatest damage done to us was on a psychological level, internalizing "Negroness" as negative and generally being brainwashed into a Western (American, British, French, Jamaican, etc.) delusion. The education platform that he created was the perfect example of the model of Black independence that Malcolm sought to build in the OAAU.

Malcolm railed against the abysmal state of schooling that Black children were receiving: "Our children are being criminally short-changed in the public school system of America. The Afro-American schools are the poorest run schools in the city of New York. Principals and teachers fail to understand the nature of the problems with which they work and as a result they cannot do the job of teaching our children."[26] The primary problem he drew attention to was that Black children "learn nothing about us other than that we used to be cotton pickers." In order to have a love for themselves and each other, to grow up to be productive members of the Black community, they needed to be taught about the greatness of our history. Malcolm rejected out of hand the proposed plan to integrate the schools in New York, arguing that the problem was not that Black and White students were separate but the actual schooling that they were receiving. Today, New York has the most segregated schools in the United States, so Malcolm was right to be suspicious of that plan.[27]

But his rejection of integration was not only because he knew it was not achievable. More importantly, he understood that the solution to the problem facing Black young people was not to change the population of the schools but to take over the schools entirely. Malcolm and the OAAU demanded that 10 percent (representing the Black population of the city) of the New York schools be turned over to their organization so that they could run them instead. He explained, "We want Afro-American principals to head these schools. We want Afro-American teachers in these schools. Meaning we want Black principals and Black teachers with some textbooks about Black people. We want textbooks written by Afro-Americans that are acceptable to our people before they can be used in these schools."

Independence was about changing not just the color of the people running the schools but the nature of what was taught. Taking over the schools in New York was meant to be a showcase for the power of Black education and a model that could be replicated across the nation. Malcolm also called for parents to boycott the schools until the demand for Black independent education was met. As well as direct action, Malcolm outlined a plan for the OAAU to "select and recommend people to serve on local school boards where school policy is made and passed on to the Board of Education" to ensure that the right goals were achieved. Alongside taking control of the schools, the OAAU was interested in adult education, providing us with the skills in math and science to be able to fulfill all the needs of Black communities.

Education extended beyond schooling, with Malcolm insisting that "we must launch a cultural revolution to un-brainwash an entire people."[28] This was true not just for Black children but for the wider community at large, who had already been victims of the biased school system. Malcolm declared that "armed with the knowledge of our past, we can with confidence charter a course for our future. Culture is an indispensable weapon in the freedom struggle." The OAAU envisioned Black creatives being at the vanguard of the revolution. One of the aims of the organization was to "work toward the establishment of a cultural center in Harlem, which will include people of all ages and will conduct workshops in all of the arts, such as film, creative writing, painting, theater, music, and the entire spectrum of Afro American history."[29]

Culture has long been used to support revolutionary movements, from the Vodou religion and drums of the Haitian Revolution to

Emory Douglas's cartoons in *The Black Panther* newspaper. There are few better ways to make an idea plain than to use the arts. Malcolm saw culture as a tool to reeducate the masses. Central in this quest was to get Black people to "identify with Africa culturally, philosophically, psychologically and the 'life' or new spirit will give us the inspiration to do the things necessary to better our political and economic and social life there in America."[30] The centrality of culture to Malcolm's practice has allowed false prophets to step in and claim his mantle. We covered Ron Karenga in Chapter 6 and his nonsensical belief that adopting a supposedly African lifestyle was a solution to our problems. This notion has unfortunately been picked up in movements like Afrocentrism, which proposes that being culturally "African" is resistance to White supremacy.[31] These civic religions offer individual salvation at the expense of revolutionary politics, in the same way that you accept the status quo if you think God is going to solve your problems for you. Culture was never the solution for Malcolm; it was a vital "weapon" to be used in the pursuit of liberation. This is an important distinction, because as revolutionary movements have declined, often all that is left is cultural nationalism, the empty idea that we can find freedom in a cultural connection with our roots. Malcolm's Africanism is the source of his radicalism, not a conservative, regressive agenda that seeks to police how we present ourselves.

LONG-RANGE PROGRAM AFRICANISM

So far in this chapter, most of the practical program of the OAAU looks like it would fit squarely within a liberal civil rights agenda: registering voters, organizing rent strikes, and boycotting the schools to ultimately change the education of Black children. Alongside these activities, the OAAU proposed a cultural center and to try to eliminate the social ills within Black communities. It is easy to see how the Malcolm myth could lead us to the conclusion that he had converted to the civil rights mainstream, especially when he admitted that "local leaders of civil rights" groups were "supportive" and it was only the "national leaders who are controlled by their White paymasters."[32] In truth, if the entire program of the OAAU were the national campaigns outlined above, then it *would* have been little more than a civil rights organization: a militant civil rights organization that sought to cause as much unrest as possible to achieve its goal, but still very much a civil rights organization. But we must understand this phase of the OAAU as the short-range program designed to bring the Black community together in America as a first essential step toward revolution. At the founding rally, Malcolm made his ambitions clear: "[We] start in Harlem with the intention of spreading throughout the state, and from the state throughout the country, and from the country throughout the Western Hemisphere." The idea was to build a global organization that was directly connected to the African continent. Enshrined in the constitution was that "Africa will not go forward any faster than we will, and we will not go forward any faster than Africa will. We have one destiny and we've had one past." From its very founding, the Organization of Afro-American Unity put the struggles of those on the continent at the heart of its political program, shattering the restrictive barriers of the nation-state. This is ever more important now that token integration means that most of us in the West are firmly in the plantation house. We can be truly radical only if we are concerned with those in the field; redeeming the African continent simply cannot be done with civil rights solutions.

Malcolm spent much of his last year traveling across Africa trying to get support for the OAAU. On his travels, he was treated as a foreign dignitary, being hosted by leaders including Sékou Touré (Guinea), Julius Nyerere (Tanzania), Kwame Nkrumah (Ghana), and Nnamdi Azikiwe (Nigeria). He spoke at the African Summit Conference in August 1964, representing the OAAU, and made the following plea: "We in America are your long-lost brothers and sisters, and I am here only to remind you that our problems are your problems. As the African Americans 'awaken' today, we find ourselves in a strange land that has rejected us, and, like the prodigal son, we are turning to our elder brothers for help."[33]

Malcolm specifically wanted the African heads of state to assist in bringing the problem of Black Americans before the UN. At the time that African Summit members were organizing against the horrors of apartheid South Africa, he sought to make the leaders see the plight of Africans in America in the same light. In fact, he argued that America was worse, because it was a "hypocrite." In typical Malcolm fashion, he pointed out that "South Africa preaches segregation and practices segregation. She, at least, practices what she preaches" and dubbed South Africa the Wolf to America's Fox. Demonstrating his disdain for the nation-state container that our politics are usually boxed in, Malcolm argued that "if South Africa is guilty of violating the human rights of Africans here on the mother continent, then America is guilty of worse violations of the 22 million Africans on the American continent. And if South African racism is not a domestic issue, then American racism also is not a domestic issue."

Malcolm was practicing what he was preaching by trying to connect the OAAU to the independence movements in Africa. We discussed the limitations of Malcolm's appeals to the UN in Chapter 5, but his links to the continent went beyond trying to get support for taking America to the so-called world court. Malcolm used the three hundred years of experience of Black people in America to tell the African leaders that this gave him a unique vantage point to understand the nature of the beast. He warned of the dangers of "benevolent colonialism" when he advised the summit they should not "escape from European colonialism only to become even more enslaved by deceitful, 'friendly' American dollarism."[34]

Malcolm saw his work in America as an extension of the liberation struggle in Africa, and he was impressed by the strides that had been made toward independence, explaining to an American audience that "just ten years ago, on the African continent, our people were colonized. They were suffering all forms of colonization, oppression, exploitation, degradation, humiliation, discrimination, and every other kind of -ation. And in a short time, they have gained more independence, more recognition, more respect as human beings than you and I have."[35]

Malcolm's faith in African leadership stemmed from his connection to those with a revolutionary vision, in particular Kwame Nkrumah, the first president of Ghana. Nkrumah was a staunch revolutionary Pan-Africanist who wanted to unify the continent so that it could stand independently from the rest of the world; like Malcolm, Nkrumah was strongly influenced by Marcus Garvey. The black star in the middle of the Ghanaian flag is taken from the name of the Black Star Line shipping company that the Universal Negro Improvement Association bought to return Afro-American ex-slaves to the African continent. Nkrumah was among the first to outline the dimensions of neocolonialism in Africa, describing the "Alice in Wonderland craziness" of the economic oppression that was maintained there after its so-called independence.[36] Malcolm met Kwame Nkrumah when he introduced the Ghanaian president to a Harlem rally in 1958. The two kept in contact by letter, and Malcolm visited Nkrumah on both of his African trips in 1964. He heaped praise on Nkrumah, saying that "there is probably no more enlightened leader on the African continent than President Nkrumah."[37]

Malcolm was not as enamored with every African leader. After all, he dubbed Moise Tshombe, who murdered the first and rightful president of Congo, Patrice Lumumba, an Uncle Tom. In a warning we should have heeded about Nelson Mandela, Malcolm cautioned against looking up to any African leader who was a darling of the Western press: "Our yardstick in measuring these various leaders is to find out what the Americans think about them. And these leaders over here who are receiving the praise and pats on the back from the Americans, you can just flush the toilet and let them go right down the drain."[38]

Nkrumah certainly measured up by this yardstick, as he was vilified for his radical positions. Malcolm's embrace of Nkrumah further demonstrated that unity was not enough without revolutionary politics. The sad history of Pan-Africanism is that the elite, Western version of it, where different African nation-states loosely collaborate in their own oppression, is the format that won out. Leaders like Nkrumah were disposed of in coups or assassinated, and Western puppets were installed. So while Malcolm praised the African countries for "submerging their differences" to try to work together, he was also clear that "any African leader who fails to co-operate in the inevitable establishment of a union government will be doing a greater service to the imperialist than Moise Tshombe."[39] Malcolm was staunchly in favor of the continental revolution, the radical vision of an Africa united that could take itself out of the racist political and economic order. For Malcolm, the independence of former colonies was a first step toward continental unity. Echoing the revolutionary Pan-African imagination of the time, Malcolm declared that "if Congo falls, Mozambique and Angola must fall. And when they fall, suddenly you have to deal with Ian Smith [in present-day Zimbabwe]. He won't be there for long once you can put some troops on his borders. Which means it will be a matter of time before they will be right on the border of South Africa and then they can talk the type of language that the South Africans understand."[40]

Everything that happened on the African continent was OAAU business. This is how we have to understand Malcolm's rejection of nonviolence. In America, violence was for self-defense, but on the African continent violence was necessary, "talk[ing] the type of language" that would be needed to liberate Congo, Mozambique, Zimbabwe, and South Africa. Reclaiming "Africa for the Africans" was a project that demanded to be fulfilled by "any means necessary." Make no mistake, in his long-range program, Malcolm envisioned the ex-slaves returning to the motherland to participate in a truly independent Africa because he knew that we could never find freedom in the wicked system of the West. The domestic organizing of the OAAU has to been seen as part of this much larger project to redeem Africa as the route to true independence.

Given the importance that Africa held in Malcolm's program of revolution, it is right to question why he did not remain on the continent. An independent Africa was the solution, and the puppet leaders installed by the West clearly could not be trusted to fulfill that mission. After leaving the NOI, Malcolm also knew that his life was in danger in America and seriously considered moving to the African continent with his family. He would not have been the first Black activist to do so. W. E. B. and Shirley Graham Du Bois had already emigrated to Ghana, the same nation where Malcolm had met Maya Angelou. A former Communist and Pan-Africanist, the Trinidadian George Padmore had made the move in the early twentieth century. In his diary written during his travels, Malcolm ultimately rejected the idea, admitting that "moving my family out of America may be good for me personally but bad for me politically."[41]

For Malcolm, the potential political damage was twofold. First, he felt a responsibility to those he had organized in the Nation of Islam. Remember that when Malcolm joined the organization it only had a handful of members, and it was due to his work and leadership that its ranks had swelled to up to seventy-five thousand by the time he departed. Initially, he had pledged not to overlap with the NOI in his work in the political arena that Elijah Muhammad was so allergic to. But his stance changed once he realized how regressive the group was, and he felt responsible, regretting that "I built a criminal organization."[42] Malcolm felt the NOI was conning Black people by promising a dead-end solution and profiting from the community. His attacks on Muhammad and the Nation of Islam were principled; his aim was to peel away the members he had recruited and bring them onto a righteous revolutionary path. Malcolm knew the wrath this would cause within the NOI and that its leadership would have no problem with killing him for it. But his principles meant that, even though he should have, he couldn't let it lie. "Make it plain" was more than just about engaging with the masses; it was about telling the truth no matter the consequences. Not long before he was assassinated, Malcolm was asked if he was afraid of death, and he replied, "I live like a man who is dead already. I have no fear whatsoever of anybody or anything."[43] This bravery is why we love Malcolm, but it also contributed to his death. Not taking on the Nation of Islam and moving to Ghana might have saved his life, but it would also have undermined the uncompromising politics that defined him.

More importantly, Malcolm did not abandon America because, although he understood that the ultimate revolution would be in Africa, we in the diaspora had an important part to play. For him, the existence of millions of ex-slaves in the West added considerable heft to the revolutionary movement on the African content. He argued that the West was "more concerned with the revolution that's taking place on the African continent than they are with the revolution in Asia and in Latin America. And this is because there are so many people of African ancestry within the domestic confines or jurisdiction of these various governments."[44]

We were the enemy within, which meant we could leverage our position to support the African revolution. But first we needed to be able to wield our collective power, which is why the OAAU had to build its membership up. Malcolm spent so much of his time traveling that he was "wondering increasingly how things are going in the States and if I'm overplaying my hand by staying away too long."[45] The work in America was vital to the overall project. This is what made the organization radical: The goal was never solely to improve conditions in American society or elsewhere in the diaspora so that more of us could earn enough money to join the house. The point was to build a mass organization with the resources and power to support the global revolution that could create a new and truly free society.

Only a minority of the OAAU's activity was in the traditional political arena, but Malcolm insisted that the organization was "just as political as any other organization in Harlem."[46] By this he meant that every action taken to organize together and improve the conditions that we face is political. We need to remove the shackles from our minds and imagine a new political and economic system. To do so, we have to abandon the false hope of an electoral system designed to oppress us and build one that allows us to thrive. This is the promise of the OAAU: to unite us together to unlock our collective power for liberation.

11

YOU LEFT YOUR MIND IN AFRICA

So far, I have outlined Malcolm's radical analysis and revolutionary solution, using his own words to bust the myths built around him and make plain his vital mission. The purpose of this book is not just to understand him but to pick up his legacy and run with it today. Malcolm spent a good deal of his time lambasting the Uncle Toms leading us astray because he knew they posed the most danger to building the revolutionary movement. It would be an injustice to Malcolm to present his vision without invoking his work to call out the modern-day Uncle Toms. You also need this energy to understand why Malcolm's work was so hard-hitting. It is easy (and fun) to call out the Black right-wingers, but they aren't the real danger because their coon shows are not meant for us. Malcolm spent his time railing against the Uncle Toms, those with credibility who were pretending to speak for us but leading us into the clutches of the smiling Foxes. Remember, it was King that Malcolm reserved most of his ire for, at a time when the good reverend was probably the most popular Black person alive.

To truly understand Malcolm's analysis, we need to call out those whom you might not be expecting. For instance, the myriad Black authors peddling easy-to-engage-with Racism for Dummies are one cohort of his modern-day Uncle Toms.[1] We are meant to follow the best-selling Pied Pipers of racial literacy to our continual doom. Apparently, you can journal your way through your White supremacy, experiment until you find your piece in the "social justice puzzle," or even interracially date to resist this wicked system.[2] We are told that terms like structural racism are unhelpful; we just need to commit really hard to becoming an "anti-racist," as though it is like a fight with a dependency on alcohol.[3] The fact that so many of us think these populist, so-called anti-racist delusions have any validity would have Malcolm breathing fire if he were alive today. There was nothing that angered him more than the White-appointed spokesperson for Negroes leading us astray. The only problem with the Uncle Tom metaphor is that it is gendered. One of the actual benefits of token integration is that we now hear more Black women's voices, many of whom have been able to access universities and journalism and take advantage of new media. We must cite Black women and draw on the excellent work that is produced, but equally we should be able to criticize and outright reject House Negro nonsense no matter which gender is producing it. Nowadays we need an appropriate word for the female collaborators. Others have used Aunt Jemima, but the racial stereotype of the food packages is more akin to a coon show than the Uncle Tom figure. I am at a loss—Malcolm would no doubt have come up with something! But I will include a trigger warning here, because the following chapter will include criticism of Black women who, Malcolm would have declared, have "left their minds in Africa."[4] Channeling the work of Malcolm, this chapter is reserved for calling out the well-meaning Black folk who are nevertheless leading us astray. I have focused on those ideas that I have most come across over the years of trying to apply Malcolm's vision in my activism. Before we can embrace radical practice, we need to remove the clutter preventing us from seeing the clear revolutionary picture.

AMERICAN DREAMING

Since the death of Malcolm and the decline of the Black Power movement, there has been a gaping hole left in the conscious community. This has been filled with a range of false prophets. We have regressed so far on some ideas that I would not be surprised if Malcolm is haunting the dreams of many of the pretenders in fits of rage. One of the latest (and most depressing) developments is to rally around the definition of the Foundational Black American (FBA), which includes "any person classified as Black, who can trace their bloodline lineage back to the American system of slavery," with particular stress being placed on the fact that "if a person's matrilineal and patrilineal lineage traces back to slavery in the Caribbean, then they are not considered a Foundational Black American."[5] To enforce their American status, the Foundational Black Americans even have a flag that incorporates the stars and stripes. The premise of the FBA is that Black people have been resisting in America since 1526, for five centuries. It should be obvious how illogical this idea is, given that for the majority of that time there was no United States of America and the system of slavery that brought Africans to the Americas was the exact same one that took Africans to the Caribbean. Until 1777, it was the British slave system that dominated what is now the United States. The FBA definition also rules out perhaps the most influential person and organization for Black America, Marcus Garvey and the UNIA, because he was Jamaican. This is so idiotic that even the FBA recognizes that Garvey was an icon, despite his non-FBA status. They refer to Malcolm as half-FBA because of his Grenadan mother!!!! House Negro, please! Apparently, half-FBAs can only be legitimate spokespeople for the group if their non-FBA parent immigrated to America before 1965, when more middle-class Africans and Caribbeans began migrating. This is all so ludicrous I'm in tears reading it as some kind of comedic irony. I would love to be able to dismiss it, but unfortunately it is powerful. Tariq Nasheed is the false prophet of the Foundational Black American idea who rose to Black fame with his film series *Hidden Colors*. The movies are a dangerous mix of truth and nonsense but have been wildly popular with Black folk. He has come over to Britain a number of times to speak to sellout (pardon the pun) crowds.

The FBA agenda is attractive because it draws on the xenophobic fears that drive all too much of the current political moment. The promises of liberation have not been met, and millions of Black Americans are rightly frustrated with the limits of token integration. With the lack of progress, people like Nasheed can see more recent migrants from the Caribbean and Africa entering America and having success. The reason he reveres Garvey and the pre-1970 immigration is that the class dynamics were very different then, with poor Caribbeans joining Black Americans in the urban ghettos and then melting into African America, with everyone being in the same economic boat. But restrictions on immigration mean that it is now only the talented tenth of Caribbean (and, increasingly, African) immigrants who are let in. Those groups come to the United States with money and advantage and have been filling the diversity quotas of universities and top companies that have a strategy of "any Black will do."[6]

In Britain, we have had a similar dynamic with the conflicts between African and Caribbean communities. Windrush-generation migration—which began in 1948 when the steamship *Empire Windrush* landed in Britain from Jamaica—from the Caribbean had few restrictions placed on it, meaning that many poor and poorly educated migrants came over. My father had only completed two years of schooling when he migrated in 1960. Caribbean migrants were forced into low-paid work and segregated into the inner cities. Most African migration tended to start a decade or two later and was initially made up of West African students, who obviously had class privilege, given that they had the resources and were permitted entry to study at British universities. African migrants were (and still are, if you take some accounts) the so-called model minority, whereas Caribbeans were seen as the rowdy ghetto dwellers descended from the enslaved. There were genuine tensions about this all the way into the 1990s. But as African migration has diversified, and more people are born in Britain, those have eased considerably. It is ironic for us here to see Caribbean migrants being viewed as the "model minority" in America, but that has become the reality, given that the immigration changes mean poorer migrants (in the Garvey mold) can no longer enter America from that region.

What this tells us is that, when we consider race, we cannot forget class. This is very easy to explain using Malcolm's framework. At one point, the Caribbeans moving to America were from the field, and now they are from the house. In that sense they are no different from the so-called FBAs, who also have managed to gain slightly more class privilege. But Nasheed and his ilk want to see FBAs as a uniquely different ethnic group that requires special protection. Of course, the resentment comes with large doses of xenophobic attitude. For example,

Nasheed argues that one of the things holding back Black community unity is the "Negro bed wench" mentality, where some Black women will sleep with the modern master to boost their individual privilege at the expense of the rest of the community. Of course he insists, with no evidence but his own self-assurance, that this "mentality is most prevalent among non–Foundational Black American females."[7] Due to the sowing of this kind of division between Black populations in America, the FBA might as well be funded by the FBI. Unfortunately, Nasheed is not the only one peddling this dangerous idea of Black African American exceptionalism.

In 2014, I was part of a debate about the legacy of Barack Obama, which we recorded in front of a live BBC audience, but the corporation decided not to broadcast (this was pre–George Floyd, after all). I had not noticed at the time but was recently told that one of my fellow critics of the White House Negro was Yvette Carnell, one of the founders of the American Descendants of Slavery (ADOS) movement. ADOS uses the same definition as FBA to define who is truly Black American, and it calls for the president to "designate descendants of chattel slavery in the United States as a protected category" by executive order. The purpose of this would be to ensure that other Black immigrants are "barred from accessing affirmative action and other set asides [funding]."[8] This is clearly nonsensical, given that, for the most part, long-standing Caribbean communities in America have become indistinguishable from those of African Americans in terms of experience and outcomes. Culturally, the best example of this is hip-hop, Black America's most successful export, which emerged in the 1970s after Jamaican DJ Kool Herc started "toasting" or rapping over break beats.[9]

The idea that there is some special Black America separate from this immigration is as untrue as it would be to claim that there is a

White America that was not influenced by the various migrants that came there in the nineteenth and twentieth centuries. It is understandable that there could be some ill feeling from Black American populations who have seen little or no progress and are now watching well-off migrants from the Caribbean and Africa come into the country and take advantage of affirmative action programs. But Malcolm would warn us that the problem isn't *who* is benefiting from government programs but the fact that we think such token integration is any kind of solution at all. The reality is that affirmative action has mostly benefited White women, and the Black people who have profited from it often flee their community, taking their slightly elevated wealth away with them. The ultimate dead end of trying to join them is that this opportunity is only available to a limited number of us. Turning our ire against a handful of migrants is the definition of a House Negro mindset that will keep us all stuck on the plantation. The fundamental issue Malcolm would have taken with both FBA and ADOS is their embrace of America. Unfortunately, these are not the only high-profile examples of American dreaming.

The 1619 Project was released by *The New York Times* with much fanfare to mark five hundred years since the first slave ship trafficked Africans into what is now the United States. Journalist Nikole Hannah-Jones brought together an impressive collection of historians and commentators to tell the stories of the Black people who were forced into building the nation. The subsequent book project captures the depths of the terror that Black folk have experienced at the hands of what Malcolm would call the "American nightmare."[10] From slavery to Jim Crow to police brutality, the noncitizen status of the ex-slaves could hardly be made clearer throughout the project. The 1619 Project has become a source of rage in the Whitelash against

Black intellectual thought in America, with the work being banned by a number of schools because it is so critical of the racism that built the nation. Ironically, no matter how useful the historical details are, Hannah-Jones's framing was so pro-American that I could feel Malcolm shifting in his grave.

In her introduction to the series, Hannah-Jones describes how uncomfortable she felt as a young person in describing herself as an American. She recounts a tale of being given the task of drawing her national flag and picking a random African country because she felt no allegiance to the red, white, and blue. After learning about the truth of just how important Black Americans were to building the nation, she regretted that feeling, explaining, "I wish that I could now go back to the younger me and tell her that her people's ancestry started here, on these lands and to boldly, proudly draw the stars and stripes of the American flag. We were once told, by virtue of our bondage, we could never be American. But it was by virtue of our bondage that we became the most American of all."[11]

I listened to her text as an audiobook and honestly had to rewind that section about three times to ensure that I had heard it correctly. The end of the passage was so bizarre I barely noticed her claim that "her people's ancestry started here," entirely neglecting our African roots. "It is by virtue of our bondage that we became the *most* American of all."[12] In other words, *because* we were enslaved, we are now apparently the ultimate super-Americans. This might be the most anti-Malcolm and dangerous position I have ever heard. I'm still flabbergasted that anyone would look at this history of slavery, terror, and abuse and conclude that made you *more* of an American. The other illogic to justify this is that Black people have been in America before most White people, making our claims to citizenship even stronger.

But Malcolm warned against this trap: "Just because you're in this country doesn't make you an American. No, you've got to go farther than that before you can become an American. You've got to enjoy the fruits of Americanism. You haven't enjoyed those fruits. You've enjoyed the thorns. You've enjoyed the thistles. . . . You have fought harder for the fruits than the White men have but you've enjoyed less."[13]

We shouldn't look at our oppression as some kind of payment for our citizenship. We should understand that it means we have never and will never be anything but ex-slaves, second-class citizens, colonial subjects. As Malcolm made absolutely plain, "The 'Negro' must realize that he is not American, in the Constitutional sense, not in the other ways that White people are American. How can any 'Negro' feel American, begging on his hands and knees for what White Americans take for granted?"[14]

Using bondage as some kind of currency for citizenship is a bizarre BDSM approach to activism. The more you beat us, the more we are yours. We can see the same sadomasochism at work in claims that we are British. Tory peer, and pioneer of the modern-day British coon show, Tony Sewell caused outrage when the government commission he chaired declared that institutional racism was a thing of the past in wonderful Britannia. It was so appalling we dubbed it the Sewage Report. He was mostly unrepentant but had to add a footnote explaining what he meant in the passage where he proclaimed that the commission sought to create "a new story about the Caribbean experience which speaks to the slave period not only being about profit and suffering but how culturally African people transformed themselves into a re-modelled African/Britain."[15] The idea that the horror of slavery forged a new evolution of African British identity (perhaps African 2.0) rightly caused an outrage. Sewell added a footnote explaining that "this is to say that in the face of the inhumanity of slavery, African people preserved their humanity and culture. This includes the story of slave resistance."[16] Talk about too little, too late, but at least Sewell was challenged, unlike Hannah-Jones's similarly dangerous ideas.

The desire to claim the nation that has oppressed us is not reserved only for those on right (more accurately the "wrong") side of the political spectrum. Worse still, Foreign Secretary David Lammy insists that the fact he was born in England and his "sensibilities are English" means that he wants to "claim that heritage."[17] America kept Black people out of citizenship, first through slavery, then with segregation, and finally with racial inequality. Britain locked us out by enslaving us remotely in the Caribbean or colonizing our homelands. The British then exploited us to build the wealth of the empire, and once we started to migrate to the mother country after the Second World War, made the colonies independent and restricted immigration. Immigration policy is the racist policy in Britain because, prior to the Windrush generation, which began in 1948, there was an extremely small number of us on the British Isles, and ever since we have been migrating they have been trying to "keep Britain White."

Ironically, although a vast number of racialized minorities live in England, Englishness has become heavily tied to Whiteness. David Lammy is one of the only Black people, either in private or in public, I have ever heard declare themselves as proud to be English. The English flag (white background with a red cross) is our version of the Confederate flag: If it is flying over a pub or a house, you know you are not welcome. But Lammy was still keen to lay claim to this mythic identity. It is doubly ironic, given that Lammy was one of the loudest voices ringing the alarm about the Windrush crisis, when thousands of Caribbean people who had migrated to the United Kingdom as children had become subject to losing their jobs, detention, and deportation because they could not prove their right to be in the country.[18] This was the logical result of Britain's increasingly racist immigration legislation that was meant to make the nation a "hostile environment" for illegal immigrants. Members of the so-called Windrush generation were perhaps the most British of the British, falling into the delusion that Britain was the benevolent mother country who would look after all of her colonial children. They survived the harsh reality of life in racist Britain only to have their position as colonial subjects, rather than citizens, confirmed alongside their precarious status. It is as true in Britain that slavery built the nation, and the ex-slaves have just as much, and perhaps even more, right to claim the fruits of our collective labor than the supposedly indigenous population. But that entirely misses the point. We have been frozen out of the prosperity that we produced *by design*. We can never be anything but ex-slaves or neocolonial subjects in nations that were built to oppress us. But even if we could fully enter the house and claim our seat at the master's table, we should have absolutely no desire to do so.

As Malcolm taught us, the West *is* racism, a White supremacist hellscape built and sustained on the slavery, genocide, and colonization of Black and Brown people worldwide. Malcolm warned us that we have moved into a period of benevolent colonialism, which mostly lacks the guns and bombs but still kills nine million Black and Brown people a year through food insecurity. White society remains as devilish as it ever was, so the absolute last thing we should want to be is American or British. Any effort to do so is ultimately the politics of the House Negro: No matter how much punishment we endure, where can we get better treatment than this? We should not want to find a place in the big house but to burn it down to the ground and rebuild from the ashes. This message is just as important to take on board as are our claims for reparations from the evils that we have survived.

THE KNIFE IS STILL IN OUR BACK

The ADOS Advocacy Foundation puts reparations demands firmly at the heart of its agenda, rightfully arguing that American society owes a debt to the ex-slaves. As usual, Malcolm used the perfect metaphor to justify reparatory justice, explaining that "if you stick a knife in my back 9 inches and pull it out 6 inches, there's no progress. If you pull it all the way out, that's not progress. The progress is healing the wound that the blow made. And they won't even admit the knife is there."[19] Slavery was the knife in our backs, and emancipation did *not* remove the blade, let alone heal the wound. Continued racial oppression means that the knife is still firmly in our backs and to heal the wound a massive transfer of wealth would be necessary.

There is no good argument against reparations for enslavement, given the devastation wrought on the enslaved and the wealth that we generated, so the ADOS Advocacy Foundation is justified in seeking damages. But the foundation argues that this money should be allocated only for ADOS, or FBA, or whatever other acronym for the ex-slaves in America. ADOS quotes figures from academics William A. Darity Jr. and A. Kirsten Mullen, who have written something of a reparatory justice manifesto for the movement. In *From Here to Equality*, Darity and Mullen argue that the source of reparations should be the US government, given the role that slavery played in the building of the nation.[20] They recognize that individuals and corporations were also guilty but rationalize that seeking recourse through the government would mean that all the guilty parties would pay through taxation. Of course, they use the FDA/ADOS criteria to determine who would be eligible for reparations payments. Carnell put it bluntly that Haitian immigrants' "issue is with the French," and Darity and Mullen similarly conclude that immigrants should petition their original nation-state for redress. But this spectacularly misses the global nature of racism. If, as Carnell argues, reparations are also due for Jim Crow and twentieth-century racial terrorism, then how could America not be indebted to Haiti for the devastation US intervention (including occupation) has wrought since the Haitians set themselves free?

Similarly, White historians called transatlantic slavery the "Atlantic system" because of the intrinsic connections between the constituent parts. A person might have been enslaved on a British ship, sold to a Dutch island, and eventually purchased by an American slave owner. British-based Lloyd's of London has been sued in the US courts because of the way it secured its wealth by insuring slave ships. Plantation owners made huge profits from enslavement, but the companies that purchased goods like cotton turned the products of slave labor into commodities that powered whole economies. The city of Liverpool in Britain became the European hub of the slave trade due to its importation of cotton produced by the enslaved on American plantations. The textile industry that built the city of Manchester became possible only after a canal connected the city to the slave port of Liverpool, so that Manchester merchants could procure the produce from the enslaved.[21] Liverpool was so pro–US slavery that the city organized a Confederate Bazaar in 1864 to raise money for Southern prisoners of war. The event was attended by thousands of people including a local member of Parliament, John Laird, and raised £20,000 (more than £2.5 million in today's money) for the cause.[22] This is just one city that benefited from the profits of apparently "American" slavery, therefore it is entirely illogical to only claim reparations from the US government. But this is the danger of being blinded by the idea of the nation-state. The larger problem when framing reparations in national terms is that it ends up becoming just another form of token integration.

Darity and Mullen argue not only that reparations should solely be sought from the government but that the amount should be determined by the size of the Black-White wealth gap. The illogic here is that slavery and continued exploitation created the yawning economic disparities and that these should be reset to create a level playing field. While there is always something to appreciate in the simplicity of an idea, this is such a narrow one that it ends up not addressing the problem. Let's imagine for a moment that this transfer of wealth has taken place, and that Black people have more wealth; many people's lives would certainly improve. But the broader system of racial inequality would not change. We would still be underemployed, hyper-policed, and likely find it impossible to buy a genuine seat at the table. There is a chance that we would pool this wealth to create Black businesses that could generate more economic opportunities outside of the current racist ones. But now, let's be honest, it's far *more* likely that this injection of wealth would be a stimulus to the existing economy. Any time we spent our reparations, invested, or bought property, we would mostly be giving the money back to White people. The system itself is racist; having more money to spend in it doesn't alter that very fact. If we don't transform the system, we would just find in fifty years that the wealth gap had returned, and we would have no one to blame but ourselves, because we had received reparations. More problematically, even if this reparatory justice fixed the racial wealth gap, there would still be millions of Black Americans living in poverty and hundreds of millions of us in the underdeveloped world suffering extreme poverty so that we could live the American delusion. Not to mention that millions of so-called non-FBA/ADOS Black people would have been excluded, meaning a good proportion would be left out from any potential dividends. A reparations plan that leads to token integration or House Negrodom is no real kind of reparations.

The limit of the reparations movement is that we ultimately end up relying on the system that has put the knife in our back in order to heal ourselves. We try to solve our oppression by using the profits produced by our exploitation and exclusion. This doesn't just limit those movements for reparations in the former colonies or settler colonial nations like America. The Caribbean Community (CARICOM) has a collective campaign for reparations from its member states to their former European colonizers. These may seem like spaces outside of the master's house, where a wealth transfer could create real systemic change. But Malcolm claimed all Black people in the West as Afro-American because he understood that Caribbean nations offered no more promise than token integration in America. The Caribbean is a series of former slave colonies, where the natives were erased and the ex-slaves lived in even worse conditions than those in America. Their present-day so-called independence is nothing but a PR exercise to keep the people from revolting. Neocolonial economics ensure that the economy of the region is controlled by the West (and increasingly China), and the coming climate catastrophe is only adding to the region's structural crisis. Wealthy Caribbeans are migrating to America to escape the former slave colonies and to find greater opportunities in the big house.

In this context, the CARICOM reparations plan is nothing of the sort. It is essentially a request for an aid package from the benevolent West. As well as calling for a "formal apology," the CARICOM Reparations Commission called for specific funds to be given to various initiatives including education, health care, and cultural restitution.[23]

CARICOM is demanding $33 trillion after a report by the Brattle Group tried to quantify the debt owed.[24] This may sound like a staggering number of dollars, but even if it were ever paid, just like with the American example above, it would become mainly a stimulus package for the West. Aid projects have a reputation for filtering money back into the West via those who are commissioned to carry out the necessary work, which only increases the ongoing dependency of the people it intends to help.[25] Taking money from the racist system only to feed it back in will cement racial inequality. A chicken can never lay a duck egg. . . even if you give it trillions of dollars to do so.

I have the utmost respect for reparations advocates and the work of people like Sister Esther Stanford-Xosei, who has been at the forefront of the Stop the Maangamizi campaigns in Europe. Reparations campaigns are vital, because they expose the continued debt that is owed to us by this wicked system. But the uncomfortable truth is that we can never remove the knife from our back, let alone allow the wound to heal, while we remain within a system built on our oppression.

The most absurd logic of the FBA/ADOS mentality I came across in relation to reparations came from Black activist Deadria Farmer-Paellmann, who had previously brought a lawsuit against Lloyd's of London for slavery reparations. Continuing to scratch her litigious itch, Farmer-Paellmann sued the Smithsonian Institution in order to *prevent* it from repatriating its collection of Benin Bronzes to Nigeria. The bronzes were stolen from the kingdom of Benin (in modern-day Nigeria), after the British killed the oba (king) and then burned down and looted the capital in 1897. The theft was so bloody and brazen that it is widely accepted the bronzes should be returned (although there is no agreement on how to do this).[26] The Smithsonian is one of many Western museums in discussion about returning their bronzes to the newly built Edo Museum of West African Art in Nigeria (although the Western museums have displayed the audacity to suggest they should loan out their stolen goods on a rotation system!).

The Smithsonian has made arrangements to repatriate twenty-nine out of its thirty-nine bronzes (of course, it has to keep hold of some of the loot), but Farmer-Paellmann not only filed her suit to get an injunction but also launched a campaign that included a petition and encouraged supporters to call the former president and vice president on its behalf. Her issue with the bronzes is that they were often made from gold that was procured by selling people into slavery. Therefore, the treasures stolen from Benin were built from the profits of evil enslavement, and Farmer-Paellmann argues that, rather than the bronzes being returned, they should be part of the reparations claim for those descended from the enslaved in the Americas. The suggested wording of the call to the leaders of the nation is:

> I'm calling to urge President Biden and Vice-President Harris to stop the transfer of the Benin bronzes from the Smithsonian to Nigeria and the Benin kingdom heirs of slave traders. They must be shared with the heirs of the people the kingdom enslaved in exchange for the manilla currency they melted to make the bronzes—over 40 million African Americans and Caribbeans![27]

At least Farmer-Paellmann's group is recognizing that slavery took place in the Caribbean, a positive step up from the FBA/ADOS mire. But the poisoned logic remains the same.

It's one thing to raise the difficult issue of the bronzes being made off the backs of those enslaved, but entirely another to tie this into a reparations claim. On the petition website, Farmer-Paellmann argues that by returning the bronzes, the "slave trader heirs will get a second chance to benefit from their ancestors' selling people into transatlantic slavery."[28] This is to fall so deeply into distortions of history that it is impossible to get out. The astronomic profits from enslavement were not generated in the trade of Africans, even in the West. It was putting our ancestors to work on plantations to mine and grow the key commodities from which capitalism was built that produced the staggering wealth of the West. On the African continent, slave traders were relatively rich in relation to other Africans, but that wealth was a literal dead end. Slavery destroyed the development of the African continent, draining out the most important resource by taking millions of us away and killing millions more in the pursuit of Black flesh. The result was that Africa, which was once ahead of Europe, became underdeveloped, and the European nations were able to colonize almost the entire continent and later extract considerable mineral wealth from it, a process that is still ongoing. African slave traders' minor wealth has been completely extinguished by that created from European colonialism, which was made possible by the slave trade. Africa did not benefit from slavery, but the exact opposite, which is why the Organization of African Unity had a reparations demand in 1990, and in 1999 the African World Reparations and Repatriation Truth Commission demanded $777 trillion to repay the debt owed to the continent.[29] Not only did Africa not benefit from slavery, but most Africans did not sell other Africans. Resistance was so fierce on the continent that slave ships eventually had to dock off the coast and wait for months as they filled up because they were afraid of liberation raids upon their human cargo.[30]

There certainly needs to be a discussion between the diaspora and the continent about the complicated history and how we move forward together, but it should be done as one, not in competition with each other. Malcolm would surely be in tears watching a so-called Negro petitioning the American government to prevent the return of cultural artifacts to Africa. Unfortunately, this kind of nationalist thinking is all too common in progressive circles. Even when efforts appear to be revolutionary, too often they are guilty of the same fundamental sin.

MAGICIANS, SCRIBES, AND PHARISEES

While he was alive, Malcolm expended a lot of energy taking down his Black academic critics. He opined that "the educated Negro will get me angrier than the White man any day. I don't get angry when the White man attacks me. He is doing what is in his nature and his guilt forces him to do. A dog is supposed to bark. But I get excited if a cat starts barking."[31]

While in the Nation of Islam, he attacked the "modern-day 'magicians, scribes, and Pharisees'" used to "ridicule" the organization and its leader.[32] The wrongheaded Black intellectuals were more dangerous than the White ones because Black people might be convinced by them. With the advent of token integration, there is now a critical mass of Black academics, and by the nature of being trained in one of the Whitest of professions, many of us have certainly left our senses back on the African continent. Again, I am going to ignore those who, looking through Malcolm's eyes, are cooning for White audiences, like the undistinguished professor of White racism Thomas Sowell. If you recognize his name but can't place him, it is likely from a Twitter encounter you have had with a troll. He is the name rolled out with some quotation attacking affirmative action, or the author of the line I get sent all the time: "Racism is not dead . . . but is kept alive by race hustlers." Sowell isn't writing for us, so I won't waste any more time on him. There are Black intellectual movements that present themselves as radical that Malcolm would have had far more problems with.

At first glance, Afropessimism is off-putting because of the instant negativity that comes from the name. Revolutionary politics, by their very nature, are always the most hopeful ones because they understand the scale of the problem and yet still believe that freedom is possible. When Malcolm declared that it was impossible to gain freedom in this system, he was nonetheless never resigned to second-class citizenship. He warned his pragmatic detractors that they were "dealing with Black people who don't care anything about [the] odds" of success.[33] This is the most common misconception about radical politics: that we are pessimistic. I cannot count the number of times I have been told that by telling young people the system is racist I am robbing them of ambition. It is an utterly ludicrous suggestion, of course. We inspire people by showing them that the system is against them *and* that we can rally to overcome it nevertheless. I would never want to dismiss an idea simply because of its name, but what you choose to call something is more fundamental than the cover of the book you slap it on. The bigger problem with Afropessimism is that the name is the perfect indicator of its fatally flawed theory.

Frank B. Wilderson III is the name most notably associated with the movement, so I paid particular attention to his book *Afropessimism*.[34] I will admit that it was a very entertaining listen, but that was because it read more like anti-racist fan fiction rather than offering any clarifying insights. It's always fascinating to read people's experience of racism, but when he likened one of his various encounters with White academics to a "lynching," I honestly put a series of eye-roll emojis into my notes. It was abundantly clear that Wilderson was suffering from the chronic condition of spending too much time writing for White academia. Being fertilized in the academy means he cannot organically engage with the radical struggles of Black communities.

Wilderson makes specific claims that his work is rooted in activism, highlighting his work for the African National Congress in South Africa and his grassroots campaigning.[35] But in truth, the framework is one born in the academy, which explains his foregrounding of pessimism. Wilderson continues where Black academic Orlando Patterson left off when he argues that slavery was a form of "social death."[36] If we are nothing but ex-slaves, then it follows that our condition has not transformed since emancipation. The problem is that Wilderson thinks that "Blackness cannot exist other than slaveness," so to be Black is to be socially dead.[37] We discussed the disastrous results of conflating race and Blackness in Chapter 8. Malcolm would completely reject the notion that Blackness is "slaveness." Remember that he declared the "new type of Negro" to be free from the constraints of the White imaginary and as one who would lead the charge to revolution. The Negro is slaveness; Blackness is our way to combat it.

Afropessimism also rejects Malcolm's politics of solidarity with all oppressed people because it engages in an Oppression Olympics, where Black people are the nonhumans that every other group defines itself in relation to. Similar to the FBA/ADOS appeal, the fact that Afropessimism draws specific attention to anti-Blackness is attractive to many. But when there is even debate about whether Afropessimism is anti-Palestinian, then we know something is seriously wrong. Anti-Blackness is absolutely a feature of the world, and we cannot just rely on collective solidarity because we are all not White. But we do not need the dead end of Afropessimism to understand the relationship we hold with other oppressed peoples. Malcolm insisted on Black organization and liberating Africa because he knew that we had to have our own power base even as we supported other struggles. Afropessimism only detracts from this idea, with an ADOS-like focus on the exceptionalism of the American so-called Negro.

Wilderson turns Malcolm's revolutionary politics on its head by opining the pessimism that we can never be free, because to end Black suffering would "mean the end of the world."[38] This is of course true, but also the point of the revolution: to end the world as it is and build it in a new image that can produce liberation. Afropessimism is seductive because it contains the ingredients of Black radical politics; unfortunately, it has not followed the right recipe. Being academics, we can rail against the system while retaining the significant benefits that it has bestowed upon us. Wilderson gets to have the best of both worlds, feeling transgressive from his bougie perch. The revolution would end the extremely comfortable world of the professor, which is why he can't be trusted to develop the revolutionary theory. The bankruptcy of the endeavor became even more apparent to me after watching a video of Wilderson speaking at Duke University. He couldn't even conceive of trying to use his work to liberate Black people, scoffing, "I would never go to Harlem and organize everyone for the end of the world. That's ridiculous."[39] What is ridiculous is that he has created a supposedly intellectual movement that rejects any responsibility for engaging with the real world. He sounded more like a hustler when he explained that "the game is to produce a language of what it means to suffer, not what it means to alleviate suffering because that is going to come from Black people in the streets and not professors." He actually admitted it: We can sit back getting paid to tell you the problem, but you will have to work out how to fix it.

I am self-aware enough to know that I am in almost exactly the same position as Wilderson, but I offer two defenses. First, I am writing this book to show just how important Malcolm's vision and mission for revolution remain. It is certainly my interpretation of his work, but I take no credit for it. If you have read, or go on to read, any of my other work, it should be apparent how fundamental Malcolm's analysis has been to all my academic output. One of my main issues with Afropessimism is that there is very little that is new in the so-called theory: a revolutionary framework rooted in overcoming anti-Blackness already exists. We would be better following Malcolm than reaching the dead end that the Afropessimists march us down. Second, my self-awareness extends to a severe discomfort with my role as professor. I have gone on record a number of times saying that I view the title "professor" as no different from that of "chief of police": Both are roles designed to maintain White supremacy. Malcolm would probably have described my role as that of the slave preacher, someone put in a position of relative authority by the system in order to lead Black people astray. You could argue that—with what central higher education has become, which only dampens the rebellious spirt of young people—we are the ultimate modern-day Uncle Toms, leading the way in molding the future generations into neoliberal ex-slaves. In the past, most slave preachers played their role in perpetuating White supremacy, teaching the flock that God would "wash you White as snow" in the afterlife, so there was no need to worry about rebellion. But others used their positions to resist. People like Nat Turner in America and Samuel Sharpe in Jamaica used their ability to travel between plantations and talk to large groups and their elevated position in society to organize large-scale rebellions. It *is* possible to use our pulpits to lead others to revolution, but improbable, so we have to always be wary.

I don't want to be too hard on Afropessimism because the radical analysis is there, and the revolutionary practice is just one step away. I know multiple people who are die-hard Afropessimists, and my argument is that we are mostly in agreement, but Malcolm offers a much better blueprint for revolution. There are some ideas, however, that have no utility, and those we should just abandon. The problem with academics is that our ideas are usually confined to the university. The academic who connects with the broader Black community is rare. The most popular, best-selling, and most dangerous ideas are often found outside of academia.

I have previously been extremely skeptical of anything that suggests we should avoid the harsh realities of resistance. After all, it's called the "struggle" for a reason. But I can also attest to the damage that can be done when you work too much, constantly trying to fit everything into an impossible schedule. Burnout is a real thing, and we are no use to anyone if we have broken ourselves. So, I genuinely went into listening to Tricia Hersey's *Rest Is Resistance* with an open mind. I started listening on my commute to work, which is only about half an hour, but that was enough for me to be exasperated by the time I started teaching one of my classes. I think the students are still laughing at my ranting when I made it into the classroom. Again, we do need to rest, but the notion that to rest is in and of itself an act of resistance is to misdiagnose the nature of the threat. Hersey has her sights set on upending the "grind culture" that insists we work ourselves into illness and even death for capitalism. When the system is telling you to grind, the logic goes that it is resistance to rest instead.

There was genuine resistance on the plantation when we broke implements or worked more slowly to reduce production and therefore the value attached to the exploitation of our labor. Emancipation in the British colonies was hastened in part because it had become less profitable due to Black women refusing to birth the future generations of the enslaved, slave rebellions, and less output caused by the counterproductive tactics of the enslaved.[40] But the plantation is a metaphor, not a literal continuation today. On the plantation, there were no wages, but now that we are "free," far too many of us work in low-paid employment with an hourly wage. It isn't a choice to work multiple jobs but a necessity to "grind." Hersey cites her grandma's closing of her eyes on her commute as an important rest practice. It is certainly an essential tactic to survive, but that is no kind of resistance. Hersey is head of the Nap Ministry, which organizes communal napping experiences. I am not against napping, but the truth is it is a luxury that many cannot afford. When I am working from home writing, I can easily schedule in a good half-hour nap, but I don't have to take public transport to work a shift in an Amazon fulfillment center. Hersey annually takes a sabbatical for the whole month of November. Even my bougie professor self can't afford that kind of indulgence! The sad reality is that the very mechanisms that create our individual privileges ensure our collective oppression.

The grind is problematic when we are killing ourselves for the master. But when we are working for freedom, the grind is liberating. One of the most astounding things I truly appreciated from writing this book is just how hard Malcolm worked. From when he left prison and joined the Nation of Islam, he crisscrossed the country, building up that organization from a handful of members to more than seventy-five thousand when he left to continue his revolutionary work. By all accounts, he barely slept and took little regard for his personal wealth, even turning up to events with holes in his shoes. When Malcolm realized the NOI was truly intent on killing him, he made efforts to stay away from his family and others, insisting that he should remain the only one on the stage before he was actually killed there.[41] He literally died for the people, and we are meant to believe that napping is a form of resistance? I doubt Harriet Tubman, who suffered debilitating seizures after being attacked by a slave owner, thought that her resting after escaping from slavery was resistance. Or that Nanny of the Maroons, who fled from slavery in Jamaica to organize raids on slave plantations, centered rest in her rebellious practice. Revolution is a grind, and a valuable one. Rest is just rest, absolutely essential but not resistance. The way that this narrative has often played out in my experience is that people continue to grind at the work that pays them and then take a rest from the unpaid slog of trying to organize. People need to work to eat, so it's easier to use your spare time to rest *rather* than to resist.

Probably the most dangerous part of the book is when Hersey talks about the value of daydreaming. She recounts the vision she had in a thirty-minute daydreaming session, where she imagined her braids grew into propellers and flew her to a planet that "has never experienced racism. People sleep up to eighteen hours a day like cats. . . . The planet is a sanctuary for Black people whose bodies have been destroyed on earth. . . . Trayvon Martin is there, Rekia Boyd is there, George Floyd is there. They are all together wearing white while smiling and resting." The value of the daydream was that it helped her in her grieving process. As she explained, "It soothed me." I am sure that daydreaming can be a useful therapeutic process, but it is not a way to resist the system of White supremacy, and it is a mockery of the word "revolution" to use it in the same sentence. The daydream soothed *her*; it helped *her*. It did absolutely nothing for Trayvon, Rekia, or George—nor to dismantle the system that killed them and will continue to destroy Black bodies. Making ourselves feel better about living in this wicked system is the most damaging thing we can do if we want to get free. As

Malcolm told us, it's only when we feel like we're on a "hot stove" that we jump up and resist.

I have tried my best to channel my inner Malcolm in exposing the false prophets and Uncle Tom ideas that are pulling us in the wrong direction. There is no doubt Malcolm would have spent at least half of his time dragging the names of the Toms, magicians, scribes, and Pharisees deluding the Black masses through the mud. I have only selected the broad themes of the most dangerous ideas, but I wanted to give an honorable mention to some who didn't quite make the cut. Academia is full of scribes doing the master's work, but Cornel West is someone who stands out: the esteemed former Harvard professor who was so damaged by being dissed by the White House Negro he thought it was a good idea to run for president himself. But then again, he has made several spoken-word albums in the past, so his judgment has always been impaired. West has managed to present a veneer of criticality while cashing those academic checks. In his ego project of running for office, he has exposed the limits of his ideas. Electoral politics is not the answer to the question of how to get freedom. So West is accepting the honorable mention on behalf of all those who try to lead us from positions within the rotten political system itself.

Apologies to Dr. Umar Johnson, but anyone who calls themselves the "King Kong of Consciousness" really can't be trusted. The school psychologist turned self-proclaimed prince of Pan-Africanism has become a meme with his hotep hot takes. He has a large following (in fact, one of the largest crowds I've ever seen come out for anything in my hometown of Birmingham appeared in order to meet him). Dr. Umar often makes sense, but the entire package is more ego than substance, and he also appears to have lost the memo that we were supposed to leave the misogynoir in the 1970s. If he ever builds the school for which he has spent over a decade fundraising and campaigning, he might come off the list. But to be honest, if he did manage to open one school just for Black boys in thirteen years (and counting), I'm not sure Malcolm would be impressed.

Ridiculing the pretenders is relatively easy, and certainly fun, but also hugely important. We need to see through the hype and the fake prophets who stand in the way of us working together for our freedom. But the Malcolm myth holds that he was great at throwing stones but had no alternative political program. Now that we have cleared the way, we can focus on rolling our sleeves up and doing the work of revolution that Malcolm truly pointed us toward.

12

NOBODY CAN GIVE YOU FREEDOM

Over six decades since Malcolm's death, the myth built up around him has prevented us from truly understanding his analysis and putting his program into action. The empty symbol of Malcolm has been used to support a range of projects so contradictory that he has been reduced to little more than the *X* on Spike Lee's film merchandise. When Clarence Thomas and Tariq Nasheed can both claim his legacy, you know that something has gone seriously wrong. There is no doubt that Malcolm is turning restlessly in his grave, dumbstruck at how the sixty years since his death have turned out. Not only did we drive full speed down the dead-end street of token integration, but many of us imagined we were following his directions. But it is never too late to realize our mistake, pop a U-turn, and get back on the road to revolution. Malcolm made it plain what the stakes were and the action we needed to take, and so it is up to us to pick up the mantle.

After reading this book, you might disagree with Malcolm, his approach, and his solutions. If so, I would advise keeping the book at hand for when the realities of the nature of racism hit you. There is a moment when we all must confront the fact that no matter how hard we try, a chicken can never lay a duck egg. The fact that sixty years after he died we are still having to remind the world that Black lives matter should hopefully have woken a few of us up. If this book has only reaffirmed your passion for Malcolm, then I implore you to pick up the baton and follow his revolutionary program. If we are not building the equivalent of the OAAU, then we should not claim Malcolm's legacy. He wasn't just speaking for our entertainment or even solely for our empowerment. He wasn't just an excellent quote for a poster or hip-hop lyric. Malcolm was trying to organize us for the revolution that is both as necessary and as possible as it was when he was slain in a hail of bullets. Of course, neither he nor his political thought was perfect. We are going to have to refine and evolve some of his diagnosis and prescription six decades after his death. But he has provided the clearest radical program that should lay the basis for any of us who want to overturn this wicked system.

POLITICAL REEDUCATION

Malcolm's words remain powerful because they break through the delusions that we have been tempted into. He is still the most uncompromising, no-nonsense speaker that we have been blessed with. This skill was absolutely essential because, as he explained, "the greatest mistake of the movement has been trying to organize a sleeping people around a specific goal. You have to wake the people up first, then you'll get action."[1] Following on its use by activists like Malcolm, the word "woke" was originally used by Black Americans to signal being awake to the realities of racism. In the current environment, being "woke" has somehow become an insult, but we need to wake up from our slumber. We have not only been sleeping but stuck in the American, British, Jamaican (or whatever relevant nation-state) dream. Just like waking up from the simulation in *The Matrix*, waking up to the real world is harsh, cold, and deeply uncomfortable. But we can never be free when we are swimming in delusions and while the system is feeding off our energy. Malcolm's "program of political reeducation" is indispensable if we are going to mobilize the support necessary for the revolution. The last thing we should do in trying to wake our people up is to pretend that we have all the answers or condemn those who are trapped in the delusions.

Malcolm neither took any prisoners nor suffered fools lightly. He was uncompromising, cutting, and loved nothing better than publicly dragging a "modern-day Uncle Tom." The previous chapter is an ode to Malcolm, who would have had made it his mission to rebuke those leading us astray. Even so, he stressed that we should "not be in a hurry to condemn because he doesn't do what you do or think as you think or as fast. There was a time when you didn't know what you know today."[2] For the most part, we are not sleeping because we want to but because the system is set up to make us believe the daydreams. If you only get your information from schools, universities, and the media, you will be stuck in the Western coma, let alone dream.

One of the by-products of token integration is that we are now even more dependent on mainstream sources for how we understand the world. In America, one of the main impacts of the infamous *Brown v. Board of Education* decision has been to close Black-led schools and make Black teachers unemployed. Black children were supposedly integrated into the White schools, shuttering the Black ones, which were simply underfunded rather than underperforming. Considering schools are more segregated now than they were before the decision, perhaps the *only* result of the ruling has been to trap millions of Black children into under-resourced schools under White control.[3] In Britain, we used to understand that the schools were "colonizers" that we could never rely on for the education necessary to sustain us. We built a robust "supplementary school" movement where we could teach the Black studies that were absent in the mainstream. But we bought into the inclusion delusion and thought we could transform the schools, leaving the movement to decline and our children firmly in the clutches of a racist school system.[4] Even in the former colonies, where we now have control over the schooling, nations often use the mother countries' exam boards for assessments and the students are clamoring to get into Western universities to make it into the house.

Even where we have the illusion of independence, we end up recreating schooling in the image of oppression. So we cannot blame anyone who is asleep to the realities of this wicked system. We need to create a program of political education so that there is no excuse not to know—then staying asleep will be a choice that we can critique. This is why Malcolm spent so much time decrying those who had the opportunity to know better, those who put themselves forward as trying to solve the problem while marching us further into the mouths of the hungry Foxes and Wolves. But even if we must call an Uncle Tom an Uncle Tom, we should also remember, in the words of Kwame Ture, that "every Negro is a potential Black" person.[5] When Malcolm was chastising the sellouts and coconuts, it wasn't because he hated them; it was very much part of his "love teaching." He was reaching out, extending the metaphorical slap to the face to awaken them to the truth. The unrelenting problem for those who choose to shuck, jive, and coon their way to success is that you are still Black: an ex-slave or colonial subject, a second-class citizen. You might be fortunate to make it through life without this realization sinking in, but for most the "nigger moment" is not so far away, and when it comes, we should be there with open arms. This obviously does not extend to everyone. Once you cross certain thresholds, there is no coming back; let's call it the Tshombe line of no return. But the reason we have so much ire for those who look like us and promote White supremacy is the disbelief that they could do us and themselves so much harm.

It is utterly essential for us to own this program of political reeducation, independently, separate from any mainstream efforts at schooling. We must acknowledge that schooling and education are two very different projects. Schooling is meant to train children in how to make it in society. When we accept that the system is fundamentally racist, then we can only conclude that the primary role of the schools is to teach White supremacy. The Eurocentric curriculum is not a problem to be overcome but the basic operating system of the schools. I don't want to pour too much cold water over the efforts to decolonize school curricula, because there has been excellent work done around the world. But we have to see the backlash against African American studies in American schools and universities as an inevitable correction to the modest gains of token integration. We may be able to win some battles in this arena, but we cannot win the war. The best we can ever get in the mainstream schools is token decolonization; we should never rely on the system to educate our children in the radical Blackness that will transform the world.

One of the most important contributions of the Black Power movement was education, enabling us to see the world differently. Malcolm's popularity was in large part rooted in his role as teacher, exposing audiences to new ways of thinking. I grew up within the British Black Power movement, and my parents' stories of having to curate books for reading groups and bookshops are a testament to the struggle for education. My dad took trips to America, hunting for the Black Power specialist with new books to read. Before the Black book sections in White bookshops, there were Black-owned book-shops and the book stalls at Black political and cultural events that fed the people. When I was younger, I would go to events solely to buy books we couldn't get anywhere else. Now we are spoiled, with the major retailer that will ship any book to your door within a day or two. In the 1960s and 1970s, activists were curating libraries, opening bookshops, and even printing books themselves. *How the West Indian Child Is Made Educationally Sub-normal in the British School System*, by Bernard Coard, remains the foundational book on racism in Brit-ish schooling. He wrote it because the community pressured him into exploring his experiences teaching in a school for discarded, mostly Black children. Britain's first Black bookshop, New Beacon, published the book, and even after its fiftieth anniversary it has still never been published by a mainstream press. It is this energy we need to tap into; we must educate ourselves, which is why it is essential that we build the organizational capacity to do so.

SELF-HELP

Self-help is much more than the individual healing prescriptions that the snake-oil salespeople are peddling. Malcolm's message was that we cannot wait for the system, or those lovely allies, to save us. We didn't create the mess we are in, but we are rolling in the muck all the same. There is no good pretending that we have progressed, have moved beyond the stereotypes, and are blazing a new trail. Black lives matter, but they are worth less, which is why we are continually having to struggle. No matter how many times we march, protest, or boycott, "nobody can give you freedom"; we will have to take it.[6] This was Malcolm's problem with the civil rights movement, that it was aimed at trying to get White people to give us concessions: We demand the right to eat with you. Give us the chance to vote in the racist system. We must have access to jobs that will exploit us. As powerful as the Black Lives Matter summer was (I have even heard it referred to as "revolutionary"!), it has mostly awakened us to a new civil rights movement.[7] Protests that demand police accountability and legislative change are helpful in the short term, but they can never address the reality that the system is itself the problem. Terms like "defund the police" or "abolition" may have a militant zeal, but these are really just civil rights campaigns dressed up in edgy-sounding language. Yes, we need the police to stop killing us and to get access to better services. But survival is not revolution, and none of these strategies can lead to liberation. Access to a wicked system is the definition of a dead end, and the only reforms we will ever get are just tinkering on the margins. Rather than continually seeking recognition and acceptance in a system that is opposed to our very being, Malcolm argued that "we need a self-help program, a do-it-yourself philosophy, a do-it-right-now philosophy, an it's-already-too-late philosophy."[8]

I was tempted to call the book *It's Already Too Late*, but I didn't want to put you off, thinking it was going to be negative. But Malcolm did not use this phrase in a defeatist context; he was telling us it was already too late to keep looking for the same token gestures. We need to build a new world, and that is only possible if we give up on the old one. We need to meet the urgency of the moment and take it upon ourselves to transform the world. Malcolm declared that instead of waiting for the White man to come and straighten out our neighborhood, we'll straighten it out ourselves. This is where you make your mistake. An outsider can't clean up your house as well as you can. An outsider can't take care of your children as well as you can. An outsider can't look after your needs as well as you can. And an outsider can't understand your problems as well as you can. Yet you're looking for an outsider to do it. We will do it, or it will never get done.[9]

For Malcolm, this was somewhat inevitable because "once we see that all of these other sources to which we've turned have failed, we stop turning to them and turn to ourselves."[10] But this is one of the few predictions that he got wrong. Sometimes it seems that the more we are let down, the greater we feel the need to seek out so-called allies. It's as if we have been brainwashed into believing that we can't succeed without the helping hands of White people. If there is anything you take from Malcolm's work, please let it be that we are enough. He told us that, yes, "we need some friends," but "we need some new allies" from within our communities and the Black nation around the globe.[11]

We used to understand that we had to rely on ourselves for the basics, but one of consequences of token integration is that we now expect the state to provide. I understand that we are technically citizens, pay taxes, and *should* receive basic services from the state. But the brutal reality is that we remain ex-slaves, colonial subjects who will *never* be treated fairly in this wicked system. Before the civil rights "revolution" of the 1960s, we were mostly kept in the field: open and hostile discrimination in America, no protections by law in Europe, and colonial subjects in the colonies. We were just as deserving of state support, but we knew we could not expect it. Just as with supplementary schools, in Britain, we organized housing associations, legal advice clinics, health awareness groups, and even collective economic schemes to overcome the lack of bank lending. The same was true in America; for all the images of gun-toting men, the Panthers were mostly about proving education, food, medicine, and services to Black communities. Self-help is the mentality of the Field Negro, understanding that we will never receive fair treatment on the plantation, so we have no choice but to provide for ourselves. But as we get used to the shelter of the house, we begin to think that massa is going to look after us.

Self-help extends beyond the survival programs to keep us afloat—it also applies to our liberation. Malcolm was a Garveyite, so I will invoke his mentor's pronouncement that "there shall be no solution to this race problem until you, yourselves, strike the blow for liberty."[12] We don't need to look to White allies, and if it is White people who are in a position to give us a helping hand, then we are looking to get to the wrong place. The area where allyship is most prevalent is in the corporate world, where there are so few of us that we have to seek White support to get in and move up. Believe me, I could not have gotten to where I am in one the Whitest professions without the support of what Malcolm would have called the odd "good White man." But the professions are the house, and the more we ingratiate ourselves into them, the deeper we sink into the delusions. There is nothing more dangerous than a good salary to end revolutionary ambitions. Now, it would be hypocritical of me to tell you not to try and get a good job, but I do ask that you consider what it means to "make it." Remember, I am the slave preacher trying to use my position to overturn the system that gives me the privileges that I enjoy. Liberty can only come when we organize outside the mainstream. The best we can do while we remain inside is to leverage our position and resources to the movement. But make no mistake, the university, corporation, government agency, or whatever neocolonial entity pays your wages can never be part of the revolution.

GLOBAL ORGANIZATION

In order for us to help ourselves, we need to be able to act as a collective, independent unit. Malcolm is remembered as a great speaker, but he was also a tireless organizer. For all the faults of Marable's *Life of Reinvention*, it does chronicle how Malcolm went from city to city building the Nation of Islam, temple by temple. By the time he left, he had turned the NOI from a cult into a national organization, and he was planning to do the same with the Organization of Afro-American Unity, but on a global scale. We need an organization that can represent our interests if we are to be able to wield our collective power. To quote Malcolm's inspiration, Garvey, again, "The greatest weapon used against the Negro is disorganization."[13] We have simply failed to collectively organize into a force that can liberate ourselves. It is testament to Garvey's vision, and the lack of foresight since, that the UNIA was the largest Black organization that ever existed. It successfully organized millions of Black people around the world more than a hundred years ago. In many ways, we should be ashamed at how little we have built on that legacy. The UNIA was plunged into chaos by Garvey's imprisonment and deportation from America on bogus charges, but that does not explain why the organization collapsed. The UNIA still exists today, but for all the people I have heard invoke Garvey's name, I have seen very little support for his legacy. Part of this is due to the conditions that we face today being different from Garvey's time. In the 1920s, we were almost all in the field; it would have taken very little to convince your average Black person that we needed a radical change. But following token integration, many of us are now in the house or firmly believe we can get into it, so it is much more difficult to prosecute the need to escape. The irony is that the easier the mechanisms for achieving global Black unity become, with cheaper travel and internet access, the harder it is to make the argument in its favor.

Individualism reigns supreme in the struggle to get into the house. Now, I do not want to suggest that there are no organizations fighting for Black people; there are countless ones, doing invaluable work, but there is no organization of Black people that can represent Black people. Without coordination there can be no power, because we cannot speak as a people. White power is reflected through a range of global organizations. At first it was the various empires that were fighting over who would reap the most benefit from our oppression. Now it is the Group of Twenty, the UN, the World Bank, the World Trade Organization, etc., that set the global system of racism. There is a myriad of differences within these organizations, but there is a collective pursuit of White supremacy. We have no organization and therefore cannot respond *as* Black people, which is why we can never fully mobilize our power. The Organization of African Unity was supposed to be the body that allowed Africa to act in unison, but it very quickly became just another global institution that facilitated White supremacy. This has only become more apparent with its transition into the African Union. The problem of the AU is structural: It is locked into the colonial nation-state system that prevents any real unity, breaking up the continent into manageable pieces for the Foxes and Wolves to gobble up. Therefore, we must tweak Malcolm's OAAU to fit the modern day.

He imagined that the OAAU would link up with the OAU because he had far too much hope in the leaders who had brought about so-called independence to the African continent. Rather than working with the OAU, now AU, a new and truly radical organization has to supplant it and the colonial nation-state. We cannot accept the borders imposed by Europeans as a rational way to organize our lives in Africa. Therefore, the governments and leaders are illegitimate, and any revolution must replace them. It is not enough to get more progressive leaders; we need to abandon the nations themselves. We should think of the OAAU as the government of the global Black nation. Its membership fee would be gained from taxation, and its different departments would be organized around issues like education, health, and defense. Rather than working with existing governments, the goal of the organization should be to bypass them, by starting branches in every city across the continent and linking them up with those in the diaspora. If Malcolm had lived to see the regression of the OAU, he would undoubtedly have understood the importance of moving beyond the limitations of the colonial nation-state. We have to acknowledge that the structures where we can be free do not exist, so we have to build them. Ghana, Kenya, Nigeria, Jamaica, and the rest are not tools that can liberate us—they are mechanisms to control us.

Once we think of the organization as a government, then we can start to see how we can manage the vast array of differences across the Black nation. We all currently pay taxes to the state and accept that the government will make key decisions around policy and services, whether we voted for them or not. This does not mean we agree on every aspect, nor that we just sit back and let the politicians decide the course of our lives. We continue to organize, and when the system works best, we work with government agencies and draw down resources to do the work we see as important. Committing to a global Black organization does not mean leaving our other work behind but bringing what we are already doing into a larger framework. This clarification is essential, because one of the barriers to the kind of unity that we need has been the feeling of the loss of control once we form an overarching organization. The common refrain against Nkrumah and his vision for a United States of Africa was that he wanted to be *the* leader, and others did not want to give up their power. That remains the seduction of the colonial nation-state: the pomp, ceremony, and illusion of power that being in charge of your own country brings. Once this has happened, it doesn't matter that the independence is a mirage and that it is the economic powers outside your borders that are truly dictating your policy.

On a local level, we have also seen these dynamics play out, where organizations compete for scant resources and there are far too many egos at work wanting to protect their patch. Malcolm attempted to solve this issue by preaching a "gospel" of "Black nationalism," which allowed everyone to be involved. In his "Ballot or the Bullet" speech, he looked to the work of White Christian preacher Billy Graham, a famous televangelist who was welcomed into churches of all denominations despite the bitter divisions and acrimony within the larger Christian body. Malcolm explained that his popularity was because he went around preaching about "White nationalism," which was something that White Christians could agree on across all their differences. Malcolm aimed to take the same approach in building the necessary Black political coalition: "You can stay right in the church where you are and still take Black nationalism as your philosophy. You can stay in any kind of civic organization that you belong to and still take Black nationalism as your philosophy. You can be an atheist and still take Black nationalism as your philosophy. This is a philosophy that eliminates the necessity for division and argument."[14]

The OAAU mobilized this philosophy in practice by creating a structure that allowed everyone to stay in their organization, church, group, or association. The aim was to build membership and bring people together to work on the issues that impact us. For instance, if we had a chapter in Birmingham, we would have an education department that brought together those interested in the issue. We would audit the work already being done and decide priorities as a department. This could involve supporting existing work or creating new projects that are missing. No one needs to stop what they are doing; we are just trying to coordinate our efforts in a way that should benefit existing organizations while creating a collective body. Imagine that model replicated across thousands of cities across the world, all working together to support the uplift of Black people—that is what the revolution looks like. It's not a romantic, violent rage but a step-by-step, block-by-block movement that eventually builds into a global organization where we can mobilize our collective power.

YOU CAN'T WRITE YOUR WAY UP ON SOME FREEDOM

It's all well and good theorizing the revolution, and I do hope you have taken a lot of out this book. But ultimately it is never enough to make the argument or to simply nod your head in agreement. My biggest frustration with academia is that we have largely accepted the Western notion that thought is separate from action. The played-out maxim that "I think, therefore I am" was actually a racist notion to separate the rational White race from the lower animallike species. To be rational was to be above the fray, looking down on the social world from the ivory tower. We need to do away with such White supremacist logic and embrace the intellectual legacy of Malcolm and myriad other activists, past and present. The knowledge that can liberate us will never be created in the university; that is as possible as a chicken laying a duck egg. Malcolm's theory seems like uncannily accurate prophecy because he was on the ground, directly engaged in the struggles he was analyzing. If there is any lesson we in the academy should learn from Malcolm, it is that we can only generate useful theory from the trenches. If our work is not organically connected to Black communities, then it can never be fit for purpose, let alone revolution.

Especially with the advent of social media, we are in the age of the talking head. I am self-aware enough to know that I am very much part of the genre, being regularly invited to share fodder for the social networks. Malcolm said to never refuse a platform, and there is nothing wrong with using all means available to get the message out there. But one of the shifts that has taken place in the era of token integration is that our spokespeople are increasingly in the house. It's always been the case that famous Black people have been asked about race issues, and unfortunately the trend of giving the mic to actors, musicians, and sports stars has continued. I have spent the last few years savaging the best-selling books on racism that make it seem that, if we can all just get along, we will be OK. But I have excluded the ex–sports stars because the books are so appalling they are not worthy of commentary. Ex–NFL player Emmanuel Acho's best-selling *Uncomfortable Conversations with a Black Man* was so terrible that I couldn't even finish it. It's so embarrassing that it could be used as evidence for the catastrophic impact of football on the brain. But I don't blame him; it really is the publishing houses that treat our lives and issues with such disdain that they think being famous and Black is enough credential to write a book. Of course, the White public laps up the nonsense because it makes them feel good to be comforted by a Black face they recognize. There certainly are Black sportspeople and celebrities who have sensible things to say about Black communities, but they are the ones who have been struggling along with us.

Academics can break through the ivory tower to have mainstream appeal, and we now have award-winning journalists and even so-called equality and diversity experts who have risen to acclaim. Given my earlier critique of the 1619 Project, it is worth thinking through the journalist's role in the radical struggle. Journalism has always been a central ingredient to Black political mobilization. Making people aware of the realities of racism and publicizing the resistance are both vital tools for activism. Ida B. Wells's campaigns around lynching are the perfect example; she toured the South documenting the atrocities and sharing the details in articles for all to see.[15] The UNIA grew to prominence through its paper, *The Negro World*, which was circulated around the globe, evading the bans on it in many of the colonies.[16] Malcolm established *Muhammad Speaks* as a vehicle to spread the word of Muhammad and to grow the NOI. There are countless other examples, including Claudia Jones working on the Communist Party newspaper in America and then establishing the first Black newspaper in Britain, the *West Indian Gazette*.[17] (A small side note, Malcolm and Jones never met, but he respected her work and there is a picture of him holding up the issue of the paper with her obituary in it on one of his trips to London.) This journalism was organically connected to the wider struggles for justice that the journalists were all part of. This is very different from journalism for mainstream outlets, where the reporting is the end point of the work. Don't get me wrong; there are some excellent Black journalists out there covering important stories. But being a witness to events is of a different nature from participating in them.

The example of the "witness" that always comes to mind is one of Malcolm's friends, the legendary James Baldwin. My mom is my biggest influence, and she identified Baldwin as one of her first inspirations to engage in Black politics. Carole Andrews was born in Britain before the Windrush generation really began arriving in large numbers, so the landscape was very White. Baldwin was one of the few Black authors readily available at the time, and his rich, captivating stories of Black life were the spark that ignited her political awakening. Leila Hassan Howe, former editor of the anti-racist publication *Race Today* and a Black Power activist, also told me the same story when I did a profile on her for *The Guardian*.[18] Baldwin's work was often fiction, but he was serving the same function as a journalist, shedding light on the realities of the Black experience, and he inspired a generation. Baldwin famously debated with Malcolm and also wrote about his supposed alter ego, King.[19] In Baldwin's writings and speeches, he shared insights into American racism and the movements seeking liberation, but he was never truly part of any of them. When racism in America became too hostile for him, he could retreat to France, unlike Malcolm, who was always compelled to confront the problem. This isn't even a criticism of Baldwin; it is just important to acknowledge the role that he played. It was a vitally important one; we need the witnesses to describe and shed light on the situation, but we should never look to them for how to chart a way through it.

We need to learn this lesson when looking at the 1619 Project. Nikole Hannah-Jones did excellent work to get *The New York Times* to support a project that so clearly outlined the deeply racist history of the nation. It was truly groundbreaking to see Black studies knowledge shared so widely. It had such a large impact that it triggered a Whitelash of resentment. Just like with Baldwin's work, the project is going to have reached and inspired many to get involved in Black politics. But Hannah-Jones is a witness, and so we should not embrace the solutions she has offered, especially when they involve draping yourself in the American flag—as though this could ever offer some kind of protection.

Similar to the limits of culture, the witness is "crucial to revolution, but not revolution."[20] This is what Malcolm meant when he said you "can't write your way up on some freedom."[21] Our written work must be an extension of the struggle if we want it to be liberatory. This is why Malcolm's words resonate so long and far after his death. It may seem an ironic quotation for me to pick out, given that you are reading my book, but this project is part of my work to build Malcolm's legacy on a practical basis. I want you to read this and then work together to build the global organization that is our only route to freedom. I am not standing on the sidelines but drawing up the plays from inside the huddle.

"YOU MUST FIGHT UP ON SOME FREEDOM"

The only way to generate the knowledge that can free us is in the process of fighting for liberation. Nobody can give you freedom, and no one can write you a step-by-step manual for revolution. Expecting a magical solution is part of our problem, if we are waiting for someone to wave a wand and show us the path to liberation. Revolution is not a set destination at the end of a maze; it is a process where we collectively build a new world. Malcolm left behind a framework for revolution, but we will have to work to forge the route to freedom. As we come together, we will need to work through the details, the specifics that we encounter, using the revolutionary blueprint as the basis for how we go forward. Malcolm died sixty years ago. He obviously can't answer every question and development that has happened since. But he did leave behind the most clear-eyed analysis and method for revolution that we must pick up and continue.

The global Black nation is the only revolutionary route to freedom. We need to be able to utilize our power by creating an organization that ignores colonial nation-states' borders. Revolutionary unity means building a collective that is flexible enough to work at the local grassroots level and on the global scale too. This will take a lot of work and struggle to come together, but this *must* be the project. Malcolm was not saying that we should ignore the fires that we need to put out on a daily basis, but that we must understand those within the broader context. Every single problem we face as Black people is produced by us having to live in a White supremacist society. Therefore, if we want to cure the disease rather than just treat the symptoms, we have to create the organization where we can build a revolutionary future. To do so, we need to connect the grassroots struggles and strategize together. How we build this unity is the biggest problem that we must overcome, especially when we have already created so many divisions between ourselves.

Unity was an underlying theme of Malcolm's work, hence the *U* in the OAAU. During his travels in Africa, he questioned in his diary if he could "change the image and destroy tribalism, create unity."[22] Whether it be nation, tribe, religion, color, gender, sexuality, class, or a variety of other areas, Black people have found unlimited ways to put up partitions between each other. Remember, Malcolm was not asking us to all be the same or to forget our differences, but to come together on the fundamental issues that impact all of us. Malcolm was imploring us to reach beyond the divides to move forward together. But he never did so at the expense of ideology, always retaining fire for the Uncle Toms looking to lead us astray. We must also take this approach to those groups and ideas within the movements that by their nature cause divisions that undermine the unity necessary for revolution. In doing so, we can address one of the glaring gaps in Malcolm's revolutionary thought that needs development.

As we discussed in Chapter 6, Malcolm very rarely talked about gender, and when he did it was often to chide men for not offering the proper protection to "our women." In truth, Malcolm never really spoke about "men" either, although he did appear to speak constantly *to* the Black man. Despite this, I have tried to show that his mission and political vision are inclusive for all Black people. Having said that, we must acknowledge the deficits not just in Malcolm's understanding of gender and sexuality but in Black political movements more generally. It's impossible to do so without directly addressing the issue, which is why Black feminism and Black queer studies emerged.[23] It is vitally important to consider Malcolm's work through different lenses, to take an intersectional approach. We can see some clear lessons that come through applying the practice of radical unity.

The story I recounted in Chapter 6 about Kimberlé Crenshaw and the #SayHerName activists—who were shouted down at a Black Lives Matter protest for raising up the names of Black women killed by the police—is instructive. We can theorize unity, but if the reality on the ground is division, then we have a serious problem. Any program of political reeducation needs to have a strong intersectional focus to ensure that we do not continue to reproduce the patriarchy. But we also need to deal with the issue now, to ensure that we are creating inclusive activist spaces. Not everyone at the march was heckling the #SayHerName campaigners, but we are all collectively responsible. Malcolm would have told us that we are all in the same boat, and the fact that we even needed a separate #SayHerName campaign is indicative of the lack of necessary unity. Crenshaw and the African American Policy Forum only started the movement because Black women were being left out of the campaigns against police brutality. Not heckling the campaign is not enough. We should have been campaigning for Black female and queer victims of police violence from the beginning. We have interpreted issues like police violence as somehow male, even though all Black people are disproportionately likely to be subject to abuse. We have to remember that "we are all in the same boat, all catching the same hell," and therefore need to respond no matter the gender or sexual orientation of the victim.[24] The fact that this even needs stating tells us just how divided we have become.

There is another fundamental issue that Malcolm's experience raises, which is one about intersectional unity. It is not a coincidence that Malcolm expressed the view that women must be at the forefront of the OAAU after he left the Nation of Islam. That organization had, and retains, deeply patriarchal ideas about the role of women that could never support Malcolm's intersectional vision for the OAAU. For all his calls for unity, Malcolm's split from the NOI was bitter, and thereafter he sought to save the members he had recruited to what he then called the "criminal organization."[25] He understood that the NOI was revolutionarily bankrupt and therefore could not be part of the struggle for liberation. Although Malcolm's departure was hastened by the revelations that Muhammad was sexually harassing his young secretaries, Malcolm did not develop a critique of the Nation of Islam's politics because of that. But the group's regressive views on women are just as important as its political inaction while waiting for Armageddon. In fact, both issues are rooted in the fundamental flaw of the NOI: the belief that if you follow the "correct" way of living, a higher power will save you. But nobody can give you freedom—that includes God or any other spiritual force you can tap into.

Much of the sexism and homophobia that plagues our communities comes from this desire to avoid so-called deviations in the pursuit of a liberated life. But we have to accept that there are some ideas that are incompatible with revolution and abandon them. Just like Malcolm told us to avoid any "Negro church with a White Jesus and a White Mary and some White angels," we have to understand and then shun the organizations that limit the role of women or reject the rights of Black LGBTQ+ communities. On an immediate and practical level, that means being clear about who we include in our Black united front. We can't be united if some of those involved exclude others. We wouldn't invite into the organization those cooning their way to mainstream success or the Toms leading us astray. We need to reserve the same energy for the misogynists and homophobes. We do this while remembering that every Negro is potentially Black, but we have to insist that radical Black politics is by its nature intersectional, as is the revolutionary future we are seeking to build. Revolutionary unity cannot be forged by sacrificing our principles for artificial unity. So we are going to have to accept that everyone cannot be on board at first. As we progress, we can engage and bring more people along with us. But if we try to bring everyone on board, we will dilute the politics so that they will not be strong enough to overturn the system.

We also need to accept that the mechanism for our liberation does not exist and set about building the global Black nation. We need to do this step-by-step, joining together the work we are already doing and creating an organization that has the capacity to move us toward freedom. The OAAU is the blueprint that Malcolm laid out, drawing on Black radical history. Those of us who want to carry on his legacy must work to build that organization, which will have chapters across Africa and the diaspora all working in harmony. So that no one can say I wasn't clear on how we get free, it starts with the creation of the modern OAAU, an organization that brings together the Black masses, who pay a membership fee and are organized into different departments around areas including education, defense, economics, and culture. Without such an organization, we will never have the power to reshape the world. It may sound fanciful now, but imagine if we could connect the grassroots work from around the world, uniting the millions of us into a force with resources, one organically linked to the African continent. From there, we would be able to radically overhaul the system and create a world free from White supremacy. If it sounds like a pipe dream, that is only because we have been conditioned into believing that there is no alternative. Malcolm died only sixty years before this book was published. When he died, revolution was not a fantasy; it was sparking across the globe, and it was by no means certain that the West would win. That is why token integration happened, to dampen the revolutionary spirit by letting some more of us into the house. It took just a few decades to quash the revolutionary movements, via tokenism and violence, so completely that we no longer believe another world is possible. If we plan and build correctly, sixty years from now the world could be very different. Malcolm stressed the urgency to act, but this does not mean we expect everything to change overnight. We need incremental change, but we must be sure we are moving in the right direction. The problem with the liberal, civil rights approach is not the pace but the direction. If we carry on trying only to edit the existing system, we will find ourselves having the same conversation in sixty, six hundred, or six thousand years. Freedom does not lie at the end of the road of token integration. As we build, though, we have to be careful that unity does not cause us to continue to travel down the wrong road.

Malcolm acknowledged the importance of the direct needs of the community, the "short-range program," which included electoral politics and working with civil rights groups. This makes practical sense in building a grassroots organization. Alongside my late wife, Nicole, and a group of other activists, we tried to do this in 2013 when we launched the Harambee Organisation of Black Unity (based on the OAAU) and tried to build it up from Birmingham in the UK. The aim was to connect the work being done in the city and then open chapters in different places, including, eventually, across Africa. There are enough reasons for a whole other book on why progress stalled, but one of the most important lessons learned from this organizing has been the impact of token integration. In the West, we are either in the house, like myself, or mostly organizing to bring more of us into the house as well. When you try to bring together those engaged on the front lines, then it is very easy to offer strategies for alleviating the symptoms rather than treating the disease. My experience has shown it is extremely difficult to attract people who are interested in the long-range program, so there is a danger that, in practice, the organization actually becomes a civil rights group. Imagine if we were able to build a mass organization in Britain, America, or any other Western state that had hundreds of thousands of members and resources running programs in education, economics, health, and culture. We would be improving the conditions of our communities by helping more of our people to get into the house and therefore making the revolutionary work more difficult. The uncomfortable truth we have to deal with in the West is that the very nature of our privilege is the mechanism of our collective oppression around the globe. Our success here is just as dependent on the racism that kills children on the African continent as is that for any of the White population. The reality is that unity can be used for a variety of purposes, and for the most part Black activism in the West has heavily focused on access to the plantation house.

Building an organization that supported token integration must have been Malcolm's ultimate nightmare. The only way to ground the movement in radical principles is to try to include the Field Negro from the outset. In Malcolm's time, there were plenty of Field Negroes in Harlem, but today the majority are in the underdeveloped world, locked out from even the scraps from the master's table. We can't wait any longer to build the global organization; we must do this from the outset. We need to have local chapters and address their issues, but we need to do this through a global structure. We have the technical resources to do this through the internet and travel. We are so much more connected to each other that I can only imagine what strides Malcolm would have made today. Reaching the grassroots, particularly in the underdeveloped world, will still take time and work, but this needs to be our mission from the beginning. Once we come together, we will realize that nothing short of a revolution can free all of us from this wicked system.

The legacy of Malcolm X is what we make it. Reject the myth that he was all hot air and going to join in King's march to token integration. Malcolm left us a radical analysis and revolutionary solution for the problems that we face. We cannot wait for those in power to treat us fairly. We must take up Malcolm's mantle and build the global Black nation into a force that can liberate us all. This is up to us, a choice we need to make and commit to. As he told us, "Nobody can give you independence. Nobody can give you freedom. Nobody can give you equality or justice or anything. . . . If you can't take it, you don't deserve it. Nobody can give it to you."[26]

ACKNOWLEDGMENTS

Writing this book has been more difficult than I thought because all of my work over the past several years has been based on the political mission of Malcolm X. If you have read any of my previous books, it will be obvious how I am bringing the receipts to support what I've been saying for years. I am thankful to Malcolm not just for the material for this book but for opening my eyes to the nature of the world and framing my entire approach to moving through it. Malcolm gave his life for us, standing firm and making it plain when others would have shied away. We all owe him a debt and this book is a tribute to his tireless pursuit of freedom for Black people worldwide. I know it must be difficult given how poorly we have picked up his legacy, but I hope he is resting in power.

This is the first book I have written without the support of my late wife Nicole Andrews, who always offered advice and sharpened my work. Hopefully there is no noticeable dip in quality without her supportive hand. Even though she was not there when I typed the words, this is a book more than a decade in the making when we were living, loving, and organizing together. It would not have been possible without Nicole's support and input. I remember her putting up with my constant playing of Malcolm speeches on a loop when I was preparing the "What Would Malcolm Say?" talk that I gave in 2015, which was the inspiration for this book. Conversations with her always made me see clearer, and the insights contained here would never have emerged without Nicole.

Nicole was also on the front lines, at the very first meeting of the Organisation of Black Unity, which we founded in 2013 after learning about Malcolm's Organization of Afro-American Unity. In a community center in Birmingham, Nicole was by my side as we explained the idea to the crowd and then helped with all the paperwork and organization necessary to actually make it a reality. Nicole worked harder than anyone else to build up the organization and refurbish the Marcus Garvey Centre. She fell out with friends over the OBU, so strong was her commitment. This book is not simply theory; it is based on the years trying to put Malcolm's vision into practice, and Nicole was there for every step of that journey.

Thank you to everyone who has been involved in OBU and later Harambee OBU once we merged with the long-standing Harambee Organisation. Every interaction, negative or positive, has shaped this work. Everyone who volunteered, came to an event, or even made promises you couldn't keep has influenced this work.

As always I have to pay special thanks to my parents, who introduced me to Black radical ideas and Malcolm in particular. Carole and Maurice Andrews were two stalwarts of British Black Power who were inspired by Malcolm and established the Harambee Organisation in Birmingham in the seventies. I was fortunate to grow up under the wing of their leadership and activism. Without their guidance, there is little chance that this nincompoop with a PhD would not have been lost in the delusions of House Negrodom. I just hope I can do them proud.

Writing this book as a single parent also has meant having to draw more heavily on my mom, sisters—Nzinga and Zakiya—and Nicole's mom, Sonia, and dad, Derek. I could have neither carried on the work nor written the book without this support, so thank you. It takes a village to write a book.

Thanks also to my editor at Penguin Hana Teraie-Wood for the suggestions on how to improve the book. Also to my copy editor Louisa Watson for the painstaking efforts and genuine engagement with the book. It is a much better piece of work due to your input. Also a massive thank-you to Anupama Roy-Chaudhury and the Bold Type family, especially Liz Dana and Michelle Welsh-Horst for seeing the value of the book and for all the hard work.

Thanks also Sarah Chalfant, Emma Smith, and Sam Sheldon at the Wylie Agency for all the support in getting the book published and in my career. Hopefully there is still much more to come.

Finally huge thanks to everyone who has read and supported my work. I will thank you in advance for joining the movement for Black liberation. The purpose of this book is to explain the need for the Harambee Organisation of Black Unity. So I thank you all for supporting Malcolm's revolutionary vision for change. Nobody can give you freedom. We have to take it.

NOTES

Preface

1. Malcolm X and A. Haley, *The Autobiography of Malcolm X* (New York: Penguin Books, 1965), 170.

2. Malcolm X (el-Hajj Malik el-Shabazz), *The Diary of Malcolm X* (Chicago: Third World Press, 1964).

3. L. Payne and T. Payne, *The Dead Are Arising: The Life of Malcolm X* (New York: Liveright, 2020).

4. T. Martin, *Race First: The Ideological and Organizational Struggles of Marcus Garvey and the Universal Negro Improvement Association* (Dover, MA: Majority Press, 1976).

5. S. Carmichael, *Stokely Speaks: From Black Power to Pan Africanism* (New York: Vintage Books, 1971), 198.

6. Malcolm X, lecture at Muhammad Temple No. 7, New York, August 16, 1959, YouTube, accessed November 26, 2024, www.youtube.com/watch?v=q4GSnCiFoz8.

Chapter 1: Make It Plain

1. A. Cleage, "Myths About Malcolm X," in *Malcolm X: The Man and His Times*, ed. J. H. Clarke (Trenton, NJ: Africa World Press, 1990), 13–26.

2. J. E. McNeil, "The Sword and the Shield: The Revolutionary Lives of Malcolm X and Martin Luther King Jr.," review, *Friends Journal*, October 1, 2021, www.friendsjournal.org/book/the-sword-and-the-shield-the-revolutionary-lives-of-malcolm-x-and-martin-luther-king-jr/.

3. Malcolm X, speech at New York Harlem Youth Opportunities Unlimited (HARYOU) Forum, December 12, 1964, YouTube, accessed November 26, 2024, www.youtube.com/watch?v=9s-XvPZeUfA.

4. Malcolm X, "The Race Problem," Michigan State University, January 23, 1963, MSU Archives and Historical Collections, accessed November 26, 2024, https://onthebanks.msu.edu/Object/162-565-2359/malcolm-x-speaks-at-michigan-state-university-1963/.

5. Malcolm X, "We Have to Learn How to Think," interview with Marlene Nadle, February 25, 1965, in *The Final Speeches: February 1965* (New York: Pathfinder Press, 2003), 250.

6. Malcolm X, "The Oppressed Masses of the World Cry Out for Action Against the Common Oppressor," speech at London School of Economics, February 11, 1965, in *The Final Speeches: February 1965* (New York: Pathfinder Press, 2003), 50.

7. J. Gonclaves, introduction, *The Political Legacy Of Malcolm X* (Richmond, CA: Pan Afrikan Publications, 1983), 7–12.

8. M. E. Dyson, *Making Malcolm: The Myth and Meaning of Malcolm X* (Oxford: Oxford University Press, 1996), 176.

9. J. Ball and T. S. Burroughs, *A Lie of Reinvention: Correcting Manning Marable's Malcolm X* (Baltimore: Black Classic Press, 2012).

10. M. Marable, *Malcolm X: A Life of Reinvention* (London: Penguin Books, 2011), 484.

11. C. Condit and J. Lucaites, "Malcolm X and the Limits of the Rhetoric of Revolutionary Dissent," *Journal of Black Studies* 23, no. 3 (1993): 291–305; R. E. Terrill, "Colonizing the Borderlands: Shifting Circumference in the Rhetoric of Malcolm X," *Quarterly Journal of Speech* 86, no. 1 (2000): 67–85.

12. I. Reed, *Malcolm and Me* (Audible Original, 2020), ch. 5.

13. M. Marable, *Living Black History: How Reimagining the African-American Past Can Remake America's Racial Future* (New York: Basic Civitas, 2011).

14. T. Parry, "The Politics of Plagiarism: *Roots*, Margaret Walker and Alex Haley," in *Reconsidering: Roots, Race, Politics, and Memory*, eds. E. Ball and K. Jackson (Athens: University of Georgia Press, 2017), 47–62.

15. X, "The Race Problem."

16. Marable, *A Life of Reinvention*, 9.

17. G. Brockwell, "MLK's Famous Criticism of Malcolm X Was a 'Fraud,' Author Finds," *Washington Post*, May 10, 2023.

18. Malcolm X, "Secret Recording: The FBI Tries to Bribe Malcolm X," February 4, 1964, YouTube, accessed November 26, 2024, www.youtube.com/watch?v=z1vEBvi90e8.

19. L. Martin, *The Gospel of J. Edgar Hoover: How the FBI Aided and Abetted the Rise of White Christian Nationalism* (Princeton, NJ: Princeton University Press, 2023), 257.

20. J. Haas, *The Assassination of Fred Hampton: How the FBI and the Chicago Police Murdered a Black Panther* (Chicago: Lawrence Hill, 2010).

21. T. Doherty, "Malcolm X: In Print, on Screen," *Biography* 23, no. 1 (2000): 43.

22. X and Haley, *Autobiography of Malcolm X*.

23. N. R. Mandela, *Long Walk to Freedom* (London: Abacus Books, 1996).

24. K. Andrews, *The Psychosis of Whiteness* (London: Penguin Books, 2023), 196.

25. "Carmichael Blasts Lee on 'Malcolm,'" *Los Angeles Times*, January 1, 1993, www.latimes.com/archives/la-xpm-1993-01-01-ca-3150-story.html.

26. B. Shabazz, "The Legacy of My Husband Malcolm X," *Ebony*, June 1969, 172–182.

27. J. Longoria, host, *More Perfect*, podcast, "Clarence X," WNYC Studios, May 18, 2023.

28. J. Jeffries, "Only the Ques Would Debate Malcolm X: The Civil Rights Movement's Big Six and the Safe Distance at Which They Kept America's Foremost Militant," *Journal of African American Studies* 26 (2022): 413–435.

29. C. Rubin, "Clarence Thomas Wants a Man Executed Before DNA Testing Is Done," MSNBC, April 23, 2023, www.msnbc.com/deadline-white-house/deadline-legal-blog/clarence-thomas-rodney-reed-supreme-court-rcna80978.

30. T. Marshall, speech at retirement press conference, June 28, 1991.

31. J. Blake, "Here's Why Many Black People Despise Clarence Thomas. (It's Not Because He's a Conservative.)," CNN, September 11, 2023, https://edition.cnn.com/2023/09/11/politics/clarence-thomas-black-people-blake-cec/index.html.

32. S. Smith, "Clarence X?: The Black Nationalist Behind Justice Thomas's Constitutionalism," *NDLS Scholarship*, 2009, https://scholarship.law.nd.edu/law_faculty_scholarship/550.

33. X, "The Race Problem."

34. P. Williams, "Clarence X," in *Color—Class—Identity: The New Politics of Race*, eds. J. Arthur and A. Shapiro (New York: Routledge, 1996), 88–97.

35. Payne and Payne, *The Dead Are Arising*.

36. M. Sawyer, *Black Minded: The Political Philosophy of Malcolm X* (London: Pluto Press, 2020), 21.

37. K. Andrews, *The New Age of Empire: How Racism and Colonialism Still Rule the World* (London: Allen Lane, 2021).

38. Sawyer, *Black Minded*, 33.

39. X, "The Race Problem."

40. M. Angelou, interview in *Malcolm X: Make It Plain*, directed by O. Bagwell (PBS, 1994).

41. P. Hill Collins, *Black Feminist Thought: Knowledge, Consciousness, and the Politics of Empowerment* (London: Routledge, 2000).

42. X and Haley, *Autobiography of Malcolm X*, 179.

43. C. J. Robinson, *Black Marxism: The Making of the Black Radical Tradition* (London: Zed Books, 1983).

44. Malcolm X, "A Summing Up: Louis Lomax Interviews Malcolm X," 1963, Teaching American History, accessed November 26, 2024, https://teachingamericanhistory.org/document /a-summing-up-louis-lomax-interviews-malcolm-x/.

Chapter 2: That Wicked Race of Devils

1. E. U. Essien Udom, *Black Nationalism: A Search for Identity in America* (New York: Dell Publishing, 1970).

2. Marable, *Living Black History*.

3. Anti-Defamation League, "Profile: Nation of Islam," September 1, 2021, accessed November 26, 2024, www.adl.org/resources/profile/nation-islam.

4. X and Haley, *Autobiography of Malcolm X*, 170.

5. Malcolm X, "Interview on 'City Desk,'" WNBQ-TV Chicago, March 17, 1963, YouTube, accessed November 26, 2024, www.youtube.com/watch?v=sVbdpc-u4aY.

6. X and Haley, *Autobiography of Malcolm X*.

7. Malcolm X, "There's a Worldwide Revolution Going On," Audubon Ballroom, New York, February 15, 1965, ICIT Digital Library, accessed November 26, 2024, www.icit-digital .org/articles/malcolm-x-speech-there-s-a-worldwide-revolution-going-on-feb-15-1965.

8. M. S. Handler, "Malcolm X Splits with Muhammad; Suspended Muslim Leader Plans Black Nationalist Political Movement," *The New York Times*, March 9, 1964.

9. Malcolm X, "The Ballot or the Bullet," speech at King Solomon Baptist Church, Detroit, Michigan, April 12, 1964, American RadioWorks, accessed November 26, 2024, https://american radioworks.publicradio.org/features/blackspeech/mx.html.

10. Malcolm X, "God's Judgment of White America," December 1, 1963, in *Malcolm X: The End of White World Supremacy: Four Speeches*, ed. B. Goodman (New York: Merlin House, 2020), 121–148.

11. X, "Interview on 'City Desk.'"

12. X, "God's Judgment of White America," 139.

13. "Malcolm X Scores U.S. and Kennedy; Likens Slaying to 'Chickens Coming Home to Roost,'" *The New York Times*, December 2, 1963.

14. Handler, "Malcolm X Splits with Muhammad."

15. Payne and Payne, *The Dead Are Arising*.

16. Malcolm X, "Educate Our People in the Science of Politics," Ford Auditorium, Detroit, February 14, 1965, BlackPast.org, accessed November 22, 2024, www.blackpast.org /african-american-history/speeches-african-american-history/1965-malcolm-x-speech -ford-auditorium/.

17. Malcolm X, "One Big Force Under One Banner," interview with Gordon Parks, February 19, 1965, in *The Final Speeches: February 1965* (New York: Pathfinder Press, 2003), 240–242.

18. Malcolm X, "I Think with My Own Mind," interview with *The New York Times*, February 18, 1965, in *The Final Speeches: February 1965*, 176–179.

19. Handler, "Malcolm X Splits with Muhammad."

20. Malcolm X, "Black Man's History," December 23, 1962, in *Malcolm X: The End of White World Supremacy: Four Speeches*, ed. I. B. Karim (New York: Merlin House, 1971), 23–66.

21. Ibid., 52.

22. Ibid., 56.

23. Ibid., 57.

24. Ibid., 57.

25. Ibid., 51.

26. Ibid., 58.

27. W. E. Cross, "The Negro to Black Conversion Experiences," *Black World* 20 (1971): 13–27.

28. X, "Black Man's History," 26.

29. Malcolm X, "Harlem Unity Rally," August 1963, New York, YouTube, accessed November 29, 2024, www.youtube.com/watch?v=MiqO6LBmG54.

30. Malcolm X, "Interview with A. B. Spelman," 1964, in *By Any Means Necessary: Speeches, Interviews and Letters by Malcolm X*, ed. G. Breitman (New York: Pathfinder Press, 1970), 4.

31. Malcolm X, "Interview with Pierre Berton," Canadian Broadcasting Company, January 19, 1965, ICIT Digital Library, accessed November 25, 2024, www.icit-digital.org/articles/pierre-berton-interviews-malcolm-x-january-19-1965.

32. X, "Black Man's History," 62.

33. X, "Harlem Unity Rally."

34. Ibid.

35. Ibid.

36. Ibid.

37. X, "Black Man's History," 65.

38. Marable, *A Life of Reinvention*.

39. L. Farrakhan, "Saviours' Day Speech," February 26, 2017, quotation at Anti-defamation League, accessed November 25, 2024, www.adl.org/resources/backgrounder/farrakhan-his-own-words.

40. X, lecture at Muhammad Temple No. 7.

41. Ibid.

42. X, "Harlem Unity Rally."

43. X, "Black Man's History," 35.

44. Ibid.

45. Ibid.

46. Malcolm X, "The Black Revolution," April 8, 1964, ICIT Digital Library, accessed November 25, 2024, www.icit-digital.org/articles/malcolm-x-on-the-black-revolution-april-8-1964.

47. Malcolm X, "Message to the Grassroots," Negro Grass Roots Leadership Conference, Detroit, Michigan, December 10, 1963, BlackPast.org, accessed November 24, 2024, www.blackpast.org/african-american-history/speeches-african-american-history/1963-malcolm-x-message-grassroots/.

48. X, "God's Judgment of White America," 137.

49. I. Wilkerson, *The Warmth of Other Suns: The Epic Story of America's Great Migration* (New York: Random House, 2010).

50. X, "Harlem Unity Rally."

51. Ibid.

52. Ibid.

53. Malcolm X, speech at the University of California, Berkeley, October 11, 1963, ICIT Digital Library, accessed November 21, 2024, www.icit-digital.org/articles/malcolm-x-at -uc-berkeley-october-11-1963.

54. X, "The Ballot or the Bullet," King Solomon Baptist Church.

55. Malcolm X, speech at the University of Columbia, May 20, 1963, ICIT Digital Library, accessed November 21, 2024, www.icit-digital.org/articles/malcolm-x-at-columbia -university-november-20-1963.

56. X, speech at the University of California, Berkeley.

57. X, "God's Judgment of White America," 137.

58. X, "Educate Our People in the Science of Politics."

59. Malcolm X, "Letter from Mecca," April 20, 1964, ICIT Digital Library, accessed November 21, 2024, www.icit-digital.org/articles/malcolm-x-s-letter-from-mecca-april-20-1964.

60. Ibid.

61. X, "Interview with Pierre Berton."

62. X, "Letter from Mecca."

63. Malcolm X, interview with Robert Penn Warren, June 2, 1964, RedSails.org, accessed November 21, 2024, https://redsails.org/x-and-warren/.

64. X, "Educate Our People in the Science of Politics."

65. Malcolm X, "The Importance of Unity," interview on being barred from France, February 9, 1965, in *The Final Speeches: February 1965*, 34–41.

66. X, "Interview on 'City Desk.'"

67. Malcolm X, speech at Harvard Law School Forum, December 16, 1964, accessed November 22, 2024, https://newspapers.digitalnc.org/lccn/2015236558/1990-10-22/ed-1/seq -4.pdf.

68. X, lecture at Muhammad Temple No. 7.

69. X, speech at the University of California, Berkeley.

70. "Malcolm X in Debate with Bayard Rustin," WBAI Radio, New York, November 1960, ICIT Digital Library, accessed November 22, 2024, www.icit-digital.org/articles/malcolm -x-at-bayard-rustin-debate-november-1960.

71. X, "Harlem Unity Rally."

72. X, "A Summing Up."

73. *Malcolm X: Excerpt from Interview with Louis Lomax*, March 8, 1964 (Greenwood, IN: Educational Video Group, 1964).

74. X and Haley, *The Autobiography of Malcolm X.*

75. X, "The Race Problem."

76. J. Barnes, "Evolution of Malcolm X's Views on Women," *The Militant* 74, no. 18 (2010).

77. X, "Interview with Pierre Berton."

78. Malcolm X, "I Live for Change and Action," interview with *Flamingo* magazine, February 10, 1965, in *The Final Speeches: February 1965*, 42–44.

79. X, "Interview with A. B. Spelman," 9.

80. X, "The Ballot or the Bullet," King Solomon Baptist Church.

Chapter 3: Stop Singing and Start Swinging

1. L. Lomax, *To Kill a Black Man: The Shocking Parallel in the Lives of Malcolm X and Martin Luther King Jr.* (Los Angeles: Holloway House Publishing, 1968).

2. X, "The Oppressed Masses Cry Out for Action Against the Common Oppressor," 47.

3. X, "There's a Worldwide Revolution Going On."

4. Malcolm X, interview with Eleanor Fischer, 1961, WNYC, accessed November 22, 2024, www.wnyc.org/story/87636-remembering-malcolm-x-rare-interviews-and-audio/.

5. Malcolm X, "On Police Brutality," Los Angeles, May 20, 1962, *The Melanin Project*, accessed November 27, 2024, www.themelaninproject.org/tmpblog/2020/2/11/malcolm-x -may-20-1962-speech-on-police-brutality-in-los-angeles-california.

6. R. Williams, *Negroes with Guns* (Detroit: Wayne State University Press, 1998).

7. L. Hill, *The Deacons for Defense: Armed Resistance and the Civil Rights Movement* (Chapel Hill: University of North Carolina Press, 2004).

8. C. Cobb, *This Nonviolent Stuff'll Get You Killed: How Guns Made the Civil Rights Movement Possible* (Durham, NC: Duke University Press, 2015).

9. M. L. King, *Where Do We Go From Here? Chaos or Community?* (Boston: Beacon Press, 1968), 57.

10. X, speech at Harvard Law School Forum, December 16, 1964.

11. X, "There's a Worldwide Revolution Going On."

12. X, "Educate Our People in the Science of Politics."

13. X, "The Ballot or the Bullet," King Solomon Baptist Church.

14. M. Wallace, *Black Macho and the Myth of the Superwoman* (New York: Dial Press, 1979).

15. Malcolm X, debate with James Baldwin, April 25, 1961, *Democracy Now!*, accessed November 22, 2024, www.democracynow.org/2001/2/1/james_baldwin_and_malcolm_x_de bate#:~:text=On%20April%2025th%2C%201961%2C%20two,rare%20recording%20 of%20their%20debate.

16. X, "Message to the Grassroots."

17. Malcolm X, Oxford University Union debate, December 3, 1964, YouTube, accessed November 22, 2024, www.youtube.com/watch?v=auWA7hMh5hc.

18. X, "Message to the Grassroots."

19. X, "Educate Our People in the Science of Politics."

20. Malcolm X, "Answers to Questions from the Militant Labor Forum," in *By Any Means Necessary: Speeches, Interviews and Letters by Malcolm X*, 22.

21. X, "Message to the Grassroots."

22. Ibid.

23. X, debate with James Baldwin.

24. X, "Interview with A. B. Spelman," 6.

25. X, "Interview with Pierre Berton."

26. X, speech at the University of California, Berkeley.

27. X, "On Police Brutality."

28. X, "Message to the Grassroots."

29. X, "Harlem Unity Rally."

30. X, "The Black Revolution."

31. X, "The Ballot or the Bullet," King Solomon Baptist Church.

32. X, "Message to the Grassroots."

33. X, "Educate Our People in the Science of Politics."

34. Ibid.

35. G. Younge, *The Speech: The Story Behind Martin Luther King's Dream* (London: Guardian Books, 2013).

36. X, "Message to the Grassroots."

37. X and Haley, *The Autobiography of Malcolm X*.

38. X, "Message to the Grassroots."

39. X, "The Black Revolution."

40. Ibid.

41. X, "Educate Our People in the Science of Politics."

42. E. M'Buyinga, *Pan Africanism or Neo-Colonialism? The Bankruptcy of the OAU* (London: Zed Books, 1982).

43. Malcolm X, "Not Just an American Problem, but a World Problem," February 16, 1965, ICIT Digital Library, accessed November 27, 2024, www.icit-digital.org/articles/malcolm-x-on-not-just-an-american-problem-but-a-world-problem-feb-16-1965.

44. Ibid.

45. X, "On Police Brutality."

46. X, "Message to the Grassroots."

47. Ibid.

48. Malcolm X, "The Ballot or the Bullet," Cory Methodist Church, Cleveland, Ohio, April 3, 1964, Social Justice Speeches, accessed November 27, 2024, www.edchange.org/multicultural/speeches/malcolm_x_ballot.html.

49. X, "The Ballot or the Bullet," King Solomon Baptist Church.

50. X, "The Black Revolution."

51. X, "On Police Brutality."

52. Ibid.

53. Malcolm X, "Malcolm X Introduces Fannie Lou Hamer," Williams Institutional CME Church, New York, December 20, 1964, *The Complete Malcolm* X, accessed November 27, 2024, https://malcolmxfiles.com/collection/malcolm-x-introduces-fannie-lou-hamer-december-20-1964/.

54. Malcolm X, "The Harlem Hate Gang Scare," 1964, in *Malcolm X Speaks*, ed. G. Breitman (New York: Grove Press, 1965), 66, 68.

55. X, "The Ballot or the Bullet," King Solomon Baptist Church.

56. Ibid.

57. X, "The Black Revolution."

58. *Malcolm X: Excerpt from Interview with Louis Lomax.*

59. Malcolm X, "On the Barry Gray Show," WBNY Radio, September 20, 1960, YouTube, accessed November 27, 2024, www.youtube.com/watch?v=6b34FU53phw.

60. X, "Interview with A. B. Spelman," 6.

61. Ibid.

62. J. Reed, "Newton-Cleaver Rift Threatens Panthers," *Harvard Crimson*, March 23, 1971.

63. C. Condit and J. Lucaites, "Malcolm X and the Limits of the Rhetoric of Revolutionary Dissent," *Journal of Black Studies* 23, no. 3 (1993): 310.

64. Malcolm X, "Why I Came to Selma: Remarks to the Press," February 4, 1965, in *The Final Speeches: February 1965*, 23–25.

Chapter 4: A Chicken Can Never Lay a Duck Egg

1. X, "On Police Brutality."

2. A. Davis, *Women, Culture and Politics* (New York: Vintage Books, 1990).

3. D. Bell, *Faces at the Bottom of the Well: The Permanence of Racism* (New York: Basic Books, 1992).

4. White House, "Executive Order on Combating Race and Sex Stereotyping," September 22, 2020, https://trumpwhitehouse.archives.gov/presidential-actions/executive-order-combating-race-sex-stereotyping/.

5. African American Policy Forum, "Welcome to the #TruthBeTold Campaign," accessed November 27, 2024, www.aapf.org/truthbetold.

6. House of Commons, Black History Month, debated on October 20, 2020, *Hansard* 682, https://hansard.parliament.uk/commons/2020-10-20/debates/5B0E393E-8778-4973-B318-C17797DFBB22/BlackHistoryMonth.

7. X, "On Police Brutality."

8. R. D. G. Kelley, "House Negroes on the Loose: Malcolm X and the Black Bourgeoisie," *Callaloo* 21, no. 2 (1998): 420.

9. Louis Farrakhan, interview with Jamilah Lemieux, *Ebony* magazine, 2016.

10. M. Marable, "Black Fundamentalism: Farrakhan and Conservative Black Nationalism," *Race and Class* 39, no. 4 (1998): 1–22.

11. X, "Harlem Unity Rally."

12. Ibid.

13. X, "On Police Brutality."

14. Ibid.

15. X, "Not Just an American Problem, but a World Problem."

16. E. Anderson, "The Iconic Ghetto," *The Annals of the American Academy of Political and Social Science* 642, no. 1 (2012): 8–24.

17. X, "On Police Brutality."

18. Ibid.

19. Ibid.

20. X, "Message to the Grassroots."

21. X, "The Ballot or the Bullet," King Solomon Baptist Church; X, lecture at Muhammad Temple No. 7.

22. X, "Harlem Unity Rally."

23. X, lecture at Muhammad Temple No. 7.

24. X, "Harlem Unity Rally."

25. Malcolm X, speech at the Militant Labor Forum, May 29, 1964, YouTube, accessed November 27, 2024, www.youtube.com/watch?v=Ux_zQnD0WfY&ab_channel=Ntwadumela.

26. X, "The Harlem Hate Gang Scare."

27. K. Andrews, *Back to Black: Retelling Black Radicalism for the 21st Century* (London: Zed Books, 2018).

28. Malcolm X, "At the Audubon," December 1964, Teaching American History, accessed November 26, 2024, https://teachingamericanhistory.org/document/at-the-audubon/.

29. C. Robinson, "C. L. R. James and the World-System," *Race and Class* 34, no. 2 (1992): 61.

30. X, speech at the Militant Labor Forum.

31. If you do want to go down that particular rabbit hole, then J. Barnes, *Malcolm X, Black Liberation, and the Road to Workers' Power* (New York: Pathfinder Press, 2009), is as good a place as any.

32. X, "Answers to Questions from the Militant Labor Forum," 17.

33. Ibid., 33.

34. Ibid.

35. Malcolm X, "Interview on Boston Radio," June 25, 1964, *ACCRA [dot] ALT* (blog), accessed November 27, 2024, https://accradotalt.tumblr.com/post/103740500460/malcolm-x-boston-radio-interview-june-251964.

36. Bell, *Faces at the Bottom of the Well*, 3.

37. Malcolm X, speech at Harvard Law School Forum, March 24, 1961, ICIT Digital Library, accessed November 22, 2024, www.icit-digital.org/articles/malcolm-x-at-harvard-law-school-forum-march-24-1961.

38. X, "The Black Revolution."

39. X, speech at the University of California, Berkeley.

40. X, "Interview with A. B. Spelman," 12.

41. X, "The Ballot or the Bullet," Cory Methodist Church.

42. X, "The Ballot or the Bullet," King Solomon Baptist Church.

43. X, lecture at Muhammad Temple No. 7.

44. X, "Not Just an American Problem, but a World Problem."

45. X, "The Importance of Unity," 39.

46. X, "Interview on Boston Radio."

47. X, "The Ballot or the Bullet," King Solomon Baptist Church.

48. X, "Not Just an American Problem, but a World Problem."

49. X, "Interview on Boston Radio."

50. *Malcolm X: Excerpt from Interview with Louis Lomax.*

51. Bell, *Faces at the Bottom of the Well*, 198.

52. X, "The Ballot or the Bullet," King Solomon Baptist Church.

53. W. E. B. Dubois, *The Souls of Black Folk* (Oxford: Oxford University Press, 2008).

54. Malcolm X, "The Ballot or the Bullet," Washington Heights, New York, March 29, 1964, AMDOCS: Documents for the Study of American History, accessed November 27, 2024, www.vlib.us/amdocs/texts/malcolmx0364.html.

55. X, "Harlem Unity Rally."

56. X, "The Ballot or the Bullet," King Solomon Baptist Church.

57. *Malcolm X: Excerpt from Interview with Louis Lomax.*

58. X, "The Ballot or the Bullet," King Solomon Baptist Church.

59. X, "Message to the Grassroots."

60. X, "Harlem Unity Rally."

61. X, interview with Robert Penn Warren.

62. Ibid.

63. N. Guyatt, *Bind Us Apart: How Enlightened Americans Invented Racial Segregation* (Oxford: Oxford University Press, 2016), 4.

64. X, "Message to the Grassroots."

65. R. Gilmore, "Fatal Couplings of Power and Difference: Notes on Racism and Geography," *The Professional Geographer* 54, no. 1 (2002): 16.

66. C. G. Woodson, "Negro History Week," *Journal of Negro History* 11, no. 2 (1926): 39.

67. X, "Not Just an American Problem, but a World Problem."

68. X, "Malcolm X Introduces Fannie Lou Hamer."

69. X, "The Ballot or the Bullet," Cory Methodist Church.

70. X, "Educate Our People in the Science of Politics."

71. X, "Interview on Boston Radio."

72. Malcolm X, Second Founding Rally of the Organization of Afro-American Unity, New York, July 5, 1964, ICIT Digital Library, accessed November 27, 2024, www.icit-digital.org/articles/malcolm-x-at-the-second-oaau-rally-july-5-1964.

73. X, "The Black Revolution."

74. M. Alexander, *The New Jim Crow: Mass Incarceration in the Age of Colorblindness* (New York: New Press, 2010).

75. X, "The Ballot or the Bullet," Cory Methodist Church.

76. D. Bell, "Brown vs Board of Education and the Interest-Convergence Dilemma," *Harvard Law Review* 98 (January 11, 1980): 513–518.

77. *Malcolm X: Excerpt from Interview with Louis Lomax.*

78. Malcolm X, First Founding Rally of the Organization of Afro-American Unity, New York, June 28, 1964, accessed November 27, 2024, www.thinkingtogether.org/rcream/archive/Old/S2006/comp/OAAU.pdf.

79. *Malcolm X: Excerpt from Interview with Louis Lomax*

80. X, "The Ballot or the Bullet," King Solomon Baptist Church.

81. C. Anderson, *One Person, No Vote: How Voter Suppression Is Destroying Our Democracy* (New York: Bloomsbury Publishing, 2018).

82. X, "The Ballot or the Bullet," King Solomon Baptist Church.

83. Ibid.

84. X, "Educate Our People in the Science of Politics."

Chapter 5: Benevolent Colonialism

1. X, "Not Just an American Problem, but a World Problem."

2. Ibid.

3. X, "The Ballot or the Bullet," King Solomon Baptist Church.

4. X, "The Black Revolution."

5. Malcolm X, "The Black Muslim Movement: An Assessment," WINS Radio, February 18, 1965, *The Final Speeches: February 1965*, 237.

6. X, lecture at Muhammad Temple No. 7.

7. W. E. B. Du Bois, "A Negro Nation Within the Nation," *Current History* 42, no. 3 (1935): 267.

8. "The Power of the Black Community: How Brands Can Tap into $1.4 Trillion in Buying Power," *Blavity*, May 17, 2023, https://blavityinc.com/black-buying-power/.

9. X, *The Diary of Malcolm X*, 48.

10. Andrews, *The New Age of Empire*.

11. X, "The Ballot or the Bullet," King Solomon Baptist Church.

12. Ibid.

13. Malcolm X, speech at the University of Ghana, May 13, 1964, ICIT Digital Library, accessed November 28, 2024, www.icit-digital.org/articles/malcolm-x-at-university -of-ghana-may-13-1964.

14. S. Carmichael and C. Hamilton, *Black Power: The Politics of Liberation in America* (Harmondsworth, UK: Penguin Books, 1968), 26.

15. W. K. Tabb, "Race Relations Models of Social Change," *Social Problems* 19, no. 4 (1971): 431–444.

16. X, "The Black Revolution."

17. Z. Kondo, *Conspiracies: Unravelling the Assassination of Malcolm X* (Addis Ababa, Ethiopia: Nubia Press, 1993).

18. R. Jeffries, "Britain's Most Racist Election: The Story of Smethwick, 50 Years On," *The Guardian*, October 15, 2014, www.theguardian.com/world/2014/oct/15/britains-most -racist-election-smethwick-50-years-on.

19. Kelley, "House Negroes on the Loose," 414.

20. "Peter Griffiths—Obituary," *The Telegraph*, November 27, 2013.

21. X, "I Live for Change and Action," 43.

22. Malcolm X, "Afro-American History," January 24, 1965, *International Socialist Review* 28, no. 2 (March–April 1967): 3–48, www.marxists.org/reference/archive/malcolm -x/1965/01/afro-amer.html#:~:text=And%20the%20thing%20that%20has,of%20 knowledge%20concerning%20the%20past.

23. K. Andrews, "Guy Reid-Bailey: The Man Who Sparked the Bristol Bus Boycott and Then Fought to Desegregate Housing," *The Guardian*, December 17, 2020, www.theguardian .com/world/2020/dec/17/guy-reid-bailey-the-man-who-sparked-the-bristol-bus-boycott-and -then-fought-to-desegregate-housing.

24. X, "The Black Revolution."

25. W. Chodkowski, "The United States Information Agency: Fact Sheet," American Security Project, November 2012, www.americansecurityproject.org/ASP%20Reports/Ref %200097%20-%20The%20United%20States%20Information%20Agency.pdf.

26. Malcolm X, "Homecoming Rally," November 29, 1964, in *By Any Means Necessary: Speeches, Interviews and Letters by Malcolm X*, 139.

27. J. Bevins, *The Jakarta Method: Washington's Anticommunist Crusade and the Mass Murder Program That Shaped Our World* (New York: Public Affairs, 2020).

28. X, speech at the University of Ghana.

29. X, "Educate Our People in the Science of Politics."

30. Andrews, *The New Age of Empire*.

31. A. S. Layton, "International Pressure and the U.S. Government's Response to Little Rock," *Arkansas Historical Quarterly* 56, no. 3 (1997): 257.

32. Ibid., 258.

33. K. Andrews, "Minnijean Brown-Trickey: The Teenager Who Needed an Armed Guard to Go to School," *The Guardian*, November 26, 2020, www.theguardian.com/society/2020/nov/26/minnijean-brown-trickey-little-rock-nine.

34. Layton, "International Pressure and the U.S. Government's Response to Little Rock," 262.

35. Ibid., 264.

36. J. F. Kennedy, "Statement upon Signing the Order Establishing the Peace Corps," March 1, 1961, John F. Kennedy Memorial Library and Museum, accessed November 28, 2024, www.jfklibrary.org/archives/other-resources/john-f-kennedy-speeches/peace-corps-establishment-19610301#:~:text=President%20John%20F.&text=This%20Corps%20will%20be%20a,the%20end%20of%20the%20year.

37. Malcolm X, "Time Is on the Side of the Africans Against Exploitation and Oppression," Council of African Organizations, February 6–8, 1965, in *The Final Speeches: February 1965*, 31–33.

38. X, "The Oppressed Masses Cry Out for Action Against the Common Oppressor," 50.

39. Andrews, *The New Age of Empire*.

40. "Powering Human Connection," Peace Corps, accessed November 28, 2024, www.peacecorps.gov/what-we-do/our-mission/.

41. X, "The Oppressed Masses Cry Out for Action Against the Common Oppressor," 50; Layton, "International Pressure and the U.S. Government's Response to Little Rock."

42. Ibid.

43. X, "Not Just an American Problem, but a World Problem."

44. X, Oxford University Union debate.

45. Ibid.

46. Malcolm X, speech at the Audubon Ballroom, New York, 1964, in "Women and the Underground press," *The Spectator* (IN), July 29, 1969.

47. X, "Not Just an American Problem, but a World Problem."

48. X, "The Ballot or the Bullet," King Solomon Baptist Church.

49. X, "Answers to Questions from the Militant Labor Forum," 19.

50. Ibid., 21.

51. Andrews, *The New Age of Empire*.

52. X, "Not Just an American Problem, but a World Problem."

53. X, "The Ballot or the Bullet," King Solomon Baptist Church.

54. X, "The Black Revolution."

55. Ibid.

56. X, "Interview on Boston Radio."

57. Ibid.

58. Fundamental Rights of People of African Descent, European Parliament, resolution 2018/2899(RSP), March 26, 2019, www.europarl.europa.eu/doceo/document/TA-8-2019-0239_EN.html.

59. W. L. Patterson, ed., *We Charge Genocide: The Historic Petition to the United Nations for Relief from a Crime of the United States Government against the Negro People* (Civil Rights Congress, 1952), accessed November 28, 2024, https://depts.washington.edu/moves/images/cp/WeChargeGenocide.pdf.

60. A. Dreher and J. Sturm, "Do the IMF and the World Bank Influence Voting in the UN General Assembly?," *Public Choice* 151 (2012): 363–397.

61. P. E. Joseph, *The Sword and the Shield: The Revolutionary Lives of Malcolm X and Martin Luther King Jr* (New York: Basic Books, 2020).

Chapter 6: The Most Disrespected Person Is the Black Woman

1. Marable, *A Life of Reinvention*, 77.

2. X and Haley, *The Autobiography of Malcolm X*, 180.

3. P. Hill Collins, "Learning to Think for Ourselves," in *Malcolm X: In Our Own Image*, ed. J. Wood (New York: St Martin's Press, 1992), 59–85.

4. X, "There's a Worldwide Revolution Going On."

5. Essien Udom, *Black Nationalism*.

6. A. Y. Davis, "Meditations on the Legacy of Malcolm X," in *Malcolm X: In Our Own Image*, 37.

7. F. Griffin, "'Ironies of the Saint': Malcolm X, Black Women, and the Price of Protection," in *Sisters in the Struggle: African American Women in the Civil Rights–Black Power Movement*, eds. B. Collier-Thompson and V. P. Franklin (New York: NYU Press, 2001), 214.

8. X, "On Police Brutality."

9. K. Andrews, K. Crenshaw, and A. Wilson, *Blackness at the Intersection* (London: Bloomsbury Publishing, 2023).

10. S. Small, *Racialised Barriers: The Black Experience in the United States and England in the 1980s* (London: Taylor and Francis, 2014).

11. X, "Educate Our People in the Science of Politics."

12. X, "Harlem Unity Rally."

13. Ibid.

14. Wallace, *Black Macho and the Myth of the Superwoman*.

15. X, "Harlem Unity Rally."

16. S. Jones-Rogers, *They Were Her Property: White Women as Slave-Owners in the American South* (New Haven, CT: Yale University Press, 2020).

17. K. Lindo, "'Send Love Inna Barrel': Mixed-Media Installation, Kingston, Jamaica," *The Global South* 12, no. 1 (2018): 56–58.

18. Wilkerson, *The Warmth of Other Suns*.

19. X, "Harlem Unity Rally."

20. A. Oakley, *Housewife* (London: Allen Lane, 1974).

21. I. B. Wells, *Crusade for Justice: An Autobiography* (Chicago: University of Chicago Press, 1970).

22. Alexander, *The New Jim Crow*.

23. P. Khan-Cullors and A. Bandele, *When They Call You a Terrorist: A Black Lives Matter Memoir* (New York: St Martin's Press, 2018).

24. K. Crenshaw, *#SayHerName: Black Women's Stories of State Violence and Public Silence* (New York: Haymarket Books, 2023).

25. Shabazz, "The Legacy of My Husband Malcolm X," 180.

26. Andrews, *The New Age of Empire*.

27. Payne and Payne, *The Dead Are Arising*.

28. Shabazz, "The Legacy of My Husband Malcolm X."

29. Malcolm X, "Letter from Cairo," August 29, 1964, ICIT Digital Library, www.icit-digital.org/articles/malcolm-x-s-letter-from-mecca-april-20-1964.

30. G. Horne, *Race Woman: The Lives of Shirley Graham Du Bois* (New York: NYU Press, 2000).

31. M. Angelou, *A Song Flung Up to Heaven* (Boston: Little, Brown, 2002).

32. M. Tubbs, *The Three Mothers: How the Mothers of Martin Luther King, Jr., Malcolm X, and James Baldwin Shaped a Nation* (New York: Flatiron Books, 2021).

33. X and Haley, *The Autobiography of Malcolm X*, 1.

34. Ibid., 8.

35. Ibid., 39.

36. E. Grant, "The Last Days of Malcolm X," in *Malcolm X: The Man and His Times*, 90.

37. W. Sales, *From Civil Rights to Black Liberation: Malcolm X and the Organization of Afro-American Unity* (Boston: South End Press, 1994).

38. Wallace, *Black Macho and the Myth of the Superwoman*, 36.

39. E. Cleaver, *Soul on Ice* (London: Jonathan Cape, 1970).

40. E. Cleaver, *Post-Prison Writings and Speeches* (New York: Vintage Books, 1969).

41. S. Dawson, "Black History x Hump Day: Revisiting That Time Eldridge Cleaver Invented Penis Pants," *Madamenoir*, February 2, 2022, https://madamenoire.com/1307231/eldridge-cleaver-invented-penis-pants/.

42. P. Magnarella, *Black Panther in Exile: The Pete O'Neal Story* (Gainesville: University of Florida Press, 2020).

43. X, "Message to the Grassroots."

44. X, "There's a Worldwide Revolution Going On."

45. V. Oforka, *The Bleeding Continent: How Africa Became Impoverished and Why It Remains Poor* (Xlibris Books, 2015).

46. S. Brown, *Fighting for US: Maulana Karenga, the US Organization and Black Cultural Nationalism* (New York: NYU Press, 2005), 21.

47. Ibid., 56.

48. P. Hill Collins, *From Black Power to Hip Hop: Racism, Nationalism, and Feminism* (Philadelphia: Temple University Press, 2006), 82.

49. X, "Educate Our People in the Science of Politics."

50. X, *The End of White World Supremacy*, 91, my italics added for emphasis.

51. X, "Malcolm X Introduces Fannie Lou Hamer."

52. K. Blain, *Until I Am Free: Fannie Lou Hamer's Enduring Message to America* (Boston: Beacon Press, 2021).

53. F. Hamer, testimony before the Credentials Committee, Democratic National Convention, August 22, 1964, American Rhetoric, accessed November 28, 2024, www.americanrhetoric.com/speeches/fannielouhamercredentialscommittee.htm.

54. X, "Malcolm X Introduces Fannie Lou Hamer."

55. "Fannie Lou Hamer Interview," September 24, 1965, on KPFA Radio, Berkeley, California, American Archive of Public Broadcasting, accessed November 27, 2024, https://americanarchive.org/catalog/cpb-aacip_28-bg2h70895r.

Chapter 7: Who Taught You to Hate Yourself?

1. X, First Founding Rally of the Organization of Afro-American Unity; X, speech at the University of Ghana.

2. Malcolm X (c.1963–1965), Box 5: Unpublished chapter from *The Autobiography of Malcolm X* called "The Negro," plus untitled fragments in Malcolm X manuscripts, Sc MG 951, Schomburg Center for Research in Black Culture, Manuscripts, Archives and Rare Books Division, New York Public Library.

3. X, First Founding Rally of the Organization of Afro-American Unity.

4. X, "Harlem Unity Rally."

5. X, "Interview on 'City Desk.'"

6. M. Omi and O. Winant, *Racial Formation in the United States: From the 1960s to the 1980s* (London: Routledge, 1989).

7. X, "On Afro-American History."

8. X, Box 5: Unpublished chapter from *The Autobiography of Malcolm X* called "The Negro."

9. Ibid.

10. X, speech at Harvard Law School Forum, March 24, 1961.

11. A. Haley, *Roots* (New York: Vintage Books, 1976).

12. X, "Interview on 'City Desk.'"

13. Payne and Payne, *The Dead Are Arising*, 312.

14. X, "On Police Brutality."

15. F. Fanon, *Black Skin, White Masks* (London: Pluto Press, 1984), 8.

16. X, First Founding Rally of the Organization of Afro-American Unity.

17. X, debate with James Baldwin.

18. Ibid.

19. X, "On Police Brutality."

20. Ibid.

21. X, lecture at Muhammad Temple No. 7.

22. Ibid.

23. Ibid.

24. X, "On Police Brutality."

25. C. G. Woodson, *The Mis-education of the Negro* (Trenton, NJ: Africa World Press, 1933).

26. Ibid., 71.

27. B. Coard, *How the West Indian Child Is Made Educationally Sub-normal in the British School System* (London: New Beacon Books, 1971), 30.

28. K. Andrews, *Resisting Racism: Race, Inequality and the Black Supplementary School Movement* (London: Institute of Education Press, 2013).

29. X, Second Founding Rally of the Organization of Afro-American Unity.

30. X, "Answers to Questions from the Militant Labor Forum," 16.

31. K. B. Clark and M. P. Clark, "Skin Color as a Factor in Racial Identification and Preferences in Negro Children," *Journal of Experimental Education* 8 (1940): 161–163.

32. "A Revealing Experiment: Brown v. Board and 'The Doll Test,'" Legal Defense Fund, accessed November 28, 2024, www.naacpldf.org/brown-vs-board/significance-doll-test/.

33. X, "Answers to Questions from the Militant Labor Forum," 17.

34. N. Hare, "The Battle for Black Studies," *The Black Scholar* 3, no. 9 (1972): 32–47.

35. "Confrontations—UWI Student Protest & the Rodney Disturbance, 1968," University of the West Indies, accessed November 28, 2024, https://uwi.edu/museum/exhibitions/confrontations-%E2%80%93-uwi-student-protest-rodney-disturbance-1968.

36. X, "Interview on 'City Desk.'"

37. Ibid.

38. Coard, *How the West Indian Child Is Made Educationally Sub-normal.*

39. Andrews, *Resisting Racism.*

40. B. Cosby, "Pound Cake Speech," May 17, 2004, NAACP Legal Defense Fund award ceremony for the 50th Anniversary of the Supreme Court Decision in *Brown v. Board.*

41. G. Demby, "Sagging Pants and the Long History of 'Dangerous' Street Fashion," *Code Switch*, NPR, September 11, 2014, www.npr.org/sections/codeswitch/2014/09/11/347143588/sagging-pants-and-the-long-history-of-dangerous-street-fashion.

42. L. Segall, "New York Politician Hopes to End Youths' Pants-Sagging Trend," CNN, 2010, https://edition.cnn.com/2010/LIVING/03/29/new.york.baggy.pants/index.html.

43. X, "Educate Our People in the Science of Politics."

44. X, "Not Just an American Problem, but a World Problem."

45. Kelley, "House Negroes on the Loose," 424–425.

46. X, "Harlem Unity Rally."

47. X, First Founding Rally of the Organization of Afro-American Unity.

Chapter 8: Thinking Black

1. S. Hall, "Old and New Ethnicities, Old and New Identities," in *Culture, Globalization and the World System*, ed. Anthony D. King (London: Macmillan, 1991), 55.

2. S. Biko, *I Write What I Like* (Johannesburg: Picador Africa, 1978, reprint 2004).

3. X, "The Black Revolution."

4. X, "Black Man's History," 23.

5. X, "Message to the Grassroots."

6. X, "On Police Brutality."

7. X, "The Black Revolution."

8. X, "Black Man's History," 24.

9. X, "On Police Brutality."

10. Ibid.

11. J. Parker, "Cold War II: The Eisenhower Administration, the Bandung Conference, and the Reperiodization of the Postwar Era," *Diplomatic History* 30, no. 5 (2006): 867–892.

12. Andrews, *The New Age of Empire*.

13. X, "The Ballot or the Bullet," King Solomon Baptist Church.

14. X, "I Live for Change and Action," 44.

15. X, *The Diary of Malcolm X*, 147.

16. X, "There's a Worldwide Revolution Going On."

17. X, "Educate Our People in the Science of Politics."

18. X, "The Black Muslim Movement: An Assessment," 214.

19. K. Andrews, "The Problem of Political Blackness: Lessons from the Black Supplementary School Movement," *Ethnic and Racial Studies* 39, no. 11 (2016): 1–19.

20. X, "The Importance of Unity," 40.

21. X, "Message to the Grassroots."

22. X, "The Ballot or the Bullet," King Solomon Baptist Church.

23. X, "Harlem Unity Rally."

24. Ibid.

25. X, interview with Robert Penn Warren.

26. X, "The Harlem Hate Gang Scare," 66.

27. X, "The Oppressed Masses Cry Out for Action Against the Common Oppressor," 54.

28. Malcolm X, "The Old and New Negro," 1963, in *The End of White World Supremacy: Four Speeches*, 91.

29. Ibid.

30. X, "The Ballot or the Bullet," King Solomon Baptist Church.

31. P. Gilroy, *Against Race: Imagining Political Culture Beyond the Color Line* (Cambridge, MA: Belknap Press, 2000); Hall, "Old and New Identities, Old and New Ethnicities," 53; K. Appiah, *In My Father's House: Africa in the Philosophy of Culture* (Oxford: Oxford University Press, 1992); M. Wright, *Physics of Blackness: Beyond the Middle Passage Epistemology* (Minneapolis: University of Minnesota Press, 2015).

32. K. Tsri, "Africans Are Not Black: Why the Use of the Term 'Black' for Africans Should Be Abandoned," *African Identities* 14, no. 2 (2016): 147–160.

33. X, Box 5: Unpublished chapter from *The Autobiography of Malcolm X* called "The Negro."

34. Ibid.

35. O. Sachs, *The Man Who Mistook His Wife for a Hat and Other Clinical Tales* (New York: Touchstone Books, 1998).

36. "Malcolm X in Debate with Bayard Rustin."

37. X, "The Ballot or the Bullet," King Solomon Baptist Church.

38. X, *The Diary of Malcolm X*, 19.

39. X, "On Police Brutality."

40. X, "The Ballot or the Bullet," Cory Methodist Church.

41. X, "The Ballot or the Bullet," King Solomon Baptist Church.

42. Ibid.

43. X, "Black Man's History," 25–26.

44. X, "On Police Brutality."

45. X, "Harlem Unity Rally."

46. M. L. King, speech at Illinois Wesleyan University, 1966, Illinois Wesleyan University, accessed November 28, 2024, www.iwu.edu/mlk/.

47. X, debate with James Baldwin.

48. X, First Founding Rally of the Organization of Afro-American Unity.

49. X, "Educate Our People in the Science of Politics."

50. X, debate with James Baldwin.

51. X, "On Afro-American History."

52. X, "Educate Our People in the Science of Politics."

53. X, speech at the University of Ghana.

54. A. Davis, *An Autobiography* (London: Penguin Random House, 2023).

55. X, "Black Man's History," 27.

56. Malcolm X, "There Is a Conspiracy to Kill Me," interview with the *New York Post*, February 18, 1965, in *The Final Speeches: February 1965*, 189.

57. X, "Not Just an American Problem, but a World Problem."

58. X, *The Diary of Malcolm X*, 133.

59. X, "Not Just an American Problem, but a World Problem."

60. X, First Founding Rally of the Organization of Afro-American Unity.

61. M. Garvey, *The Philosophy and Opinions of Marcus Garvey: Or Africa for the Africans* (London: Routledge, 1967), 1, 6.

62. Martin, *Race First*.

63. Carmichael, *Stokely Speaks*, 198.

64. E. Cronon, *Black Moses: The Story of Marcus Garvey* (Madison: University of Wisconsin Press, 1969), 4.

65. X, "There's a Worldwide Revolution Going On."

Chapter 9: House and Field Negro

1. T. Shelby, "Two Conceptions of Black Nationalism: Martin Delaney on the Meaning of Black Political Solidarity," *Political Theory* 31, no. 5 (2003): 667.

2. Collins, "Learning to Think for Ourselves," 67.

3. X, "Message to the Grassroots."

4. X, "On Afro-American History."

5. Kelley, "House Negroes on the Loose," 431.

6. X, "Message to the Grassroots."

7. Collins, *Black Feminist Thought*.

8. X, "Interview on 'City Desk.'"

9. X, Oxford University Union debate.

10. Social Market Foundation, "Black Graduates Get Worse Degrees and Earn Less than White Peers," news release, March 18, 2021, www.smf.co.uk/black-graduates -get-worse-degrees-and-earn-less-than-white-peers/.

11. For a full discussion, see K. Andrews, *The Psychosis of Whiteness* (London: Penguin Books, 2023), 118. Here, it will serve well enough to inform you that when Europeans migrated to South America, they did not cease to be White. Most Latinx in the United States actually identify as White; K. Taylor, *From Black Lives Matter to Black Liberation* (Chicago, IL: Haymarket Books, 2016).

12. Andrews, *The New Age of Empire*.

13. X, speech at the University of Ghana.

14. X, "Interview on Boston Radio."

15. B. Seale, *Seize the Time: The Story of the Black Panther Party* (New York: Random House, 1970).

16. Malcolm X, "The House Negro and the Field Negro," Selma, Alabama, February 4, 1965, in *The Final Speeches: February 1965*, 26–28.

17. X, "Educate Our People in the Science of Politics."

18. X, lecture at Muhammad Temple No. 7.

19. X, interview with Robert Penn Warren.

20. X, "Educate Our People in the Science of Politics."

21. X, "Interview with Pierre Berton."

22. X, "The Black Revolution."

23. Andrews, *The Psychosis of Whiteness*.

24. X, speech at Harvard Law School Forum, March 24, 1961.

25. X, "On Police Brutality."

26. K. Badenoch, in House of Commons, Black History Month, debated on October 20, 2020, *Hansard* 682.

27. K. Badenoch, speech to the Conservative Party Conference, Manchester, UK, October 2, 2023.

28. N. Waller and N. Sakande, "Majority Jury Verdicts in England and Wales: A Vestige of White Supremacy?," *Race & Class* 65, no. 4 (2024): 26–52.

29. X, "Harlem Unity Rally."

30. Ibid.

31. X, "The Ballot or the Bullet," King Solomon Baptist Church.

32. D. Height, *Open Wide the Freedom Gates: A Memoir* (New York: Public Affairs, 2005), 149.

33. X, "I Live for Change and Action," 44.

34. X, "Message to the Grassroots."

35. X, "On Police Brutality."

36. X, First Founding Rally of the Organization of Afro-American Unity.

37. X, "Homecoming Rally," 148.

38. X, "Harlem Unity Rally."

Chapter 10: A Better Word Is Independence

1. B. Perry, *Malcolm X: The Life of a Man Who Changed Black America* (New York: Station Hill, 1992).

2. Malcolm X, "Harlem and Political Machines," New York, July 4, 1964, in *By Any Means Necessary: Speeches, Interviews and Letters by Malcolm X*, 72.

3. X, Second Founding Rally of the Organization of Afro-American Unity.

4. X, "The Black Revolution."

5. K. Woodard, *A Nation Within a Nation: Amiri Baraka (LeRoi Jones) and Black Power* (Chapel Hill: University of North Carolina Press, 1999).

6. X, interview with Robert Penn Warren.

7. Malcolm X, interview on *Front Page Challenge*, 1965, CBC Archives, YouTube, accessed November 28, 2024, https://youtu.be/C7IJ7npTYrU.

8. X, "The Black Revolution."

9. X, "Interview with A. B. Spelman," 9.

10. C. L. R. James, *The Black Jacobins* (London: Penguin Books, 1938).

11. Andrews, *Back to Black*.

12. X, Second Founding Rally of the Organization of Afro-American Unity.

13. Garvey, *The Philosophy and Opinions of Marcus Garvey*, 6.

14. X, "Interview with A. B. Spelman," 7.

15. X, interview with Robert Penn Warren.

16. J. McEvoy, "David Lammy: Friend of Israel," *Declassified*, January 25, 2024, www.declassifieduk.org/david-lammy-friend-of-israel/.

17. X, *The Diary of Malcolm X*, 117.

18. X, First Founding Rally of the Organization of Afro-American Unity.

19. X, "Interview with A. B. Spelman," 13.

20. X, "There Is a Conspiracy to Kill Me," 189.

21. X, Second Founding Rally of the Organization of Afro-American Unity.

22. Ibid.

23. Ibid.

24. X, "The Ballot or the Bullet," King Solomon Baptist Church.

25. X and Haley, *The Autobiography of Malcolm X*.

26. X, Second Founding Rally of the Organization of Afro-American Unity.

27. S. Cashin, *White Space, Black Hood: Opportunity Hoarding and Segregation in the Age of Inequality* (Boston: Beacon Press, 2021).

28. X, Second Founding Rally of the Organization of Afro-American Unity.

29. X, First Founding Rally of the Organization of Afro-American Unity.

30. X and Haley, *The Autobiography of Malcolm X*, 55.

31. M. Asante, *Afrocentricity: The Theory of Social Change* (Chicago: African American Images, 2003).

32. X, "Interview with A. B. Spelman," 8.

33. Malcolm X, speech to the African Summit Conference, Organization of African Unity, Cairo, August 21, 1964, ICIT Digital Library, accessed November 28, 2024, www.icit-digital.org/articles/malcolm-x-s-speech-to-the-african-summit-conference-august-21-1964.

34. Ibid.

35. X, First Founding Rally of the Organization of Afro-American Unity.

36. K. Nkrumah, *Africa Must Unite* (London: Panaf Books, 1998), 27.

37. X, speech at the University of Ghana.

38. Ibid.

39. X, "Time Is on the Side of the Africans Against Exploitation and Oppression," 32.

40. X, "The Oppressed Masses Cry Out for Action Against the Common Oppressor," 53.

41. X, *The Diary of Malcolm X*, 48.

42. X, "There's a Worldwide Revolution Going On."

43. D. Brown, "Malcolm X Didn't Fear Being Killed: 'I Live Like a Man Who Is Dead Already,'" *The Washington Post*, February 26, 2018, www.washingtonpost.com/news/retropolis/wp/2018/02/26/malcolm-x-didnt-fear-being-killed-i-live-like-a-man-who-is-dead-already/.

44. X, "Educate Our People in the Science of Politics."

45. X, *The Diary of Malcolm X*, 14.

46. X, "Harlem and Political Machines," 72.

Chapter 11: You Left Your Mind in Africa

1. For a full discussion, see Andrews, *The Psychosis of Whiteness*, ch. 8.

2. L. Saad, *Me and White Supremacy: How to Recognise Your Privilege, Combat Racism and Change the World* (London: Quercus Publishing, 2019); C. Fleming, *How to Be Less Stupid About Race: On Racism, White Supremacy and the Racial Divide* (Boston: Beacon Press, 2018); A. M. Brown, quoted in A. Solomon and K. Rankin, *How We Fight White Supremacy: A Field Guide to Black Resistance* (New York: Nation Books, 2019), ch. 8.

3. I. X. Kendi, *How to Be an Anti-Racist* (New York: One World, 2019).

4. X, "The Ballot or the Bullet," King Solomon Baptist Church.

5. "Who Is Foundational Black American and Who Is Not?," Foundational Black Americans, accessed November 22, 2024, https://officialfba.com/.

6. S. Dovi, "Preferable Descriptive Representatives: Will Just Any Woman, Black, or Latino Do?," *American Political Science Review* 96, no. 4 (2002): 729–743.

7. T. Nasheed, *Foundational Black American Race Baiter: My Journey to Understanding Systematic Racism* (Chatsworth, CA: King Flex Entertainment, 2021), 63.

8. "Reparations," ADOS Advocacy Foundation, accessed November 28, 2024, www.adosfoundation.org/reparations/.

9. Chuck D, *This Day in Rap and Hip-Hop History* (London: Octopus Publishing Group, 2017).

10. X, "The Ballot or the Bullet," King Solomon Baptist Church.

11. N. Hannah-Jones, *The 1619 Project: A New Heritage Project* (New York: Oneworld, 2021), 36.

12. My italics.

13. X, "Educate Our People in the Science of Politics."

14. X, Box 5: Unpublished chapter from *The Autobiography of Malcolm X* called "The Negro."

15. *Commission on Race and Ethnic Disparities: The Report* (Commission on Race and Ethnic Disparities, March 2021), 8, https://assets.publishing.service.gov.uk/media/6062ddb1d3bf7 5ce1060aa4/20210331_-_CRED_Report_-_FINAL_-_Web_Accessible.pdf.

16. A. Modhin, "UK Race Commission Amends Line on Slave Trade After Criticism," April 30, 2021, *The Guardian*, www.theguardian.com/world/2021/apr/30/uk-race -commission-amends-line-on-slave-trade-after-criticism.

17. L. Campbell, "David Lammy Praised for Response to Radio Caller Who Said He Was 'Not English,'" March 29, 2021, *The Guardian*, www.theguardian.com/world/2021/mar /29/david-lammy-praised-for-response-to-lbc-caller-who-said-he-was-not-english.

18. M. Goodfellow, *Hostile Environment: How Immigrants Became Scapegoats* (London: Verso Books, 2019).

19. Malcolm X, television interview, March 1964, YouTube, accessed November 22, 2024, www.youtube.com/watch?v=cReCQE8B5nY.

20. W. Darity and K. Mullen, *From Here to Equality: Reparations for Black Americans in the Twenty-First Century* (Chapel Hill: University of North Carolina Press, 2020).

21. E. Williams, *Capitalism and Slavery* (London: Andre Deutsch, 1964).

22. J. Bennett, "The Confederate Bazaar at Liverpool," *Crossfire—The Magazine of the American Civil War*, December 1999, www.acwrt.org.uk/uk-heritage_The-Confederate-Bazaar -at-Liverpool.asp.

23. "Ten Point Action Plan," CARICOM Reparations Commission, accessed November 28, 2024, https://caricomreparations.org/.

24. P. Robinson, *Report on Reparations for Transatlantic Chattel Slavery in the Americas and the Caribbean* (Brattle Group, June 8, 2023), www.brattle.com/wp-content/uploads/2023/07/Report-on-Reparations-for-Transatlantic-Chattel-Slavery-in-the-Americas-and-the-Caribbean.pdf.

25. D. Moyo, *Dead Aid: Why Aid Is Not Working and How There Is Another Way in Africa* (London: Penguin Books, 2010).

26. Andrews, *The Psychosis of Whiteness*, ch. 6.

27. "Call to Action! Stop the Benin Bronze Transfers," Restitution Study Group, accessed November 28, 2024, https://rsgincorp.org/direct-action/.

28. D. Farmer-Paellmann, "Share the Benin Bronzes! They Belong to All of Us," September 12, 2022, Change.org, www.change.org/p/share-the-benin-bronzes.

29. A. S. Banjo, "An Overview of the Process and Politics of Reparations in Africa," *The Constitution* 3, no. 3 (2003): 50–67.

30. Andrews, *New Age of Empire*, ch. 3.

31. X, Box 5: Unpublished chapter from *The Autobiography of Malcolm X* called "The Negro."

32. X, speech at Harvard Law School Forum, March 24, 1961.

33. X, "The Black Revolution."

34. F. Wilderson, *Afropessimism* (New York: Liveright, 2020).

35. L. Park, "Afropessimism and Futures of . . .: A Conversation with Frank Wilderson," *The Black Scholar* 50, no. 3 (2020): 29–41.

36. O. Patterson, *Slavery and Social Death: A Comparative Study* (Cambridge, MA: Harvard University Press, 1982).

37. Wilderson, *Afropessimism*, 102.

38. Ibid., 107.

39. F. Wilderson, "The Politics of Pessimism in an Anti-Black World," speech at John Hope Franklin Humanities Institute at Duke University, November 9, 2020, YouTube, accessed November 28, 2024, www.youtube.com/watch?v=Tug7UWedzrw.

40. S. Dadzie, *A Kick in the Belly: Women, Slavery and Resistance* (London: Verso Books, 2020).

41. Marable, *A Life of Reinvention*.

Chapter 12: Nobody Can Give You Freedom

1. X, "We Have to Learn How to Think," 250.

2. "Quotes by Malcolm X," Malcolm X: The Official Website of Malcolm X, accessed November 28, 2024, www.malcolmx.com/quotes/.

3. G. Orfield, *Reviving the Goal of an Integrated Society: A 21st Century Challenge* (Los Angeles: Civil Rights Project/Proyecto Derechos Civiles, 2009).

4. Andrews, *Resisting Racism*.

5. K. Ture, "Free Huey Rally," February 17, 1968, LfK(S) Collectif, accessed November 28, 2024, www.lfks.net/en/content/stokely-carmichael-free-huey-rally-1968-feb-17.

6. X, "Malcolm X Introduces Fannie Lou Hamer."

7. Cashin, *White Space, Black Hood*, 182.

8. X, "The Ballot or the Bullet," King Solomon Baptist Church.

9. X, First Founding Rally of the Organization of Afro-American Unity.

10. X, "The Ballot or the Bullet," King Solomon Baptist Church.

11. X, "The Ballot or the Bullet," Cory Methodist Church.

12. In M. K. Asante, *100 Greatest African Americans: A Biographical Encyclopedia* (New York: Prometheus Books, 2002), 136.

13. Garvey, *The Philosophy and Opinions of Marcus Garvey*, 10.

14. X, "The Ballot or the Bullet," King Solomon Baptist Church.

15. Wells, *Crusade for Justice*.

16. Martin, *Race First*.

17. C. Jones, *Beyond Containment: Autobiographical Reflections, Essays, and Poems* (Banbury: Ayebia Clarke Publishing, 2011).

18. K. Andrews, "Leila Hassan Howe: 'My Life Was Made Hell. You'd Just Hear a Tirade Against Immigrants,'" October 8, 2020, *The Guardian*, www.theguardian.com/society/2020/oct/08/leila-hassan-howe-black-power-london-revolution-black-lives-matter.

19. X, debate with James Baldwin.

20. N. Warren, "Pan-African Cultural Movements: From Baraka to Karenga," *The Journal of Negro History* 75, no. 1/2 (1990): 26.

21. X, "I Live for Change and Action," 45.

22. X, *The Diary of Malcolm X*, 46.

23. Collins, *Black Feminist Thought*; E. P. Johnson and M. G. Henderson, *Black Queer Studies: A Critical Anthology* (Durham, NC: Duke University Press, 2005).

24. X, "The Ballot or the Bullet," King Solomon Baptist Church.

25. X, "There's a Worldwide Revolution Going On."

26. X, "Malcolm X Introduces Fannie Lou Hamer."

INDEX

Note: Quotes are attributed to Malcolm X unless otherwise credited.

Credit: Birmingham City University

KEHINDE ANDREWS is professor of Black studies at Birmingham City University, where he led the development of the first Black studies degree in Europe. Andrews regularly writes for *The Guardian*, *The Independent*, *Ebony Magazine*, and CNN. The author of *The New Age of Empire*, he lives in Birmingham, UK.